Anna Kutkina

BETWEEN LENIN AND BANDERA

Decommunization and Multivocality in Post-Euromaidan Ukraine

With a foreword by Juri Mykkänen

Bibliografische Information der Deutschen Nationalbibliothek

Die Deutsche Nationalbibliothek verzeichnet diese Publikation in der Deutschen Nationalbibliografie; detaillierte bibliografische Daten sind im Internet über http://dnb.d-nb.de abrufbar.

Bibliographic information published by the Deutsche Nationalbibliothek
Die Deutsche Nationalbibliothek lists this publication in the Deutsche Nationalbibliografie; detailed bibliographic data are available in the Internet at http://dnb.d-nb.de.

Cover illustration: Photo: © 2021 by Anna Kutkina, graffiti in Kyiv, Ukraine, by Aleksei Kislov and Julien Milan.

ISBN-13: 978-3-8382-1506-8
© *ibidem*-Verlag, Stuttgart 2021
Alle Rechte vorbehalten

Das Werk einschließlich aller seiner Teile ist urheberrechtlich geschützt. Jede Verwertung außerhalb der engen Grenzen des Urheberrechtsgesetzes ist ohne Zustimmung des Verlages unzulässig und strafbar. Dies gilt insbesondere für Vervielfältigungen, Übersetzungen, Mikroverfilmungen und elektronische Speicherformen sowie die Einspeicherung und Verarbeitung in elektronischen Systemen.

All rights reserved. No part of this publication may be reproduced, stored in or introduced into a retrieval system, or transmitted, in any form, or by any means (electronical, mechanical, photocopying, recording or otherwise) without the prior written permission of the publisher. Any person who does any unauthorized act in relation to this publication may be liable to criminal prosecution and civil claims for damages.

Printed in the EU

Soviet and Post-Soviet Politics and Society (SPPS)
ISSN 1614-3515

General Editor: Andreas Umland,
Stockholm Centre for Eastern European Studies, andreas.umland@ui.se

Commissioning Editor: Max Jakob Horstmann,
London, mjh@ibidem.eu

EDITORIAL COMMITTEE*

DOMESTIC & COMPARATIVE POLITICS
Prof. **Ellen Bos**, *Andrássy University of Budapest*
Dr. **Gergana Dimova**, *University of Winchester*
Dr. **Andrey Kazantsev**, *MGIMO (U) MID RF, Moscow*
Prof. **Heiko Pleines**, *University of Bremen*
Prof. **Richard Sakwa**, *University of Kent at Canterbury*
Dr. **Sarah Whitmore**, *Oxford Brookes University*
Dr. **Harald Wydra**, *University of Cambridge*

SOCIETY, CLASS & ETHNICITY
Col. **David Glantz**, *"Journal of Slavic Military Studies"*
Dr. **Marlène Laruelle**, *George Washington University*
Dr. **Stephen Shulman**, *Southern Illinois University*
Prof. **Stefan Troebst**, *University of Leipzig*

POLITICAL ECONOMY & PUBLIC POLICY
Dr. **Andreas Goldthau**, *Central European University*
Dr. **Robert Kravchuk**, *University of North Carolina*
Dr. **David Lane**, *University of Cambridge*
Dr. **Carol Leonard**, *Higher School of Economics, Moscow*
Dr. **Maria Popova**, *McGill University, Montreal*

FOREIGN POLICY & INTERNATIONAL AFFAIRS
Dr. **Peter Duncan**, *University College London*
Prof. **Andreas Heinemann-Grüder**, *University of Bonn*
Prof. **Gerhard Mangott**, *University of Innsbruck*
Dr. **Diana Schmidt-Pfister**, *University of Konstanz*
Dr. **Lisbeth Tarlow**, *Harvard University, Cambridge*
Dr. **Christian Wipperfürth**, *N-Ost Network, Berlin*
Dr. **William Zimmerman**, *University of Michigan*

HISTORY, CULTURE & THOUGHT
Dr. **Catherine Andreyev**, *University of Oxford*
Prof. **Mark Bassin**, *Södertörn University*
Prof. **Karsten Brüggemann**, *Tallinn University*
Dr. **Alexander Etkind**, *University of Cambridge*
Dr. **Gasan Gusejnov**, *Moscow State University*
Prof. **Leonid Luks**, *Catholic University of Eichstaett*
Dr. **Olga Malinova**, *Russian Academy of Sciences*
Dr. **Richard Mole**, *University College London*
Prof. **Andrei Rogatchevski**, *University of Tromsø*
Dr. **Mark Tauger**, *West Virginia University*

ADVISORY BOARD*

Prof. **Dominique Arel**, *University of Ottawa*
Prof. **Jörg Baberowski**, *Humboldt University of Berlin*
Prof. **Margarita Balmaceda**, *Seton Hall University*
Dr. **John Barber**, *University of Cambridge*
Prof. **Timm Beichelt**, *European University Viadrina*
Dr. **Katrin Boeckh**, *University of Munich*
Prof. em. **Archie Brown**, *University of Oxford*
Dr. **Vyacheslav Bryukhovetsky**, *Kyiv-Mohyla Academy*
Prof. **Timothy Colton**, *Harvard University, Cambridge*
Prof. **Paul D'Anieri**, *University of Florida*
Dr. **Heike Dörrenbächer**, *Friedrich Naumann Foundation*
Dr. **John Dunlop**, *Hoover Institution, Stanford, California*
Dr. **Sabine Fischer**, *SWP, Berlin*
Dr. **Geir Flikke**, *NUPI, Oslo*
Prof. **David Galbreath**, *University of Aberdeen*
Prof. **Alexander Galkin**, *Russian Academy of Sciences*
Prof. **Frank Golczewski**, *University of Hamburg*
Dr. **Nikolas Gvosdev**, *Naval War College, Newport, RI*
Prof. **Mark von Hagen**, *Arizona State University*
Dr. **Guido Hausmann**, *University of Munich*
Prof. **Dale Herspring**, *Kansas State University*
Dr. **Stefani Hoffman**, *Hebrew University of Jerusalem*
Prof. **Mikhail Ilyin**, *MGIMO (U) MID RF, Moscow*
Prof. **Vladimir Kantor**, *Higher School of Economics*
Dr. **Ivan Katchanovski**, *University of Ottawa*
Prof. em. **Andrzej Korbonski**, *University of California*
Dr. **Iris Kempe**, *"Caucasus Analytical Digest"*
Prof. **Herbert Küpper**, *Institut für Ostrecht Regensburg*
Dr. **Rainer Lindner**, *CEEER, Berlin*
Dr. **Vladimir Malakhov**, *Russian Academy of Sciences*

Dr. **Luke March**, *University of Edinburgh*
Prof. **Michael McFaul**, *Stanford University, Palo Alto*
Prof. **Birgit Menzel**, *University of Mainz-Germersheim*
Prof. **Valery Mikhailenko**, *The Urals State University*
Prof. **Emil Pain**, *Higher School of Economics, Moscow*
Dr. **Oleg Podvintsev**, *Russian Academy of Sciences*
Prof. **Olga Popova**, *St. Petersburg State University*
Dr. **Alex Pravda**, *University of Oxford*
Dr. **Erik van Ree**, *University of Amsterdam*
Dr. **Joachim Rogall**, *Robert Bosch Foundation Stuttgart*
Prof. **Peter Rutland**, *Wesleyan University, Middletown*
Prof. **Marat Salikov**, *The Urals State Law Academy*
Dr. **Gwendolyn Sasse**, *University of Oxford*
Prof. **Jutta Scherrer**, *EHESS, Paris*
Prof. **Robert Service**, *University of Oxford*
Mr. **James Sherr**, *RIIA Chatham House London*
Dr. **Oxana Shevel**, *Tufts University, Medford*
Prof. **Eberhard Schneider**, *University of Siegen*
Prof. **Olexander Shnyrkov**, *Shevchenko University, Kyiv*
Prof. **Hans-Henning Schröder**, *SWP, Berlin*
Prof. **Yuri Shapoval**, *Ukrainian Academy of Sciences*
Prof. **Viktor Shnirelman**, *Russian Academy of Sciences*
Dr. **Lisa Sundstrom**, *University of British Columbia*
Dr. **Philip Walters**, *"Religion, State and Society", Oxford*
Prof. **Zenon Wasyliw**, *Ithaca College, New York State*
Dr. **Lucan Way**, *University of Toronto*
Dr. **Markus Wehner**, *"Frankfurter Allgemeine Zeitung"*
Dr. **Andrew Wilson**, *University College London*
Prof. **Jan Zielonka**, *University of Oxford*
Prof. **Andrei Zorin**, *University of Oxford*

* While the Editorial Committee and Advisory Board support the General Editor in the choice and improvement of manuscripts for publication, responsibility for remaining errors and misinterpretations in the series' volumes lies with the books' authors.

Soviet and Post-Soviet Politics and Society (SPPS)
ISSN 1614-3515

Founded in 2004 and refereed since 2007, SPPS makes available affordable English-, German-, and Russian-language studies on the history of the countries of the former Soviet bloc from the late Tsarist period to today. It publishes between 5 and 20 volumes per year and focuses on issues in transitions to and from democracy such as economic crisis, identity formation, civil society development, and constitutional reform in CEE and the NIS. SPPS also aims to highlight so far understudied themes in East European studies such as right-wing radicalism, religious life, higher education, or human rights protection. The authors and titles of all previously published volumes are listed at the end of this book. For a full description of the series and reviews of its books, see www.ibidem-verlag.de/red/spps.

Editorial correspondence & manuscripts should be sent to: Dr. Andreas Umland, Department of Political Science, Kyiv-Mohyla Academy, vul. Voloska 8/5, UA-04070 Kyiv, UKRAINE; andreas.umland@cantab.net

Business correspondence & review copy requests should be sent to: *ibidem* Press, Leuschnerstr. 40, 30457 Hannover, Germany; tel.: +49 511 2622200; fax: +49 511 2622201; spps@ibidem.eu.

Authors, reviewers, referees, and editors for (as well as all other persons sympathetic to) SPPS are invited to join its networks at www.facebook.com/group.php?gid=52638198614 www.linkedin.com/groups?about=&gid=103012 www.xing.com/net/spps-ibidem-verlag/

Recent Volumes

229 *Oxana Schmies (Ed.)*
NATO's Enlargement and Russia
A Strategic Challenge in the Past and Future
With a foreword by Vladimir Kara-Murza
ISBN 978-3-8382-1478-8

230 *Christopher Ford*
UKAPISME–Une Gauche Perude
Le marxisme anti-colonial dans la révolution ukrainienne 1917 - 1925
Avec une preface de Vincent Présumey
ISBN 978-3-8382-0899-2

231 *Anna Kutkina*
Between Lenin and Bandera
Decommunization and Multivocality in Post-Euromaidan Ukraine
With a foreword by Juri Mykkänen
ISBN 978-3-8382-1506-8

232 *Lincoln E. Flake*
Defending the Faith
The Russian Orthodox Church and the Demise of Religious Pluralism
With a foreword by Peter Martland
ISBN 978-3-8382-1378-1

233 *Nikoloz Samkharadze*
Russia's Recognition of the Independence of Abkhazia and South Ossetia
Analysis of a Deviant Case in Moscow's Foreign Policy Behavior
With a foreword by Neil MacFarlane
ISBN 978-3-8382-1414-6

234 *Arve Hansen*
Urban Protest
A Spatial Perspective on Kyiv, Minsk, and Moscow
With a foreword by Julie Wilhelmsen
ISBN 978-3-8382-1495-5

235 *Eleonora Narvselius, Julie Fedor (Eds.)*
Diversity in the East-Central European Borderlands
Memories, Cityscapes, People
ISBN 978-3-8382-1523-5

236 *Regina Elsner*
The Russian Orthodox Church and Modernity
A Historical and Theological Investigation into Eastern Christianity between Unity and Plurality
With a foreword by Mikhail Suslov
ISBN 978-3-8382-1568-6

237 *Bo Petersson*
The Putin Predicament
Problems of Legitimacy and Succession in Russia
With a foreword by J. Paul Goode
ISBN 978-3-8382-1050-6

Contents

Preface by Juri Mykkänen xi
Acknowledgements xv

Introduction 1
1: Theory as 'Hegemonic' Practice 15
    Constructing multivocality 23
    The 'imagined community' 27
    Bridging 31

2: The Postcolonial Soviet 37
    Disputing othering 43
    The opposition 48
    Debating decommunization 52

3: 'Researching' Methods 61
    Interviews, visuals, texts 68
    Textual and narrative analysis 74

4: The Poster — Roots of the Lenin cult 79
    Methodology of the poster 81
    The leaders cult 86
    Historical memory 90

5: Art of the Protest 95
    Messages of the revolution 100
    The "Strike Poster" — "Страйк Плакат" 104
    Posters and the state 112
    Romanticization + realism 118
    Birth of dialogism? 121

6: Meanings of Lenin 127
   The 'Leninfall' — original multivocality 129
   Creative remembering 137
   The Lenin camouflage 145

7: Filling the 'Pedestal' 153
   Bandera and the nationalist discourse 156
   The bookshelves: mirroring decommunization 162
   "One Hundred Years of Fighting for Independence" 168
   The 'other,' the Ukrainian, and the state 176

Conclusion 185
References 195

Sources

Figure A: Map of Ukraine: visual presentation of the collected data 62
Figure B: Exponential non-discriminative snowballing sampling (Dudovskiy 2012) 63
Figure C: Layered textual analysis (Covert 2014) 75

To All Ukrainians

Preface

When the journalist Malcolm Borthwick of the Guardian visited the Chernobyl nuclear disaster site during the winter of 2019, he noted in passing that the last two surviving statues of Lenin in Ukraine are in the Chernobyl exclusion zone, as signs of time stood still.[i] A few others in small villages have since been found still intact, but the fact remains that almost every symbol of the communist past of Ukraine has been removed, demolished, or replaced, much in the fashion that is known to have taken place in all the former socialist countries of Eastern Europe. In itself, such an eradication of the past is dramatic, yet decommunization (as this refashioning of history is called) can be easily overlooked as a simple political victory over an oppressive regime and a justified removal of the visible insignia associated with the infamous past.

Anna Kutkina's study of the events surrounding the official decommunization laws of 2015, ranging from the Euromaidan demonstrations in 2013 to the frozen conflict in the Eastern Ukraine through 2018, takes us on an ethnographic journey behind the façade of history's rectification. The study reveals the contested nature of the stamped-out symbols. It highlights the processes and mechanisms of local and creative meaning-making, and its political nature beyond the official break with the Soviet past. With so many examples, Kutkina shows how complex an issue the past can be and how a symbol, despised by many, can be profoundly ambiguous, sometimes even for those Ukrainians whose experience of socialist rule was predominantly adverse.

As so often in postcommunist societies, the Ukrainian reaction towards its past has also assumed a nationalist outlook. But again, nationalism in Ukraine has many faces, sometimes hardly recognizable as expressions of nationalism. In obvious cases, amply illustrated by Kutkina, nationalist groups would paint statues of Lenin in the colors of the Ukrainian flag, thus celebrating the true Ukraine liberated from Soviet rule. But equally, others would dress Lenin in traditional Ukrainian shirts to acknowledge the potential of peaceful political transformation. The acts of transforming Soviet symbols, which at the first glance seem uniform, can therefore serve different ideas and memories of the past, and political projections into the future. In these acts, the Soviet symbols are vehicles for political expressions of multiple meanings.

A startling observation that cuts through Dr. Kutkina's study are the many voices which, in their appearance, seem to say the same thing, celebrating a reborn nation rid of the Soviet past and Russian influence, but which, on closer inspection, reveal a rather ambiguous cultural landscape. A political poster from 2016 demonstrates this point well: John Lennon's portrait overlaid with text saying, "Imagine there is no Putin." It is a clever pun, but culturally it allows more than one interpretation. It is anti-Russian and obviously relates to Russian aggression. Yet, it targets the Russian president, rather than being a blanket denunciation of all things Russian. Another political poster showing raindrops in the form of small Lenin statues also alludes to Russian aggression, but this time reminding the viewer of the totalitarian past of the Soviet Union and the similarities of Russian conduct under its present rulers. Again, the message can be read as a selective condemnation of Russian politics —or, perhaps, a more general dissociation of Ukraine from specific elements of Russian culture.

In his *On Populist Reason*, Ernesto Laclau used Gustave le Bon's classic book *The Crowd* as a starting point for his theory of signification. The important term that Laclau borrowed from le Bon was "suggestion," which le Bon used to explain the influence of words and symbols on mass behavior. For le Bon, a simple word may bring forth—or suggest —a chain of associations that grows in the minds of people into images that arouse them to action with which the original word cannot be denotatively associated. Laclau takes this as an early, yet incomplete, attempt to theorize the arbitrary nature of signification.[ii] In other words, there is no prior fixation between an expression and interpretation; instead there are many possible ways to make the connection. Yet, to say that the meanings associated with statues, street names or political posters are multiple does not indicate the radical arbitrariness of signification. Quite the contrary, the sources for signification were already in place in Ukrainian history, to be recovered and appropriated in public. If the Euromaidan still appealed to images of the European legacy, human rights and good government, the war in the Donbass region and the Russian annexation of the Crimea enacted a different nationalist imagery. It ranged from the state-sponsored war propaganda, reminiscent of Soviet style socialist realism, to the popular cult of Stepan Bandera, a controversial nationalist leader who was lethally poisoned by a KGB agent in 1959. Signification may lack an innate order, but it certainly is structured and motivated. The resulting structures may be durable but they exist side by side, sometimes competing and sometimes dominating, but never totally occupying the symbolic field.

Dr Kutkina uses an older classic, Mikhail Bakhtin[iii], to make sense of the multiple voices that seek to leave their marks on the public imagery of Ukraine's national identity. In the Bakhtinian manner, Kutkina's ethnographic study shows vividly how various voices, with their different valorization of Ukrainian culture and history, come together in a dialogue. There is no ultimate order, only clashing, conflicting, contrasting, counterposing, and partly overlapping views and understandings expressed through the creative use of symbols. In the spirit of Bakhtin, an interesting angle in Kutkina's work is her intentional disregard of social class or other sociological anchors of her subjects, the many Ukrainians engaging themselves in the interpretative acts. The symbolic dialogue that grew out of the Euromaidan was so diverse within the typical social divisions that arranging the symbolic dialogue along them would have been ill-justified.

Between Lenin and Bandera is an astute look into an unfolding scene of a symbolic struggle for national identity. It studies meaning-making as it happened and interprets political symbolism in a way that avoids the old sin of interpretative studies: the meaning of symbols is derived from the people doing the meaning-making instead of from the mind of an omnipotent observer. This is done without sacrificing analytical rigor. The study is at once deeply local and profoundly universal.

—Juri Mykkänen, February 2021

---

i   Revisiting Chernobyl: "It is a huge cemetery of dreams". The Guardian, February 28, 2019.
ii   Ernesto Laclau, *On Populist Reason* (London: Verso, 2005), p. 22.
iii   Mikhail Bakhtin, *Problems of Dostoevsky's Poetics*. Ed. and trans. Caryl Emerson (Minneapolis: University of Minnesota Press, 1984), p. 28.

Acknowledgements

This book is an outcome of an individual journey supported by the many. It was made possible and has benefited greatly from the encouragement, cooperation, wisdom, and generosity of many people—my academic mentors, colleagues, researchers, interviewees, family and friends. To proceed with any kind of a chronological order in expression of gratitude is a challenging task, since the value of every single person walking the path of this research with me is immeasurable.

I will attempt to accomplish it by putting a geographic framework on this statement and thanking Finland for becoming the scientific home of this research. This book was made possible in part by the grants of the CIMO Foundation, the University of Helsinki Research Foundation and the KONE Foundation. Four people in particular gave special feedback and encouragement to this work: Professor Juri Mykkänen, Professor Markku Kangaspuro, Professor Pertti Ahonen and Dr. Emilia Palonen. I am grateful to each of them for their unique contribution, which came of essential support during different stages of the research. I am particularly thankful to Professor Juri Mykkänen for his invaluable collaboration, for pouring his heart and tireless hours to perfect, and for being the foreword author of this book. I am grateful to Professor András László Pap, Professor Don Kalb and Professor Elena Trubina for their feedback and genuine involvement in this research at different stages of its completion.

I am most appreciative for support in many areas from my dear friends Rich Reynolds and Deema Annyk, whose assistance in proofreading and providing technical support turned numerous ideas and sketches into a written text.

Successive versions of the arguments were presented to audiences at the University of Helsinki and the University of Tampere in Finland, Columbia University in the US, the University of Ottawa in Canada, Central European University in Hungary, the University of Tallinn and the University of Tartu in Estonia, the UCL

Institute of Education in the UK, Taras Shevchenko National University of Kyiv in Ukraine, and EURAC Research in Italy and Austria. It has been a long, international journey, and I am grateful for all the comments I received on those occasions.

My sincere gratitude goes to my dear friends Lidia Antonova, Ekaterina Netchaeva, Elena Gorskaya, Marina Andretti, Yuriy Shostak, Dmitriy Zamiatin, Dmitriy Kashkan, Natalka Patsuirko, Giorgio Forghieri, Eri Nagai, Anastasia Shmeleva, Iana Kramarovskaia, Sandra Kim, Andrew MacInnis, Guss, and Svetlana Zhikharev. Their support, encouragement and love transcended both time and space, and came as a precious gift of care and lift when needed. The spring of absolute talent and kindness are my deeply loved friends from Estonia and Finland—Kristina Norman, Meelis Muhu, Liisa Kaljula, Natalia Munatajeva, Inga Skucaite, Mark Teramae, Vaslav Skopets, and David Dusseault. I am grateful to these endowed artists, researchers, and foremost, amazing individuals for their love, advice, and sincere compassion for Ukraine.

As I look back at the journey behind this book, I cannot abstain from expressing gratitude to my teachers and mentors who left an immeasurable mark in the formation of my character and my research interests. I record my particular admiration for Professor Peggy Meyer—a person of a tremendous intellectual and human scale, whose knowledge of Eastern Europe, support, and passion for research have always been a beacon. Back in 2002, probably they would not have estimated the importance of their impact on the life of an immigrant arriving in Canada from Ukraine—Ms. Meiyan Yip, Ms. R. Desrochers, Mr. R. Bloudell and Ms. Tatiana Smolina are the teachers who inspired, whose support and care are as unforgettable, as invaluable. I would also like to express deepest gratitude to Dr. Roy Cline and Dr. Donald's family for their immense, infinite impact on my life. For her thoughtfulness, the ability to listen and hear, for being so open and free, my profound gratitude goes to the Education Planning Officer of the University of Helsinki, my dear friend Marjukka Laakso. Her professionalism, energy and sense of humor added to successful completion of this book in countless ways. For years in a row, Ilari Lahtela shared the path of this research with me offering nothing but support, care and love. I am grateful to him for everything he is, for his courageous feedback, patience, and ongoing presence at all stages of this journey and beyond.

I would like to thank my family — people who make expression of gratitude a challenging process, as there are never enough words. I am grateful to my mother Nataliya Ganytska for the lessons she gave me as a teacher, as a woman of strength and a person of unique character. I am thankful to my sister Ilona Souchotte and my brother-in-law Mark Souchotte for their support, their kindness, understanding, for their acceptance and love. Finally, I am grateful to my best friend and inspiration, my father Volodymyr Kutkin. I bow to the extent of his support of my every endeavour, his delicacy, and his tremendous power of will. His unshakable faith in me and my work made this book possible.

For their time, their openness, sincerity and willingness to share what were often very personal stories, I extend special gratitude to all the research participants in Ukraine. They taught to conquer fear through perseverance and faith. Every chapter of this book carries a print of the Ukrainian's voice. I am grateful for every single one of them.

I thank God for placing this research in my life and for paving my path to complete it. It was quite a journey.

Anna Kutkina

Vancouver
June 2021

Introduction

> Pardon me, — the stranger responded gently, — but in order to govern, one needs, after all, to have a precise plan for a certain, at least somewhat decent, length of time. Allow me to ask you, then, how can man govern, if he is not only deprived of the opportunity of making a plan for at least some ridiculously short period, well, say, a thousand years, but cannot even vouch for his own tomorrow?
> — Mikhail Bulgakov, The Master and Margarita

Statistics in the USSR 'knew' everything. It recorded the number of sewing machines, ballerinas, yard keepers, doctors and filmmakers. According to Ilf and Petrov, the only thing that was not known for sure was the number of chairs in the country. However, there was one more sphere outside the statistical control — monuments of Lenin. Gigantic and small, sitting and standing, made of granite and bronze, thousands of Lenin statues penetrated every corner of the vast Soviet land. Basic extrapolation and analysis of the photos of Lenin statues in Russia prior to 1991 indicate that there were a minimum of 7000 monuments and busts of the 'great leader.' At least visually, long-time-gone Lenin continued to 'govern.'

Compared to Russia, where overall there was no in-depth data on cultural objects of the regions, the record of Lenin monuments in Ukraine was conducted more thoroughly. In 1987 the Institute of History of the Academy of Science of the Ukrainian Soviet Socialist Republic published a study — "Monuments of History and Culture of the Ukrainian SSR." This work provided data on all monuments of the republic's regions, both the pre-revolutionary and Soviet. It was stated in the foreword of the manual that there were over 4000 Lenin monuments in the republic. Out of almost 500 Ukrainian regional centres there has never been an official monument of Lenin installed in three western oblasts of Ukraine — Irshave, Volyn, and Shymske. In total, up until 1991 Ukraine has been the country with the highest concentration of communist symbols — over 5500 monuments of Lenin were raised in the cities, towns and villages. Of all Soviet republics, this makes Ukraine the host of the largest number of the 'great leader.' In his analysis of promulgation of communist statues in the USSR, Kudinov (2015) explains high concentration of Lenin monuments in Ukraine by the geopolitical and cultural particularity of the region—its geographical proximity to Europe and the re-occurring attempts of dissociation from the Russian Empire. Another popular explanation of the density of the communist symbols in Ukraine is grounded on the idea that the Soviet authorities implanted Lenin statues as means of ideological control—both physical and discursive reminders of the immortality and omnipresence of the communist rule (Michalsky 1998).

In Ukraine, the figure of Lenin has been a trigger of ambiguous sentiments since the early stages of Sovietization. Himself the symbol of the revolution and struggle against imperialism, Lenin embraces the coloniser, the Soviet Empire or the 'other'—the discursive and ideological formation that obtained particular relevance within the socio-political context of (post)Euromaidan Ukraine. Cleared from his biographical or political ideas, Lenin is nothing but a monument. With the occupation of the Crimean Peninsula and an outbreak of war in Donbas in 2014, however, the narratives on the imperial ambition of the Russian Federation became particularly acute, and with that the figure of Lenin. Popular media and state discourses of the Russian Federation on the necessity of 'restoration of the Slavic brotherhood' and intervention of Russia into domestic affairs of Ukraine propelled the desire for eradication of any form of Russian presence within the socio-political and cultural space of Ukraine. The transformation of the Soviet heritage, thereby, obtained both regional and national scale.

On April 9 2015 the Ukrainian parliament adopted a bill that became known as the "decommunization laws." The law 'On condemning the Communist and National-Socialist totalitarian regimes and prohibiting the use of their symbols' made provision for the removal of all communist monuments and symbols that "glorify functionaries of [the] Soviet totalitarian regime" (Gobert 2016). Inclined to be implemented within six months, the 'Leninfall' took over three years, and was marked by creative modes of adaptation of the statues and their pedestals to regional particularities of 'decolonization.' According to the authors of *Looking for Lenin* (2017),

Niels Ackermann and Sébastien Gobert, "there has been no consistency in handling [the statues]; they have been variously toppled and left unclaimed; stored away by the authorities; broken up or tampered with beyond recognition; or repossessed by hopeful locals." Further questions that arise from this process are on how the communist monuments, as well as empty plinths of the dismantled statues, become canvases for articulation of personal, grassroots messages of both similar and opposing nature, and how the physical space of the statues could be used to address the government, fellow citizens, the Russian aggressor and even Lenin 'himself.'

But before we proceed with further investigation, let us start from the very 'beginning.' The monuments to the leader of the world proletariat were installed as early as during his life, but it is his death that paved the way for "people's" Leniniana — systemic emergence of peculiar and unusual monuments. On January 27 1924 — the day of Lenin's burial, the Second Congress of the Union of SSR published the resolution on the monuments of the leader. Besides the popular slogans on the 'eternal life of Ilych in the minds and hearts of the fellow men and the generations to come,' and 'the heroic fight of the working class over the victory of socialism across the globe,' the resolution required Central Electoral Committee of the USSR to develop and certify projects to the monuments of Lenin in Moscow, Kharkov, Tiflis, Minsk, Leningrad and Tashkent, and set the deadline for their erection (Kudinov 2015). This document provided the foundation for an official, monumental Leniniana that would grow into thousands of stone-bronze Ilych-s sprouting for over 60 years to come.

In the late 1960s, the newspaper "The Soviet Culture" published a note — the pioneers of the Ukrainian SSR discovered a photo that captured the unveiling of the Lenin monument in Zhytomyr on November 7 1922. The photo was delivered with the following text: "Look closely at this image, the reader. What you see is the first-time monumental sculpture of the founding father of the Communist party of the Soviet state." The bust was presented next to the Palace of Labour to honor the fifth anniversary of the revolution. Made of bronze that was received from the soldiers of Nikolai

Shchors's squad who donated their collets and old weapons for the matter, the monument was announced to be the first statue of Lenin in Ukraine.

As was discovered later, however, in spring of 1919 the Kievan newspaper "Bilshovyk" has published a reference to "eight busts of the leaders of the proletariat [to be] installed: the bust to Lenin and Trotsky at the Sofiivska square, the bust to Taras Shevchenko at the former Tsar's square, the bust to Karl Marx at Dumska square, the bust to Sverdlov at Pechersk, the bust to Karl Libknekht at Teatralna square, the bust to Engels at the Vasylkivska Street, and the bust to Rosa Luxemburg at Alexandrovskaya square. However, the busts were not meant to last long. The Denikinites[1] and the Petlurovites[2] destroyed revolutionary art. Shortly after, the "Bilshovyk" would share: "...The revolutionary monuments were chopped with checkers."

According to local press of the time, sculptures and busts of Vladimir Illych were installed in the early 1920s in Kyiv, Dnepropetrovsk, Chernihiv and Sumi right after the formation of the Ukrainian Soviet Socialist Republic. Shortly after, Kharkiv newspaper "The Communist" also announced the installation of the first monument of Lenin designed by the local author Kratko. Another

---

1   The Denikinets were the voluntary soldiers of the Military White Guard Army of General Denikin, who were fighting against the Bolsheviks between 1917 and 1920. The Armed Forces of South Russia were the unified military units of the White movement in southern Russia. Accessed November 18, 2019. Source: https://kremenhistory.org.ua/tag/denikincy/

2   The term 'Petlurovites' was used toward soldiers and commanders of the Ukrainian Army led by a politician and journalist Semen Vasylyovych Peltura. Semen Petliura (1879-1926) was a Ukrainian journalist and politician, the Supreme Commander of the Ukrainian Army and President of the Ukrainian National Republic (1918-1921). A symbol of Ukraine's national struggle for independence for part of the Western Ukrainian diaspora, Petliura and his followers ("Petliurivtsi") are associated with massive acts of violence against the Jewish settlements. According to the Encyclopedia of Ukraine (Paris-New York: 1970), Petliura and his followers committed 307 (25%) of crimes against the Jewish population in Odessa only during 1981-1922, and after the fall of Russian Empire in 1917, attributed a controversial role for connection with the pogroms of the Jewish settlements in other regions of Ukraine. Accessed March 2, 2019. Source: http://www.encyclopediaofukraine.com/display.asp?linkpath=pages %5CP%5CE%5CPetliuraSymon.htm.

monument to Lenin unveiled in his lifetime was the statue in Luhansk—in 1922, it was installed by the train modellist I.P. Borunov. During the Second World War, the statue was sent to Italy to be melted down, where it was stolen and hidden by local partisans until the end of the war. In 1945, it was discovered in the National Gallery of Rome, and was presented to the citizens of Cavriago for Lenin's '100 year birth anniversary.' Back in the days, the citizens of Cavriago passed the resolution in support of "Russian Sovetists" and elected Lenin an honorary mayor of Cavriago (Kudinov 2015).

After his death, the number of Lenin-s skyrocketed—busts, statues and commemoration boards were erected at all corners of the Soviet Union. In 1969 the local newspapers published a series of articles about unique statue installed in Kremenchug:

"It happened in January 1924...The citizens were coming to Dnepr from morning till evening to see the monument of V.I.Lenin, which appeared on ice next to Fantasy island. The plinth, crafted masterly, said: "May you sleep peacefully, dear Illych. We will make your testament come true." The monument was designed by the workers of the Kremenchug port, who collected different photos of Lenin and transformed them into an ice-bust with the help of a self-taught artist. The only problem with the postament was that spring was coming soon. And so the workers decided to commemorate Ilych by collectively joining the party."

By the end of the 1920s-early 1930s, professional sculptors Kozlov, Korolev and Kotikhin created a number of monuments of Lenin that were recommended for mass distribution—the uncontrolled, peoples' Leniniada faded away, launching the beginning of the all-national, involuntary communization. Together with other republics, Ukraine has entered what the historians would call "100 years of fighting for independence"—decades-long wrestling for political and cultural autonomy from Russia.

The studies of American sociologist Ronald Inglehart prove that history matters. In his comparative analysis of the post-Soviet transitioning of Russia and Ukraine, Yaroslav Hrytsak explains the countries' shift in opposite directions by drastically different value systems—"while most Russians choose the survival values, many Ukrainians prefer values that signify self-expression." According to

Hrytsak, this difference has a historical background. As a considerable share of ethnic Ukrainian lands stood outside the Russian sphere of influence and were part of the Polish-Lithuanian Commonwealth, Ukrainians paved their way to a strong tradition of self-governance. It is for this reason that, scholars argue, political patterns that brought to power figures like Stalin or Putin are impossible in Ukraine (Hrytsak 2014; Magocsi 2010; Subtelny 2009). In the same manner, the studies also show that in societies like Russia or Ukraine, the majority can often be indifferent or rather ambivalent, while the directions for development are defined by the motivated minority. In Hrytsak's terms, "to a considerable degree, the Maidan of 2004 [for example] was the revolution of [such a minority or] the middle class" (Hrytsak 2014: 27). Should Yaroslav Hrytsak and Russian filmmaker and writer Andrei Konchalovsky ever have a discussion, there would surely be space for further reflections. In his 2014 interview to BBC News[3], Andrei Konchalovsky explains what he defines as "the two mentalities of Russia and Ukraine" by what he calls "a cultural genome"—the system of priorities a person uses when getting out of bed in the morning and all the way until he or she goes to bed." According to Konchalovsky, the middle class is "not the consumption basket, but is the bourgeoisie—the class that neither Russia nor Ukraine ever had." In this sense, Russia's-Ukraine's diversity may require additional explanation.

As Russian historian Dmitri Furman wrote, "Ukraine passed, if we can say this, an exam for democracy that we [Russians] in reality failed in October of 1993." In other words, it was a peaceful shift in power in the summer of 1994 that distinguished Ukraine from Russia, where the change of the regime arrived with fire and tanks. According to Hrytsak, this difference "played a decisive role in setting Russia and Ukraine in different paths." Whether or not we can 'detect' democracy via the prism of absence or presence of active fighting or violence is yet another question. Perhaps there is more to this point that is worth leaving for a later discussion. Bottom line, the Ukrainian identity, since the time it emerged, was

---

3   Andrei Konchalovsky. Interview. BBC News Russian. Accessed October 2, 2017. Source: https://www.youtube.com/watch?v=h7bvLGaWLCE

linked to language, culture, religion and many other aspects of one's self-identification that were distinctly local and, to some degree, exceeded the boundaries of the political. In Konchalovsky's terms, the battle for Ukraine is as 'natural' as long-last, and will continue "as long as the fight of the Latin and Greek worlds goes on, between Byzantium and Rome." What I am particularly interested in this book is to examine the democratization of Ukraine as a *domestic* phenomenon. In his famous work, *Internal Colonization: Russia's Imperial Experience*, Alexander Etkind traces colonization of many peoples, including Russians, by the Russian Empire that conquered territories and domesticated its own lands. In this book I am devoted to do the opposite—to explore decommunization or self-*de*colonization of Ukraine as an internal phenomenon that is so complex and multilayered as to, oftentimes, remain completely *local*, and yet carry the potential of international, global outcomes.

The 94 Days

In the fall of 2013 the world has once again recalled the word "Ukraine." The protest that became known as the Euromaidan Revolution started on 21st November 2013 as a response to Ukrainian government's decision to suspend signing the Association Agreement between the EU and Ukraine. It became the starting point of a dramatic political, cultural and economic change that affected daily existence of the majority of Ukrainians. Created during the first days of the protest as a name for a Twitter account, the term 'Euromaidan' consists of the two parts—"Euro," an abbreviation for Europe, and "Maidan," a Turkish term for a "square" or, symbolically, "open space." Adopted by Ukrainians during the reign of the Ottoman Empire, the term 'Maidan' became a symbol of the revolution and an ongoing desire of the country to obtain its cultural and socio-economic independence from the Russian reign. The subsequent process of decommunization is the pinnacle of what is recorded in the world's chronicles as a historic statement of Ukraine—the 94 days of the Euromaidan Revolution.

Officially lasting until 23 February 2014—the day when the Ukrainian Parliament voted to impeach President Yanukovych

(Shipenkov and Pelevina 2013: 2), the "Maidan" or "The Revolution of Dignity" claimed the lives of hundreds of people on both sides of the protest, turning into years of rivalry between Russia and Ukraine. Since spring of 2014, the annexation of Crimea by the Russian Federation and war in Donbas remain matters of both national and international dispute and attract the attention of political, media and scholarly public (Allison 2014; Gobert 2017; Mankoff 2014; Robinson 2016; Viatrovych 2015). Irrespective of the discipline—be it sociology, political science, anthropology, economics or art, the existing studies of the aftermath of the 2014 revolution are exceptional in their diversity. They vary from classical discussions of the post-Soviet space as that of "conflicting and confused identities" (Weeks 2014: 61) to those of interpretation of the post-Soviet developments as attempts of the state's "humanization" (Enwezor 2008: 12) or liberation from the Soviet or Russian empire (Shkandrij 2001: 14).

In this book I present the results of extensive fieldwork in different regions of Ukraine as of 2013-2018, as well as ample analysis of academic, media and archival sources that address both Ukraine and the broader post-Soviet space. I examine what I argue to be the core characteristic of (post)Euromaidan Ukraine—*multivocality*. An outcome of research that recorded the Maidan protests live and includes 64 interviews and videos with the protestors, civic activists, politicians, members of non-governmental organizations, soldiers, artists, and ordinary citizens of oftentimes opposing stands, this book explores decommunization as both the political and cultural component of ongoing realities of the revolution and its aftermath. It is both an ethnographic study of particular cities and people, and at the same time, an analysis of the meaning-making process related to national identities. Very simply put, I came to study data that was "raw"—the visual, interview or video material transcribed on the fly. The videos, photos and interviews were recorded in order to analyze the events and their aftermath as they happened live. Eventually, the book developed into a project that examines (post)2013 decommunization taking place at both the regional *and* national level, where the the ordinary citizens' and the government's involvement in diverse forms of the meaning-making—be it political poster exhibitions, preservation or demolition of communist symbols, or renaming of the streets—is a multivocal, sinuous phenomenon.

In her definition of Euromaidan as a space that reflects sociopolitical and cultural composition of Ukraine, the curator and analyst of *Hudrada*, Lada Nakonechna, delineates Maidan as a "multitude of completely *different* people who would never cross paths ordinarily" (Nakonechna 2014: 15). In theoretical terms, the concept of 'borderlands' has been often used to explain the emergence of socio-political and cultural diversity and provide an alternative for re-articulation of the idea of mono-ethnicity or homogeneity of the political and cultural spaces of states like Ukraine. According to Professor of comparative politics Tatiana Zhurzhenko, as for the geopolitically amorphous zones "in between," such as Ukraine, it is rather natural for "borderlands [to] generate hybrid identities and create political, economic and cultural practices that combine different, often mutually exclusive values" (Zhurzhenko 2014: 2). The units situated between the politically and culturally diverse domains, borderlands are associated with multiculturalism and cosmopolitanism. Yet, such qualities of the borderlands pose a practical challenge to governments in power, as, if not being acknowledged at the institutional level, carry potential of threatening the integrity of the state.

Particularly after the Euromaidan revolution, when multiplicity of the grassroots narratives on political and cultural evolution of the state became distinct (*Documenting Maidan* 2014), traditional usage of the concept of 'borderlands' as the theoretical framework that explains construction and weakness of national identity was no longer fully sufficient (Zhurzhenko 2014; Sakwa 2016; Snyder 2014). In her earlier work on formation of Ukraine's socio-political identity, Zhurzhenko argues that geographically close to Russia, Eastern regions of Ukraine have been "politically loyal to the Ukrainian state, [where] many of [the Russian speaking Ukrainians and Russians in eastern Ukraine] were adherent to both the Ukrainian and Russian political stands" (Zhurzhenko 2002: 2). At the same time, many of them neither wanted to accept the imposition of a

Ukrainian cultural identity based on ethnic/linguistic criteria combined with anti-Russian sentiments, nor the opposition of a 'European Ukraine' to an 'Asiatic Russia' (ibid: 2). Twelve years later, as being affirmed by the author of this quote, "every part of this sentence [had to be] reconsidered." During and after the Euromaidan revolution, with the exception of Donbas, broad ideological consensus has emerged among all regions of the country, with the anti-Russian sentiments obtaining the scale of a national rather than regional condition.

In his analysis of (post)Euromaidan Ukraine, Timothy Snyder argues that, facing the undeclared military aggression from the distinctly stronger neighbor—the Russian Federation, as the state of 'borderlands,' Ukraine has turned into 'bloodlands' (Snyder 2017: 4). Forced into circumstances where their lives were put in danger, large populations of cities like Zaporizhzhya, Kharkiv, or Kryvyi Rih opted for the Ukrainian state by "being driven by considerations of safety and fear of violence, inspired by a new sense of patriotism, or led by the pain of national humiliation and by solidarity with those fighting for the nation's territorial integrity" (Zhurzhenko 2014: 3). At the same time, both during and after the revolution, some parts of the population have sympathized with separatists and the Russian Federation. Following Zhurzhenko, they continued to do so in exchange for higher salaries, pensions, or due to political and cultural loyalty to Russia. Back in 2014, when conflict in Donbas was still at its peak, the question on 'how to live together again in one state after the war was over' was one of the most acute ones.

Considering the diversity of socio-political and cultural backgrounds of the participants of the revolution and that of the media, political and academic analysts, dozens of books and academic articles have been published on multiple aspects of Maidan and its aftermath. However, even as years went by, little attention has been paid to specific ways the political and cultural meanings in Ukraine were being constructed. Not to deny the existence of narratives on "termination of military activities in Donbas being one of the primary objectives of "correct" narration of present" (Shevel 2015), the process of de-Sovietization emerged as the dominant legislative and discursive formation of post-Euromaidan Ukraine. Officially, the 'decommunization' or massive elimination of the Soviet heritage from the physical, ideological and mental space of Ukraine has started with toppling of the monument of Lenin in Kyiv on December 8 2013. The toppled and smashed Lenin became the symbol of 'Europeanization,' triggering further acts of detachment from the Soviet legacy such as lustration of the corrupt ruling elites or banning of the Communist Party. It has taken the scale of national reforms that penetrated both the economic and socio-political domain, and affected the physical and cultural topography of Ukraine.

Since the early days of the Euromaidan revolution, the fundamental dilemma was "how to undo the legal, institutional, and mnemonic legacy of the Soviet era that mandates and institutionalizes one 'correct' interpretation of the past without repeating the Soviet approach of mandating one 'correct' interpretation and punishing the public expression of dissenting viewpoints" (Shevel 2015). The possibility of aggravating domestic divisions in Ukraine by alienating the south and east from the rest of the country, passing decommunization laws and establishing anti-Soviet narrative as the only national and legal framework has been acknowledged by both the Ukrainian and international scholars (Cohen 2016; Hartmond 2016; Hitrova 2016; Marples 2018; Soroka 2018). When it comes to taking the Soviet monuments down or renaming the streets, for instance, the studies have shown absence of any sizable public protests against the governmental policies of such kind (Portnov 2017; Shevel 2016; Viatrovych 2015). At the same time, the same studies also affirmed that "there [was] no evidence of the widespread support for decommunization in the Ukrainian society" (Shevel 2016: 3). As such, if one were to trace civic reaction to the official implementation of the 2015 decommunization laws three to four years down the line, neither support nor noticeable public objection to decommunization could be detected. The explanation of what was eventually taking place at the grassroots, ordinary citizens' level, I argue, is largely *missing*.

It always struck me as funny how easily detectable, usually media-broadcasted transformations, how easily they can distract someone who is trying to spot micro processes. The barricades, fallen communist statues, a baseball hat, green and brown tents on Maidan, tents at the borderline war zone, elegant young couples, soldiers, the internally displaced professors and university students from Donetsk, Kryvyi Rih and Crimea, exhausted men drawing casually on a pipe next to the Lenin pedestal, Cossacks with their long moustaches, parents mourning "The Heavenly Hundred,[4]" 'nationalists' marching with photos of Bandera[5], grandparents mourning "notorious Soviet past," volunteers of the ATO[6] bringing victory home, smiling, artists, journalists, more soldiers—this time in the wheelchairs, though, cursing both war and the state...And graffiti, and posters, and slogans and songs..."Ne Tvoja

---

4   The name "Heavenly Hundred" refers to deceased activists whose deaths are connected to the protests on Maidan in Kyiv, from 21 January to 22 February 2014. Volodymyr Kadygrob, #*Euromaidan: History in the Making* (Osnovy Publishing, 2014), 170-171.
5   Stepan Andriyovych Bandera (1 January 1909- 15 October 1959) was a Ukrainian politician, revolutionary and the head of a militant wing of Ukrainian independence movement. He was a leader of the Ukrainian Nationalist Organization (OUN) during and after the Second World War. Within the national context of Ukraine, he is one of the most controversial figures of the country's history. Remembered as a hero primarily in western regions for an attempt to proclaim an independent Ukrainian state, Bandera is seen as a war criminal in central and eastern oblasts. There, he is condemned for collaboration with Nazi Germany and for killing Jews, Russians and other ethnic minorities living on the territory of Ukraine. The 'Banderite' is a term (primarily of negative connotation) used to address the proponents of his figure. Accessed June 2, 2018. Source: /https://www.britannica.com/biography/ Stepan-Bandera.
6   ATO (or Anti-Terrorist Operation) is a term that was introduced by the government of Ukraine to identify Ukrainian military operations on the territory of Donetsk and Luhansk that fell under the control of Russian military forces and pro-Russian separatists. Since 2014, the term 'ATO' has been used by media, publicity and government of Ukraine as well OSCE and other foreign institutions to refer to the military activities in eastern Ukraine. Accessed September 14, 2015. Source: http://uacrisis.org/66558- joint-forces-operation.

Vijna⁷" and "Nas Kynuly⁸"....all in the same space. Eventually, inevitably...at some point one cannot but wonder 'how to make sense of it all?'

Curious about statistics or chronological reports can always find data on the number of communist statues being demolished, streets renamed, marches and protests in favor or against 'Europe' or 'Russia', or rather rarely, both. They can also find criticism of the lack of swift democratic transitioning, or on the contrary, speedy controversial de-Sovietization reforms. What I intend to do with this book is to take a step further by filling in the missing pieces on the nature, content and modes of articulation of the *grassroots* narratives on decommunization. Specifically, it will be shown how the process of regional and national de-Sovietization has taken multiple forms of political expression and can be examined as an integral part of hegemonic meaning-making. To unravel the hegemonic process, I address the regional evolution and articulation of meanings in different areas of Ukraine and reveal the complexity of the meaning-making. The book looks at public events such as posters and photo exhibitions or demolition of communist statues as effective mechanisms for exposing the multivocality of a state which, as the government of Ukraine claims, is being 'unified' in its fight for decommunization.

The theory of hegemony by Ernesto Laclau and Chantal Mouffe (1985), as well as broader intellectual framework of the international relations and historical materialist traditions (Cox 2019; Modelski and Wilkinson 1999; Thompson 2015) addresses hegemony as being "more than dominance" (Cox 2019: 366), and "being

---

7   The song "Ne Tvoya Viyna" ("Not Your War") was released by the Ukrainian rock band, "Okean Elzy," in April 2015. The song is an open statement of condemnation of Russian aggression and war in Donbas. Okean Elzy. "Not Your War." Believe Music. May 2, 2015. Music video, 4:28. https://www.youtube.com/watch?v=xwQpCA3NWyk.

8   "Nas Kynuly" ("We were dumped") is the song of Ukrainian singer, leader of the rock band "Skryabin," Andriy Kuzmenko. The song is a provocative statement toward the government of Ukraine which, as being implied, has "dumped" its people and failed to deliver its promises. Skryabin. "Nas Kynuly." #Скрябін #KuzmaForever #Кузьма. July 20, 2020. Music video, 3:30. https://www.youtube.com/watch?v=o5NH2yKh11M.

born out of conflicts and contradictions in the process of socio-political decay" (Cox 2019: 377). The ground idea of discourse theory—that of the social phenomena being mediated through discourse, with meanings being never permanently fixed, is applied further in this work to examine decommunization as a *broad* array of narratives.

Such theoretical 'reading' of de-Sovietization is particularly relevant if we are to try making sense of diversity. Its purpose is to identify different ways discourses, such as 'Europeanization,' 'de-Sovietization,' or 'Russification,' are part of the meaning-making process that is "never complete" (Cox 2019; Laclau 1985; Thompson 2015). At the same time, if we are to comprehend "heteroglossia" (Bakhtin 1981) or acknowledge the existence of different voices, it is important to examine how the discursive or physical opposition to such discourses—be it oppositional political poster exhibitions or demolition (or preservation) of the Soviet monuments—is counter-hegemonic: how it establishes particular relations and orders of meaning that are of a contesting nature. The hegemonic approach, therefore, would permit us to detect decommunization as a political and cultural struggle over the 'Soviet' past and, potentially, 'European' present and future. This 'struggle,' however, does not imply socio-political or cultural division of the country's population. As will be shown further, it involves articulation of *both* contentious and similar stands, where multiplicity of the socio-political positions is core to the meaning-making. As that of discourse analysis theory, the aim of this book is "not to discover which groups exist within the society" (Rear and Jones 2013), or to unravel particular political formations that object or support decommunization. My primary objective is to examine how the political and cultural diversity of the country's citizens is being articulated and becomes visible within the process of the discursive struggle—within the scope of this work, that of post-Euromaidan decommunization. This 'struggle' or 'contestation,' as we are to see shortly, is a continuous process of meaning-making that is being articulated both during and after the revolutionary transformation of a state. Finally, and most importantly, irrespective of the arguments presented, theories applied or data discussed, the objective is to 'study' and understand people—the Ukrainians, as they are.

1. Theory as 'Hegemonic' Practice

"Let's Talk Politics..."
—V.K.

Rewriting histories and memories is an important process in revolutionary times. Historians and political scientists have been reading these processes from different perspectives. Understanding dominant meaning-making and challenges to it, however, is an intricate task. I chose to 'run' the collected data through the prism of the theory of hegemony by Ernesto Laclau and Chantal Mouffe (1985) to explore transformations visible in political posters, communist monuments or street-naming, and to look at how they operate in different cultural and political contexts of Ukraine.

As the data-gathering process continued and multivocality of the stands on decommunization came apparent, it became important to examine 'de-Sovietization' as a phenomenon that included struggle or contestation of diverse socio-political positions, and, at the same time, did not necessarily imply "dominance" or "supremacy" of one position over the other. According to Arrighi (2010: 365), the theoretical approach of 'hegemony' "could be justified if [it is used] to emphasize the connotation of "leadership": the struggle over the country's past, present or future being that of articulation (or alternation) of both controversial and similar socio-political and cultural stands. Within such a process, the multiplicity of socio-political positions is core to meaning-making, which employs ideological or cultural concept of hegemony as being indicative of a dialogue rather than discursive and physical domination of one discourse (or ideology) over the other.

The Russian literary theorist, semiotician and philosopher, Mikhail Bakhtin, defines 'multivocality' as "co-existence of numerous voices (polyglossia) or socio-political contradictions that intersect and interanimate one another in a single language." When analyzing the collected data, I expanded on such definition of diversity with an objective to add to the theoretical discussion of meaning-making by juxtaposing the mechanisms of hegemonic articulation addressed in the discourse theory of Laclau and Mouffe (1985), and Bakhtin's work on heteroglossia. The idea was to look at how the process of hegemonic meaning-making implies the existence of counter-hegemonic formation that is 'polyglossic' or multivocal (Bakhtin 1981) and is counterposed to 'monologism' or single-thought discourse.

As different elements are being articulated or put together through fixing of meanings (Laclau 1985: 18), the emergence of dialogism (Bakhtin 1981: 28) (or multiple socio-political stands) at particular points carries a tendency of producing and explaining the socio-political and cultural transformations. This is an important addition to discourse theory that easily overlooks the question of change. When it comes to examining multiple forms of decommunization, the process that includes such measures aims towards dismantling the communist legacy of states, governments, cultures, and even the citizens' mentalities. As we are to examine further, the process of (post)Euromaidan decommunization is the hegemonic practice that is rather complex — an endeavor that forms particular relations and sequence of meanings within physical and political space.

While hegemony is about generation and maintenance of political order, it is also about challenging it — the counter-hegemony. An attempt to establish particular relations and orders of meanings, hegemonic formation presupposes existence of counter-hegemonic construction which is characterized by the contesting nature of the meaning-making process. In other words, if hegemony is deeply grounded, then counter-hegemony is addressing these grounds. Within such a framework, a multiplicity of meanings is feasible, as the process of construction of counter-hegemonic formation involves articulation of potentially diverse, both similar and contentious stands. For Laclau (1985), 'articulation' comprises the connection of possible constituents of meaning (or 'elements'), with the result that meaning arises and that these constituents become what he calls 'moments' — "signs that have their meaning fixed by discourse" (Rear and Jones 2013: 8). In other words, as an array of discourses, each structuring reality in a particular way, compete to define what is 'true' within a particular aspect of the social world (ibid: 5), meanings are being altered and reconstructed.

To address an 'outcome' of construction of hegemonic and counter-hegemonic formations within the physical and discursive space — graffiti, monuments, street names, or political poster exhibitions, for instance, I expanded on Benedict Anderson's (1983) classical theory of the 'imagined communities.' For Anderson (1991: 6), a nation is 'imagined' because "the members of even the smallest nation will never know most of their fellow members, meet them, or even hear of them, yet in the minds of each lives the image of their communion." When analysing the collected data, there emerged the necessity for examining multiple modes of articulation of the imaginings. I narrowed the point of the departure from 'nation' (Anderson 1983: 7) and looked at construction of the 'imagined communities' at different levels of the state, be it that of the government or the elites, or that of the ordinary citizens. The hegemonic meaning-making, further on, implies the existence of counter-hegemonic formations that are 'polyglossic' (Bakhtin 1981) by nature of the diversity of people's opinions.

From the perspective of politics of the meaning-making, the articulation of hegemonic formations (Laclau and Mouffe 1985; Modelski 2015; Overbeek 2019) affect (or define) the daily existence of a state's citizens. For Laclau, 'articulation' comprises the connection of possible constituents of meaning (he calls 'elements') with the result that meaning arises and that these constituents become what he calls 'moments.' Within the context of cultural studies, for instance, an example of articulation would be "the formation of a methodological framework for understanding of what a cultural study does" (Slack 2012: 18). On the other hand, Slack argues, articulation also "provides strategies for undertaking a cultural or political study" and serves as a way for contextualizing the object of the analysis. In her discussion of social reality as being constituted by an ongoing struggle over meaning, Mouffe (1985: 98) defines 'hegemony' as "the practice of articulation through which given order is created and meanings of social institutions are fixed." According to Laclau and Mouffe (1985: 105), further on, *articulation* is a "practice [that establishes] relations among elements such that their identity is modified." The renaming of streets or demolition (or preservation) of monuments that I observed throughout my fieldwork is an example of such articulation, where the government or the citizens have been using different objects of urban space to present their political and cultural stands on the past, present and, potentially, future. In this sense, the concept of *articulation* was particularly relevant, as it allowed the theoretical framework for examination of multiple modes of decommunization, which in itself was a continuously altering phenomenon.

In his analysis of *articulation* as a practice that both establishes a relation among elements and also modifies their identity, Torfing (1999: 101) argues that "the articulation of discursive elements into contingent moments within a hegemonic discourse takes place in a conflictual terrain of power and resistance, and will, therefore, always include an element of force and repression." Within the framework of data I collected, Torfing's acknowledgement of 'repression' or contestation as being part of the articulation process has certainly proven to be true. While different discourses remain part of the meaning-making process, in our case—those of Europeanization or decommunization, they operate in the political space of the state and have proven to be the powerful mechanisms of articulation of both the dialogue *and* discrepancy between the citizens and the government. If one puts all elements together, hegemony could be defined further as "the expansion of a discourse, or set of discourses, into a dominant horizon of social orientation and action by means of articulating unfixed elements into partially fixed moments in a context crisscrossed by antagonistic forces" (Torfing 1991: 101).

Within the field of discursivity, Palonen argues, "antagonisms or heterogeneity is the underlying condition of the meaning-making process" (Palonen 2018: 101). Political articulations simplify this heterogeneous space by establishing a connection between different elements and generating new meanings and dominant narratives and hegemonic formations. Furtheron, discourses are the articulated set of elements (Read and Johnes, 2013: 4) that construct a hegemonic horizon within the process of contestation. Finally, the discursive construction is further defined as the one where meanings are generated relationally through articulation: according to Read and Johnes, it is a product of meaning-making on an uneven ground. At heart there is, however, the underlying heterogeneity. Changing of the street names in Budapest or Ukraine, for instance, is one of the many examples of such meaning-making, where "layering of the political discourses upon [the country's] landscape is done by powerful social actors and groups with relational ties to the past and future eras" (Palonen 2018: 2). It involves the construction of the hegemonic horizon that is indicative of the ideological transformations of the period (Azaryahu 1996), as well as generation of a discursive universe (Palonen 2018).

Broadly speaking, according to Gramsci (1971: 55), there exist two forms of hegemony: *transformist* and *expansive* hegemony. Construction of nationality in such a way that preserves the hegemony of the ruling group while including cultural features from the subordinated groups to ensure their loyalty is an example of transformist hegemony. The successful creation of "a collective national-popular will" is the expansive hegemony. According to Torfing, both forms of hegemony involve the process of revolution-restoration — the political renewal that carries potential for a revolution being an attribute of expansive hegemony. Collecting data, I focused on application (or 'testing') of the second, expansive form of hegemony within the context of post-Euromaidan Ukraine. Here, the hegemonic reading of the data provided a model for explaining the formation of a collective will within a heterogeneous state. "An offensive strategy for building an active consensus to mobilize the masses in a revolution" (Torfing 1999: 111), expansive hegemony contains both an ideological and a political scheme which allows the evolution of particular civic demands and the expression of similarities they expose (Gramsci 1971: 132). Within the expansion of the hegemonic process, contiguity between discursive elements is obtained through re-articulation of meanings. The phenomenon of 're-definition' of nationalist symbols or groups as the discursive and physical elements of democratic transitioning of a (post)revolutionary state, for instance, is one of the examples of such hegemonic formation: it involves re-articulation of meanings to allow integration of particular citizens' (or governmental) stands.

To be added further, the Laclau-Mouffean, post-Gramscian definition of hegemony is especially valid for analysis of the processes of the re-articulation of a country's 'self' and the 'other.' Inspired by the work of Laclau and Mouffe (1996: 32), Kevin DeLuca (1999: 18) writes that "in a world without foundations, without given meanings, the concept of articulation is the means for understanding the struggle to fix meaning and define reality temporarily." Such definition of articulation is particularly important, as the process of re-articulation of the citizens' views of the past, present and future takes place through interaction and 're-construction' of multiple elements in their surroundings—monuments, political posters, or the street names.

It should also be noted that in cases such as the disintegration of a colony or an empire, hegemonic (re)articulation takes place within a rather compressed time-frame, and is often accompanied by conflict or confrontation—be it a revolution, a civil war, or any other form of the socio-political turmoil. In such terms, the reconciliation requires additional susceptibility which includes acknowledgement of the existence of *multiple* rather than homogenous stands—discourses that are *heterogeneous* in their cultural and socio-political nature. As such, this process consists of a number of discursive formations that are reflective of *multivocality* of the population. At the administrative level, however, as I illustrate when we move to discussing the data, hegemonic formations carry the potential of being limited in presentation of unilateral rather than multiple socio-political strata. Within the state where the government restrains from acknowledgement of the grassroots political and cultural multivocality, the hegemonic formations may imply further necessity of re-evaluation of regional and national policies to create social space for institutionalization of diversity.

Conventionally, after political alterations like revolutions or the collapse of an empire, we can observe hegemonic articulations emerging in diverse discursive and physical forms. They vary from graffiti, posters or monuments to laying scientific foundations for public meetings, conferences or exhibitions. The public domain of such nature provides space for establishment of heterogeneous meanings. As soon as such visual (or ideological) elements engage with the state's political or cultural context, there arises ongoing struggle over meanings — be it the definition of modern 'nation,' the 'hero,' the 'patriot,' the 'colony' or the 'colonized,' the 'self' or the 'other.' In the Laclauian perspective, the articulation of meanings is taking place in constant juxtaposition of one element against the other and, to a certain extent, even within exclusion of certain elements in the name of justification of the commonly approved political stands — for instance, banning of the Soviet symbols as means of 'Europeanization' of the state. As has been the case with the post-Soviet space, the forms of embodiment of such elements are rather diverse, and vary from a critical article, poster, or piece of intellectual property to an open protest or, on the contrary, refusal to participate in a public protest as a statement of silent demonstration. The articulation of meanings, therefore, extends beyond a particular linguistic, cultural or socio-economic group.

To some extent, the policies, departments, routines, procedures, rituals or hierarchies, therefore, may all seem insignificant at face value. However, it is the process of change of such social units that often mobilizes particular response — the government's support of discursive frameworks that goes along with existing political narrative, and its disapproval of the one objecting an individual or groups in power. This signals the importance of further analysis of the relation between discourse and affect, as well as location of hegemonic construction to involve the question on what socio-political scenarios are at work within a particular process such as that of decommunization.

In her critical stance on exploring the changing conditions of hegemony and counter-hegemony in 'postmodern and globalized times,' Carroll argues that "the process of articulation becomes more important than that which is being articulated" (Carroll 2011: 5). As concrete hegemonic projects emerge out of articulation of interests of different social groups, the process of hegemonic meaning-making carries a sense of socio-political and/or cultural accomplishment. Such sense of 'realization,' Carroll asserts further, is one of the primary factors that bears potential of making the meaning-making more significant than the final product of articulation. Within a context where the change of political, economic or cultural directories occurs as articulation of intact hegemonic constructions, however, "the perception of the term counter-hegemony as complementary to hegemony," according to Carroll, is misleading. It is delusive because there is an asymmetry between the two—hegemony and counter-hegemony, which is rooted in different forms of power that are at stake. As long as "power-over is sustained through an effective blending of persuasion and coercion, Holloway argues further, hegemony remains intact" (Holloway 2005: 2). Occurring in either direct or veiled opposition to the aspects of dominant hegemony, the counter-hegemonic struggle takes place through the oppositional politics that vary from global justice movements to local, regional revolutions. At its core, what may seem as the "celebration of fragments in a politics of difference...articulation of counter-hegemonic formations unravels the negation of closure, where fixation of homogeneity is opposed" (Kebede 2005: 12). Ideally, in practical terms, as social solidarity and political unity depend on both the ordinary citizens and the state, the articulation of similarities is to construct the baseline of the political meaning-making.

Finally, in "Universalism, Particularism and the Question of Identity," Laclau argues that "originally the societies were far more homogeneous than the present ones" (Laclau 1995: 106). For over twenty years, the claim of heterogenization of the society has maintained its relevance: the process of meaning-making, that can be observed in multiple cases of demolition of objects of urban or rural spaces, change of visual signs of discursive articulation, such as change of the street names, or installation of the political poster exhibitions, is the discursive struggle of diversity of meanings. "Different political groupings are differentiated from one another (and differentiate themselves from one another) through evaluations of the national past," Palonen (2008: 219) argues, and, I would insist further, the present, and potentially the future. As we are to examine shortly, the discursive struggle is taking place at different administrative and civic (ordinary citizens) levels, where both the discursive and physical elements compile contestation. "Street names and statues [for instance] undergo a similar process as political discourses that are created and sedimented through practices of inclusion and exclusion and inscribed through key elements" (Laclau 1990, 2005; Palonen 2006, 2008; Modelski 2018). According to Robinson, through acts of naming or renaming, construction or demolition, both the population and the government are engaged in political acts that ultimately "carry no unified medium" (Robinson 2011: 7). Rather, it is an affluence of diverse social languages—both the discursive and physical ground for multivocality or, as Bakhtin defines it, *heteroglossia* (Bakhtin 1970: 14).

Constructing Multivocality

When we come to examining decommunization as a multivocal rather than solely uniform phenomenon, Bakhtin's reading of the single-thought discourse or 'monologism' as an integral part of the 'dialogical principle' is particularly timely. Homophony, or single-voice, is "the one transcendental perspective or consciousness that integrates all signifying practices, ideologies, values and desires that are deemed significant" (Robinson 2011: 39). According to Bakhtin, in a monological world, the subjects have value only in relation to the dominant, transcendent perspective. They are reduced to the status of objects by means of not having rights as to be recognized as a separate, independent consciousness. Within such a framework, the 'truth' is being constructed abstractly and from the dominant perspective that creates a horizon of meaning that excludes the possibility of articulation of autonomous voices. Such a process leads to discursive elimination or 'death' of the other who is unheard and exists in a state of non-being. In his examination of the origins of monologism, Bakhtin provides the example of novels where characters exist exclusively to articulate the author's ideology. The characters are deprived of their distinct voices and are used by the author as a tool for establishment of a single-tone, 'flat' narrative. Taken beyond the exclusively literary circles, the scheme of monologism is applicable for a broader socio-political context of hegemonic political meaning-making. According to Bakhtin, "the closure of recognition and public articulation of different voices is that of language that [becomes] associated with nationalism" (Bakhtin 1981: 18). Such tendencies of centralization of the discursive formations and the neglect of multivocality are counterposed to construction of the linguistic or socio-political diversity.

As discursive and ideological contrast, *dialogism*, further on, countervails the establishment and implementation of monologism. Its primary characteristic, referred to by Bakhtin as 'double-voiced' or 'multi-voiced,' is the recognition of multiplicity of voices and citizens' perspectives. In literary terms, dialogism is present in a novel when each character has his or her "final word and relates to and interacts with [that] of the other character" (Robinson 2011: 42). Importantly, the discourse does not simply unfold, but rather interacts, leaving space for articulation of the multiple into a *multivocal* discursive construction. Within the framework of theories such as 'discourse analysis,' dialogism is seen as a mechanism or a scheme for construction of heterogeneous hegemonic formations — the street names, political posters, or multiple modes of toppling/or preservation of monuments that serve as physical and discursive space for articulation of diverse socio-political and cultural stands of both the citizens and the government are but a few examples of such phenomenon. In its nature, the dialogical process transcends both voice and time uniformity. It engages with and is formed by the voices of others; it obtains meanings from both the present and the past, and uses the history to articulate and construct within both the private and public domain. As means of construction of cultural and socio-political strata that is sensitive to diversity, the dialogical discourse requires not only acknowledgement, but also the interaction of 'differences.' Following Laclau and Mouffe, it is designed to generate participation and response and has a polemical quality of resisting a 'closure' — "the temporary interruption in the fluctuation of meanings" (Laclau and Mouffe 1985: 104).

For Bakhtin, all signifying practices, be it the use of language or symbols, have an ultimately dialogical objective. "Human consciousness is not a unified entity, but rather is always conflict-ridden between different consciousnesses" (Robinson 2011: 42). What emerges as a ground claim of Bakhtin's theory of dialogism is that it does not only provide space for discursive articulation of differences; if being applied within a particular political or cultural framework (such as that of Ukraine, for instance), dialogism implies practical implications of giving a particular voice — the discursive or political space — to the standpoints of many. Therefore, it assumes creation of a society that is fundamentally irreducible to dominance of the one over the many. As Robinson illustrates in his analysis of Bakhtin's *Problems of Dostoevsky's Poetics*, "[dialogism] denies the possibility of transcendence of difference...separateness and simultaneity are permanently with us" (Robinson 2011: 43). Within such a context, meanings are being established within the process of contestation, where engagement into a dialogue is the primary context for construction of a socially inclusive world-view.

In *Problems of Dostoevsky's Poetics*, Bakhtin develops the concept of *polyphony* that informs much of his literary and political work. Literally meaning multiple voices, *polyphony* develops into a single perspective that acknowledges the existence of different voices that are not subordinated to the voice of the author (be that an author of a literary work or a political leader or entity). In its basic terms, the process of the discursive struggle implies the existence of more than one voice. In *The Dialogic Imagination*, Bakhtin expands the concept of dialogism into that of *heteroglossia*. In his essays, the emphasis is made on the conjunction of diverse speech-genres. Each novel is composed in different styles to assemble multiple voices into a single text. The monological view of a novel, or a particular narration of the text is turned into a combination of diverse perspectives because, Bakhtin argues, "the language which is used has been borrowed from others." The novelistic 'scale' of heteroglossia and the discursive struggle is also the feature of the socio-political and cultural space that discloses both history and present.

For Bakhtin, the view of language as a closed system is problematic, since he sees the creation of a unified language, for instance, as a vehicle for centralization of power. By elevating a particular language to the status of 'national' or 'international' (such as English within the colonial context, for example), there occurs a suppression of heteroglossia of multiple everyday speech types (or socio-political stands) by hegemonization of a particular language (or ideology).

What we can extract from Bakhtin's theory as essentially valuable is the idea of centralizing tendencies being the process that counterposes diversity. It can be applied for examining what I argue to be the construction of the homogeneous hegemonic formation, as well as articulation of heterogeneous hegemonic domain. Articulated by the state, monologism (or homogeneous hegemonic formation) co-exists 'in line' with heteroglossia—the multivocal counter-hegemonic construction of the diverse citizens' voices. For Bakhtin, it is heteroglossia that construes the foundation of socio-political and cultural existence of the state. In broader historical terms, "monoglossic dominance is doomed to be ruptured by the return of heteroglossia, as the dominant discourse is interrupted by multiple voices of the people" (Robinson 2011: 45). As such, for the social ways of expression to occur via peaceful means, though contested and changing, the *dialogue* is the primary form for articulation of meanings.

In his analysis of history, Bakhtin uses the theory of "monologism versus heteroglossia," where he argues that "it is the emergence of dialogism at particular points of the state's course that produces cultural revolutions" (Bakhtin 1981: 15). As I examine further in more detail, the expression of multivocality within a point when the state occupies or imposes the position of monologism, in our case—Russia's dominance over Ukraine, provokes not only cultural, but also socio-political transformations. Within such a process, old forms of physical or discursive formations are given new meanings, while new social relations produce new forms of speech (or re-construct the old ones). Not necessarily new, the physical objects of daily existence, such as monuments or street names are given new meanings via articulation of particular, at times diverse, discourses into a regional (or national) hegemonic formation. Not necessarily the complementary truths, different perspectives produce new realities and novel ways of seeing. Here, according to Robinson, "it is incommensurability which gives dialogue its power."

The 'Imagined Community'

Finally, when it comes to examining the process of nation-building and the construction of the 'other,' for Benedict Anderson, the point of departure is that of "nationality, as well as nationalism and its cultural artifacts of a particular kind" (Anderson 1983: 6). The creation of such artifacts is an outcome of spontaneous abstraction of aggregated historical forces that eventually merge into ideological or physical entities for defining socio-cultural and political context of the state. In an anthropological spirit, Anderson defines a nation as "an imagined political community," where the majority of its members will never intersect or meet during their lifetime, and where yet "in the minds of each lives the image of their communion." Though indirectly, the nation is also imagined as limited due to its "finite, if elastic, boundaries" (Anderson 1983: 8). Within the scope of my research, I addressed the 'imagined communities' as the construction of both physical and cultural (discursive) space, as well as the result of the meaning-making process.

Anderson's concept of 'imagined communities' has become a major reference point within a broad spectrum of studies including sociology, nationalism, political science and geography (Anthony D. Smith 1991; Crang 1998; Gupta and Ferguson 1992; Massey and Jess 1995). In his analysis of Anderson's work, Anthony Smith pays particular attention to the general theoretical implication of Anderson's theory, where he argues that the discursive selection of the article 'the' instead of 'a' particular nation is what lays the primary foundation for the 'nation' as a theoretical, broadly applied concept (Smith 1991: 16). Articulation of social space as 'the' imagined community, therefore, "provides the foundation for addressing specific nationalist imaginings within both regional and international politics" (Derian 1993: 7). Finally, another step forward in providing the hypothesis for Anderson's use of the term 'nation' instead of 'state,' according to Smith, is the premise for Anderson's use of the term 'nation' instead of 'state.' For Smith, "it is not intended to suggest that the nation is the most definitive feature of the international system, but rather that it is an important one" (Smith 1991: 12). In such a stance, the nation 'grants' the basis for theoretical examination because it embodies individuals of diverse cultural or socio-political backgrounds who are to be represented by the state. The term is also constructing a broader spatial and time domain, where examination of a particular political system and its members could be conducted based on multiple identities shaped within a wide range of historical contexts.

Within the scope of international relations, Nikos Papastergiadis (1992: 2) refers to the work of Homi Bhabha (1990: 4), who addresses the concept of the 'nation' as to also underline the existence of cultural differences and construction of otherness in the post-colonial realm. In broader terms, according to Bhabha, the nation serves as an arena for expression of multiple forms of power relations, be it class or gender, as well as political principles, such as democracy or sovereignty. Within its physical and discursive scope, the nation is also the space for articulation of "hybrid identities" that are expressed via articulation of cultural supremacy or sovereignty (Bhabha 1990). Such "hybrid identities," Bhabha argues further, "deploy the particular culture from which the identities emerge to construct visions of a [modern] community, and versions of [the state's] history" (ibid: 212). If being juxtaposed to Anderson's definition of nation as being confined due to its "finite boundaries," Bhabha's conception of a nation, therefore, is a 'soft' one: it challenges Anderson's rendering of 'nation' and the 'imagined communities' by addressing 'nation' as a political and cultural space that is rather liquid and is open for diversity or "negotiation" of meanings of nation.

Upon further analysis of the existing critiques of Anderson's work, extensive 'geographical' application of his assertions is few. For instance, Blaut (1989) does not address Anderson's work in his analysis of Marxist theories of nationalism, and Short's (1991) *Imag-*

ined Country refers to Anderson's *Imagined Communities* as an additional reading (Barnes 2001: 16). One of the major criticisms of Anderson's work comes along the lines of his "failure to fully acknowledge or develop the implications of mobility, space and nation" (Radcliffe and Westwood 1996: 118). One of the most vocal critics of Anderson's arguments are also the postcolonial scholars who assert that Anderson is 'too linear in his explanation [of how] the political structures and institutions change from dynasties to sovereign nations through the standardized influence of print capitalism' (Said 1993; McClintock 1995). To add to existing debates, an Indian political scientist and anthropologist, Partha Chatterjee addresses the limitedness of the imagined communities by primarily European colonialism (Chatterjee 1993: 24). Nationalism and nations, Chatterjee argues, "operate only within borders articulated in Europe, and thus can only be conceptualized within the European structures." Following such a narrative, anti-colonial nationalisms oppose colonial nationalism using similar nationalist arguments. According to Chatterjee, anti-colonial nationalism could only be imaged through cultural practices. While acknowledging its importance, he challenges Anderson's definition of the processes of print capitalism as a standardized language, and argues on limitations of using such approach within the context of rather multilingual, diverse societies of the post-colonial space.

Finally, prominent critique of Anderson's work is presented by Don Mitchell who pays particular attention to definition of the concept of 'nation':

The questions that [arise] are ones about who defines the nation, how it is defined, how that definition is reproduced and contested, and, crucially, how the nation has developed and changed over time...The question is not what common imagination exists, but what common imagination is forged (Mitchell, 2000: 269).

In his work on discourse theory, Torfing (1999: 193) argues that "the homogenization and substantialization of the national space will take the form of a number of predicative statements defining what the nation is." At the same time, he continues, "the true essence of the nation escapes predication" (ibid: 194). The process of homogenization of the nation is taking place through discursive construction of the 'enemies of the nation,' which are simultaneously outside and inside the nation. Within the political and cultural context of (post)Euromaidan Ukraine, not only the symbols of 'the other,' or the oppressor, such as monuments of the communist regime, but also the concept of the 'nation' is being re-articulated. As I examine further in more detail, the homogenization and substantialization of the 'nation' includes reduction of difference to sameness, and this is what Torfing argues to be a defining feature of the nationalist discourse.

Countries such as Ukraine, in other words, could be seen as the example of homogenization of the nation, where both present and historical context of the state contains multiple instances of institutional reduction of cultural, linguistic or political distinctions to uniformity. If read within the theoretical framework of Bakhtin's 'monologism' theory (or single-thought discourse), the state is the 'voice' that articulates one transcendental perspective into the entire field, or the ordinary public. The socio-political consequences of such practice are often aggravated by the nationalist rhetoric, and vary from civic discontent to arrant military activities, or the legislative policies of decommunization.

The revolutionary events of countries in transition bring us abruptly face to face with the significance and applicability of Anderson's theory within the context of political evolution of the post-Soviet states. For instance, when it comes to explaining enthusiasm of the ordinary citizens' willingness to die for territorial integrity of their country (e.g. Ukrainians and the military conflict in Donbas), Anderson argues that "secular transformation of fatality into continuity, contingency into meaning is what justifies and *promotes* the salvation" (Anderson 1983: 11). If, as Anderson points, "nation-states are widely conceded to be 'new' and 'historical,' the nations to which they give political expression always loom out of an immortal past, and, still more important, glide into a limitless future" (ibid: 12). Though unofficially, such logic of turning chance into destiny—construction of meanings for present and future that is either based on the 'glorious' past or is liberated from the 'oppressive' elements of the present is what composes the backbone for justification of sacrifice for countries involved in armed conflict.

As Debray recounts, "yes, it is quite accidental that I am born French; but after all, France is eternal" (Debray 1988: 16). The same statement could be applied to any other state. Such narrative, endowing of uncontrolled elements of life such as place of birth, for instance, with power of predetermination of one's destiny, is commonly used by the governments as means of hegemonic establishment. The process of articulation is taking place in order to create a solid order and meaning of social institution that is fixed (Laclau 2005). Through multiple forms of articulation—political posters, toppling of the communist monuments or re-naming of the streets, for example, the 'new' political formation is being created, be it the local community or the nation as such. While the process of actual meaning-making that leads to construction of hegemony involves real acts of physical interaction with objects of political art, architecture, or cities' topoi, the final outcomes of such manipulations coin a rather phantomic, illusionary formation or the 'imagined community(ies).' Within this process, "tracing the specificity of the particular discourses introduced into the city-text" (Palonen 2018) could be one of the modes of analysis of the hegemonic formation. Another would be to identify specific mechanisms that transform the process of meaning-making into that of an ongoing compromise—the emergence of *dialogism* as means of producing socio-political alteration.

Bridging

To conclude, the process of dialogue, not only the strictly human one, but also that of interaction with objects of one's surrounding (e.g. demolition or preservation of communist symbols) is an essential element of the meaning-making process. To exist, it requires engagement of multiple voices, positions and subjects. It is the phenomenon that transforms people and carries the potential of producing physical (e.g. topographic) changes.

Analysis of a broader array of academic literature that deals with the concept of hegemony and the process of meaning-making unravels varied intellectual traditions. The fields of intellectual practices involve world-systems analysis, historical materialism, or international relations, to name a few. On the basis of an ongoing dialogue, scholars in the field strive to add to existing 'classics' of hegemony (Gramsci 1971; Laclau and Mouffe 1985) to facilitate its common understanding. In his "Approaches from a Historical Materialist Tradition," Robert Cox (2019), for instance, aligns with traditional definition of hegemony as "[being] never complete" (Laclau 1985). At the same time, he also argues that "there is always some opposition provoked by a hegemonic order, [where] some contradictions generated from within lead to its transformation" (Cox 2019: 366). For Cox, as well as other academics contributing to socio-political and cultural understanding of social change through the prism of hegemony (e.g. Chase-Dunn 2018; Gills 1994; Thompson 2015), "historically transitory nature of a hegemonic order relates to the success with which a dominant structure of power [generates] a condition of acquiescence over a vast range of the order that it is in fact...dominating." In their further examination of the nature of hegemony, followers of the historical materialist tradition, for instance, define hegemony as a 'quality of a whole, not just a relationship among the parts' (Cox 2019; Chase-Dunn 2018; Thompson 2015). For them, hegemony is more than just dominance. It is an "internalized coherence...that has been transformed into an intersubjectively constituted reality" (Cox 2019: 337). According to Destradi, within a broader domain of international relations, the term 'hegemony' is also used as synonymous to that of 'empire' (Destradi 2010: 909). Such practicum, however, makes an unequivocal identification for meaning particularly problematic (Destradi 2010; Krasner 2001).

In this book, my intention is to examine decommunization to address an existing manner of equalization 'hegemony' and 'empire.' I suggest to apply both classical analysis of 'hegemony' discussed above (Laclau and Mouffe 1985) and that of a broader theoretical framework (international relations or culture studies, e.g. Cox 2019; Destradi 2010; Hardt 2000) to explore meaning-making of states in transition—in our case, Ukraine. The definition of hegemony as a 'process that is never complete' is used as a common reference point between the school of discourse analysis and wider theoretical approaches that examine hegemony as a relationship of 'dominance' and 'subordination' (Bussmann and Oneal 2007; Cox 2019; Knorr 1985; Rapkin 2005). Here, I emphasize the transitory nature of hegemonic formations as being the ground condition for the socio-political and cultural changes within a state. The 'other' or the 'empire,' as I illustrate further, serves as an integral component and point of reference that both comprises *and* stimulates the process of meaning-making.

In the preceding discussion, theoretical parallels were drawn between the theory of discourse analysis, Bakhtin's (1981) theory of heteroglossia (and monologism) and that of Anderson's (1983) 'imagined communities.' According to Bakhtin (1981: 12), "the entire world can be viewed as polyglossic or multi-voiced since every individual possesses their own unique worldview which must be taken into consideration through dialogical interaction." He argues further that "different worldviews eventually condition one another and turn into a process which produces change through creative elaboration by ways of new and different meanings" (Bakhtin 1981: 271). It is important to note that within the framework of coexistence of multiple voices within one state, the concept of hegemony not only refers to the privileged position of a nation-state or a group, but becomes a broader construction of multiple discursive formations. The concept of monologism (Bakhtin 1981: 8) could be used further in parallel with that of a homogeneous hegemonic formation. Dialogism, on the other hand, could be juxtaposed with heterogeneous hegemonic construction that, I argue, is being formed through multiple forms of socio-political and cultural dialogue. As a step further, a dialogue can then produce a discursive response that originates actual social changes.

The task of bridging heterogeneous elements into a potentially consummated whole is the one Bakhtin, as well as Laclau and Mouffe, Destradi or Cox aim at resolving at various levels. This chapter addressed the theoretical background of the 'evolution' of multivocality — the meaning-making process that ranges from monologism to heteroglossia, the hegemonic to counter-hegemonic formation. In a broader conceptual framework, the juxtaposition of monologism to polyphony, or homogeneity to heterogeneity, could be seen as the interlocative correlation between 'I' and the 'other.'

Such interaction (or lack of such) occurs within the space of lived experiences, where establishment of the hegemonic reading remains a personal, interpretative act. It occurs through articulation and fixing of meanings — putting different elements of history, present and the potential future together. Within such a process, despite the necessity and possible desire of both individuals and the public (or state) to create a uniform, mutually-inclusive formation, it is important to remember contestation as an integral component of the meaning-making.

In the following chapters, we take off with analysis of both the informal and authorized procedure of eradication of the Soviet past from the physical and discursive space of Ukraine — decommunization — through the prism of resolving such 'tension' between homogeneity and heterogeneity, hegemony and multivocality. As we are to recall, the process of hegemonic meaning-making implies the existence of articulative operations that seek to provide fixation of a discursive field. In the case of post-Euromaidan Ukraine, decommunization is akin to decolonization. It could be seen as a hegemonic construction to the extent that it manages to redefine the terms of state-relations and set a new agenda for specific political formations, similar to those of other post-Soviets states. Identification and further juxtaposition of ordinary citizens' and government's narratives, as well as multiple processes of interaction with objects of national past, require implementation of dialogism as the effort of understanding, as "the active reception of speech [and action] of the other" (Voloshinov 1996: 45).

Ultimately, from the critical point of view, Anderson's take on nationalism as unifying a nation instead of allowing nation's multiple meanings has been acknowledged as being potentially single-minded. Whereas the question of "what common imagination exists" endures (Anderson 1983; Mitchell 2000), examination of reproduction and contestation of the 'imagined communities' is essential for further analysis of development and transformation of nation over time. In the case of Ukraine, the concept of a 'new nation' is being constructed around the 'other' — the Soviet state and that of the modern Russian Federation. The process of meaning-making emerges into hegemonic (and counter-hegemonic) formations that take multiple forms and range from toppling (or preservation) of communist statues to re-naming of streets or exhibitions of political posters. But before we proceed with empirical analysis of (post)2013 decommunization, I suggest addressing the existing debates on the postcolonial status of Ukraine together with discussing the conceptual basis of post-Euromaidan de-Sovietization.

2. The Postcolonial Soviet

> "Get up! My honey, get up!
> My honey, get up! My honey, get up!
> Come on! My dear, come on! My dear, come on!
> Demand more!"
> —Okean Elzy, "Vstavai"/"Get up"

In postcolonial studies, the term 'postcolonial' implies a set of transformative political practices, ideas and ways of thinking and doing that involve deeply considered engagement with the experience of colonialism and its past and present effects — political, economic or cultural legacy of an empire. In this context, the process of decommunization can be seen as a form of the post-colonial transformation, where 'othering' is an integral component of the hegemonic formations. Multiple overlapping of discourses and contestation of meanings occur within contexts that reflect both private (the ordinary citizens') and public (the state's) engagement with the past as a means of shaping the country's present and future.

As the spread of colonialism often implies violence and physical or ideological (cultural) coercion, the process of decolonization can be erratic and equally traumatic. The intention of this chapter is to present the analysis of the academic discussion of decommunization as a phenomenon of socio-political and cultural transformation of the state, where the process of decommunization or 'de-Sovietization' includes multiple forms of articulation of the 'colonial other.' It varies from the official legislative reforms, such as the 2015 decommunization laws in Ukraine, for example, to multiple forms of the citizens' interaction with objects of cultural heritage and the political art — monuments, street names or political posters. I intend to illustrate further how the process of 'democratic' or 'pro-European' transitioning includes debates on the necessity of post-Euromaidan decommunization — the relevance and timeliness of complete demolition of the Soviet symbols from both the physical and cultural space of the state. The tendencies of the post-colonial debates are comparable to those of the Ukrainian decommunization: as multiple forms of pros and cons continue to emerge, there exists the necessity of clear identification of what to *forget*, as much as what to *remember*.

Twenty-five years after the publication of *Orientalism*, Edward W. Said raises the question of "whether modern imperialism ever ended" (Said 1994: xxi). The process of extending power and dominion, either by territorial, socio-political or cultural control, imperialism always involves the use of power. As the phenomenon of suppression and multiple forms of domination of one political unit (or state) over the other, it is the global occurrence that knows no racial, economic or cultural limitations. It spreads from ancient times of China, Asia or the Mediterranean, to those of Europe, North or South America. For people of Central and Eastern Europe, the struggle against imperialism is also a centuries-old phenomenon. As the time of powerful landlords and foreign monarchs dominating the socio-political space of this region is long-time gone, the communist regime could be seen as the most 'recent' form of an empire that has been openly fought against in central and eastern Europe (Bremmer 2017; Glatz 1983; Pearson 1997). Particularly after the collapse of the Soviet Union in 1991, the process of decommunization has taken multiple forms and has been implemented by both the governments and ordinary citizens of the newly-formed states. Within this time-span, the reconstruction of the society through 'rediscovery' or re-articulation of the country's political and cultural heritage has been the focal point of democratization. Back in 1995, Tarifa and Weinstein argued that "the goal of post-Communist transitioning must be the creation of a new kind of society." They insisted that the probability of "history, with all of its mysteries, biases, and falsifications [playing] a significant role in reconstruction of eastern Europe [was] high" (Tarifa and Weinstein 1995: 17). As I illustrate further, their assertion is particularly relevant when decoding the collective and personal representations within periods of transition, such as the revolution or war.

When it comes to the historical legacies—the modes of reconstruction or the scale of socio-political and cultural changes that have taken place in the former communist states since 1991, there exist considerable distinctions between the countries of the post-Soviet block. In particular, scholars working on decommunization distinguish two general tendencies: "the states that have chosen a path toward democracy and those that continue the replacement of the orthodoxies of communism with orthodoxies of another kind" (Kozak 2017; Mayerchyk 2015; Tarifa and Weinstein 1995). Usually, the economic, political and cultural turbulence is the inevitable condition of the states undergoing transitioning. However, according to Tarifa and Weinstein, "the outcome of decolonization or decommunization ultimately depends on how two pressing questions are handled": '*what* should be de-communized in the societies?' and 'how should the task be accomplished?' (Tarifa and Weinstein 1995: 64). In addressing the first question, the authors assert that two alternatives are to be distinguished: "either to de-communize the body politic—the institutions, or the principles involved in governing civil society—the focus on the people, or the citizenry" (ibid: 64). The decommunization of the body politic involves demolition of the one-party state model and implementation of the democratic principles of governance—the multi-party system. The decommunization of the citizenry, on the other hand, is a "personal matter" (Kolakowski 2002: 17). The latter type of decommunization, Vogel argues, is at its root "an anti-democratic undertaking, [since] it calls attention to people's past associations in rendering judgements to the effect that some are fit to participate in the reconstruction of the society and others are not" (Vogel 1993: 2).

In the academic circles and debates, we can identify the alignment with the argument of Minchik who states that "the question of *how* decommunization is to be accomplished requires a more complex answer" (Minchik 2003: 12). The examination of implementation of decommunization as the phenomenon of both the "body politic" or institutions, *and* "personal" or ordinary citizens also has been acknowledged as particularly significant (Tarifa and Weinstein 1995; Kolakowski 2002, respectively). I align with the argument of Minchik (2003) who states that "the question of *how* decommunization is to be accomplished requires a more complex answer." Motivated by the atrocities of the past (e.g. physical or ideological purges), the process of decommunization takes diverse forms and varies from what could be seen as a democratic articulation of the ordinary citizens' stands via relatively peaceful demonstrations (e.g. decommunization of the Baltic states) to those of potential weakening of the citizens' democratic protection (e.g. decommunization laws of the post-Euromaidan Ukraine) (Kozyrska 2016; Himka 2015; Motyl 2015).

For scholars working on democratic theory and democratic transitioning in Latin America, Africa, or Asia following World War II, for instance, the death of authoritarianism rarely led to full implementation of the democratic practices (Huntington 1991; Curry 1993; Mitchell 2013). Analysing similar historical experiences, American sociologist Seymour Martin Lipset (1994) and Polish philosopher Leszek Kołakowski (2002) illustrate that conditions do not bode well for democratization efforts in the former communists states of central and eastern Europe. However, to a lesser or greater extent, old-style communism has been repudiated. Hereon, it is important to expand on the complexity of existing debates on the postcolonial status of modern Ukraine and explore both the affirmative and opposing stands on Ukraine's postcolonial nature as a scientific narrative that allows examination of the constitution of a modern community or a nation, and, at the same time, enables investigation of re-articulation of the nation's past.

As such, the process of Sovietization was the cornerstone of the socio-political evolution of the 20th century eastern and central European states. For the whole of Eastern Europe, Schöpflin argues, "Stalinism has been the central formative experience since the war, the benchmark against which all subsequent developments [have been] measured" (Schöpflin 1993: 75). The extraordinary quality of this political system originates from both its extensive ideological and geographical scope. According to Schöpflin, "it is hard to master a precedent for the experiment conducted by the Soviet Union in culturally diverse polities over such a short period of time" (ibid: 75). Within the intensity of the process of 'Sovietization,' all strata of the society, all forms of civic activity, all public and individual elements were expected to comply with a set of norms and regulations that were established by the highest echelon of administration or undergo psychological or physical persecution for failing to do so. In such terms, the desire of the ruling elites to extend and retain the authority over the people (or territories) resembles colonial formations.

Clearly, within the communist system, independent thinking or public debate were discouraged rather than supported by the state. The Marxist-Leninist apparatus established a powerful hegemony that aimed at precluding doubt and claimed at providing answers to potential questions on politics, economics, or culture. Such stance gave birth to a specific way of existence and construction of daily activities — be it approaching the task of building a bridge or composing poetry. This scheme of ideological carcass constructed political space that was hierarchical, regimented and communal. Finally, the civic feedback that would challenge the state apparatus was a rather rare phenomenon, with the past, present and future of a country being 'defined' by the state. Naturally, development of the society capable of generating initiative or multiple forms of an independent thought was rendered complex.

At least as far as the study of imperialism and culture is concerned, however, "nearly every writer of the 19th century was extraordinarily well aware of the fact of the empire" (Said 1993: 14). "The liberal cultural heroes like John Stuart Mill, Arnold, Carlyle, Newman, Macaulay, Ruskin, George Eliot and even Dickens had definite views on race and imperialism, which are quite easily to be found at work in their writing," Said (1993: 14) asserts further. Despite ideological and socio-political purges that followed those who critiqued the state, writers and poets of central and eastern Europe have also expressed their civic and cultural stands that acknowledged the existence of an empire. The 19th and 20th centuries Ukrainian poets and writers, Taras Shevchenko, Mykola Bazhan, or Mykola Khvyliovyi, or famous dissidents of the Soviet era, Alexander Solzhenitsyn, Yelena Bonner or Yuri Orlov are among such many. If, according to Said (1993: 15), the "intellectual, aesthetic, scholarly and cultural energies...have come to serve the broadly imperialist view of the world," the same cultural forces could be seen as exposing and objecting to the colonial system.

Therefore, whether over seventy years of the communist rule succeeded in breeding a politically and culturally homogeneous society of no independent thought is open for debate. However, what emerged as a general framework of most of the post-communist states is an explicit antagonism towards the state-imposed uniformity. The struggle for independence from cultural and socio-political dictate became the primary objective of movements in favor of de-Sovietization (Portnov 2014; Tischner 2005; Weiner 2001). With the exception of the majority of Russians in Russia, subjects to "powerlessness in the name of utopia" (Schöpflin 1993: 80), citizens of Lithuania, Latvia, Estonia, Hungary, Poland, Ukraine and other post-communist states expressed an explicit desire to distance themselves from the cultural and political remnants of the communist rule. The process of such detachment has taken place in multiple forms of both physical and discursive demolition of relics of the communist past. The motion of articulation and confirmation of sovereignty of these states occurred through toppling of the communist monuments as physical and ideological reminders of the colonial heritage. The process of 'decommunization' has also taken place as renaming of the streets and production of various forms of political art that served as a bridge between ordinary citizens and the newly formed governments.

In the following sections of this chapter I focus on specific examples of the meaning-making processes within the post-Soviet states like Ukraine, where construction of national identity occurs through the prism of juxtaposition of the 'self' and the 'other.' I address existing debates on credibility of defining the Soviet past as 'colonial,' and pay particular attention to the socio-political aftermath of the communist rule: corruption, poverty or weak civic institutions. Examination of 'othering' is particularly important for a broader analysis of decommunization since, as the phenomenon of socio-political and cultural transformations, it is grounded on identification of the 'oppressed' and the 'oppressor,' 'the self' and 'the other.' Multiple forms of decommunization—the Singing Revolution of Lithuania (1991), the Revolution of Roses (Georgia, 2003), the Orange Revolution (Ukraine, 2006), or the Euromaidan Revolution, are the examples of civic expression where profound post-communist transitioning faces a long-term challenge of creating both physical and discursive space for inclusion of the citizens' political and cultural diversity. Such space, as we are to discern shortly, associates remembering with the consciousness of a *tabula rasa* – provides room for new things.

Disputing Othering

Broadly speaking, the socio-political developments of states in transition have been analyzed by both European and international scholars and organizations. One tendency to be distinguished is the disposition of justifying ongoing hurdles of the country by its historical ties to the empire. In the case of most of the post-Soviet states, such empire is the eastern, Russian neighbor. In his explanation of modern nation-building, Mykola Ryabchuk insists that "it is to be set as a response first and foremost to its post-colonial status" (Ryabchuk 2013: 4). Another Ukrainian scholar working on post-colonialism and the post-Soviet domain, Maria Mayerchyk, argues further that "discourses such as feminism, nationalism, post-colonialism or (post)-Sovietness are intersected in the production of meaning within the protests and wars that follow" (Mayerchyk 2015: 19). As multiple forms of resistance to the empire, historical figures become particularly important during times of post-colonial identity construction. They are not only perceived as symbols of a new (e.g. 'European') state, but are also viewed as role models for amalgamating political and military action.

When it comes to theories that reconstruct the country's broader colonial context, Gerasimov and Mogilner address professional historical inquiry as the "postcolonial subjectivity." Any normative historical scheme embedded in one's analysis immediately raises suspicions that "certain empirical data might not have been taken into account because they do not fit into this scheme, and the rest have been interpreted from a vantage point alien to both the protagonists of the events and the conventions of the study's chosen methodology" (Gerasimov and Mogilner 2015: 12). The essentially geopolitical historical articulation ascribes meaning to selective events depending on their geocultural positioning: it depicts the post-Soviet space as a token of the historical spectacle between two global players—Russia and the United States, who compete for regional domination. One year after the Euromaidan, in winter of 2015, Timothy Snyder addressed the revolution as an outcome of historical interplay between another set of global players: the European Union and Russia, "each advancing its own historical scenario and embodying a distinctive historical (that is, civilizational) political organization." Snyder's analysis of post-Euromaidan events includes evaluation of the revolution and war as "only [making] sense when the country's history is placed within a global framework and the choices of [its] revolutionaries are understood as a response to a historical predicament." In other words, within the framework of international analysis of the Ukrainian post-2013 socio-political and cultural developments, Ukraine and the broader post-Soviet space are examined as the geopolitical sphere of influence of three major players: the USA, the EU and the Russian Federation. Most of the other countries of the former USSR are the domain of geopolitical contestation primarily between the US and Russia, however, either due to their geographic location (e.g. Georgia), or the existing membership in the EU (Estonia, Lithuania, or Poland, for instance).

Another popular assertion that exists within the analytical discourse on the 'colonial' status of the post-Soviet states is on "limitedness of options of these countries to two pre-existing historical scenarios—the fundamental choice between integration and disintegration" (Gerasimov and Mogilner 2015: 5). Evaluating the historical 'causes' of the Euromaidan Revolution, Snyder argues that "Ukraine is little more than a function of its own history, while history is a product of contention between several great powers" (e.g. "the Nazi and Soviet projects of transformation") (Snyder 2015: 8). Already in early 2014, a prominent writer and political activist, Jurii Andrukhovych expanded on the idea of Ukrainians articulating their stands on their country's geopolitical belonging. He provided an extensive definition of what 'pro-European' choice means for the citizens of the post-Soviet states: "when we are fighting 'for Europe'—that means we are fighting for our independence. It is for this reason that pro-European choice equals independent Ukraine and equals a free individual in a free country." In this context, it could be argued that for the ordinary citizens of countries like Ukraine, the question of 'disintegration' is generally eliminated from both the discursive and physical domain of the state.

The 'integration,' in Adrukhovych's terms, occurs via ideological or non-physical space, where the 'European choice' is also the possibility of re-integration or the *return* to the original, centuries-old idea of Ukraine's independence. At the end of the day, the 'international' vision of the status of the post-Soviet states as countries that are trapped between multiple empires could be defined as that of a geopolitical contestation. The Ukrainian narrative of 'its own, independent political course,' for instance, includes extensive emphasis on cultural, non-physical (re)-integration into the European socio-political and cultural domain. According to Shevel, when it comes to the political and cultural context of post-Euromaidan Ukraine, however, "the ideas of colonialism and decolonization become equal to decommunization" (Shevel 2015: 5). It is present in both the international and east European narrative. It is also what I argue to be at the core of construction of the hegemonic formations that involve articulation of diverse forms of interpretations and meanings of east European heritage.

The popular historicist stance on the post-Soviet space, even somewhat exaggerated as that of Snyder in regard to Ukraine, is geopolitical since it treats values and cultures as being spatially and civilizationally defined. "There is 'Europe,' the champion of normal decolonization and good integration, the 'Balkan model' of nationalism, successful in de-colonization but failing to provide proper social integration, and 'eastern Europe,' which in the 1930s became the space of competing colonial projections and aspirations by regional superpowers—the USSR and Germany" (Gerasimov and Mogilner 2015: 18). Finally, the clash between Germany and the Soviet Union, Gerasimov and Mogilner continue, "was also a clash between two re-colonial ideas, two notions of how to apply colonial knowledge to the center of Europe" (ibid: 21).

One of the primary cornerstones for explanation of the socio-political turmoil in the post-Soviet space is based on the classics of postcolonial theory. In his extensive analysis of Ukraine as a postcolonial state, for instance, Andrzej Szeptycki (2011) presents a number of classical definitions of colonialism. This term has been traditionally defined as 'West European powers' rule over overseas territories inhabited by other racial groups.' The colonial expansion is striving to control and turn advantage over another society via physical or cultural domination of the supreme authority. According to Kieniewicz, "a colony is thus a territory subordinated politically and economically, lying outside the colonizers' own state and their own civilization" (Kieniewicz 2003: 42). Such definition, however, Szeptycki claims further, needs to be broadened: "colonialism should be described as a protracted rule over another racial/ethnic group, coupled with a policy of economic exploitation and forced acculturation." White settlers' colonies of Canada, or the dilation of non-European powers such as Japan are but a few examples. Continuum of an empire striving to take control over a frail state is the pivotal condition. In a similar vein, the case of the post-Soviet domain is a complex phenomenon where both narrative and physical space has been used for re-articulation of the countries' colonial status. Depending on the regime in power, colonial (or anti-colonial) narratives are often contested by articulation of multiple, at times conflicting hegemonic formations.

Despite the decades-long debates on veracity of the approach, increasingly more authors have been construing the present and past of the Soviet/Russian-Ukrainian relations along the scheme of the (post)colonial paradigm (Bowen 1991; Galeotti 2014; Petro 2014; Shkandrij 2001). In addition, many journalists have also analyzed Russia's wars in the post-Soviet space through the postcolonial lenses: they argue that "Russia has taken up a new imperial mission, aimed at unifying the post-Soviet lands under its rule" (Danen 2016: 21). The Eurasian Union is being defined as one of the examples of Russia's imperial objectives. Historical legacy of the USSR, Russian imperialism, is often assumed, but, as Danen affirms, "seldom explained." Particularly in the context of the Ukrainian-Russian crisis (2013-2014) and military confrontation in Donbas (2014-present), the theoretical framework of the conflict's coverage is protean. In such state, examination of how the post-2014 Russia-

Ukraine conflict could be explained from a post-colonial point of view is integral, as the very fact of discordance in application of the postcolonial theory to modern post-Soviet context construes the heterogeneity of the meaning-making process within the political realm of eastern and central Europe.

In his prolific discussion of the disintegration of the Soviet Union, Taras Kuzio argues that "the former USSR is a perfect example of the empire" (Kuzio 2004: 45). He uses Michael Doyle's definition of an empire as being "a relationship, formal or informal, in which one state controls the effective political sovereignty of another political sovereignty." Kuzio sees the USSR "as a socio-political body with a defined core (Moscow and the Russian SFSR) and peripheries (the non-Russian republics), where the elites ruled, and the peripheries were subordinated to the core" (ibid: 48). He also draws special attention to organization of the Soviet state, where "the Russian SFSR was the only Soviet republic that possessed no republican institutions for the bulk of the Soviet era and it, alone of the 15 republics, was never portrayed as the "homeland for its titular nation" (ibid: 51). The popular discourse of the USSR on 'Russia being the elder brother,' or the 'leading nation' of the Soviet space, also commonly used by the modern Russian state, turned into a policy that deliberately confuses Russian and Soviet identities.

While one should not expect the Ukrainian-Russian relations to be fully normalized after the decades of the historical socio-political and cultural confrontations, Kuzio's parallel between Irish-English and the Ukrainian-Russian relationship in regard to civic, class-attributes of an empire, for instance, is to be re-examined in more detail. Ireland lost its language (Ukraine nearly did), Ireland and Ukraine were colonized by English/Scots and Russian, respectively. While, most certainly "the upper classes were assimilated in both countries" (Kuzio 2002: 18), it would be an exaggeration to argue that, historically speaking, the Ukrainian elites have been continuously partitioned from the peasant majority.

Already in the early 19th century, many among the intelligentsia gradually developed a sense of estrangement from the empires' establishment, and, in turn, directed their interest towards the peasant masses. Driven by the ideas of German philosopher, Johann

Herder, Ukrainian intelligentsia in both western and eastern parts of what is now modern Ukraine had a strong desire to raise the national, classless identity. In his *Ukraine*, Subtelny addresses Herder as being the first to insist that "human civilization lives not in its general and universal, but in its national and peculiar manifestations, [and though] each culture manifestation must be original, its originality is that of the national community and the national consciousness" (Subtelny 2000: 45). In other words, instead of viewing society from the narrow perspective of a nobleman, or a peasant, members of the Ukrainian intelligentsia articulated their civic stands as approaching the society as a whole and considering the interests of all. In time, "criticism of the status quo became a standard feature of the intelligentsia's discourse—so much so that in the late 19th century, a part of the intelligentsia even dedicated itself to changing the status quo at any cost and by whatever means necessary," Subtelny indicates further (ibid: 48). The claim that "Ukrainians became 'non-historical' peasant people with no ruling class" (Kuzio 2002: 12), or the outcasts of the Russian Empire, as such, is to be re-addressed. One of the key attributes of the periphery—the dismantlement of the elites from the ordinary masses, was but an exception in states like Ukraine.

The Opposition

By analysing photo, interview and video data that I collected during numerous fieldwork trips to Ukraine, I came to a conclusion that the idea of 'Ukraine being the colony of Russia' obtained particular importance *after* the Euromaidan revolution. As all salient transformations, it needed both time and space. Preeminently, it turned into a mode of *unification* of the state against the external aggressor—the Russian Federation. Considering the political framework of the time, 2014-2018—the occupation of Crimea by Russia and war in Donbas, the re-assessment of the past and contestation of the definition of an 'enemy' have also become tangibly relevant.

In "The Postcolonial is Not Enough," Yaroslav Hrytsak objects to the traditional view of Ukraine being a colonized state. He argues that it was specifically during the interwar period that the idea to defend their autonomic rights to rule their republic was articulated by some of the Soviet Ukrainian leaders. Though the contrariety was demolished together with the defenders of postcolonial discourse, "the situation took another turn after World War II and the death of Joseph Stalin, when a unified and placated Ukraine was granted the role of a "younger brother" to Russians in the administration of the Soviet Union" (Hrytsak 2015: 15). According to the author, both within the Russian Empire and the Soviet Union, Ukraine was *more core* than a colony. "Colony fits the Ukrainian lands of the Habsburg monarchy better. From Vienna's perspective, these lands were political and economic backwaters. In contrast to their compatriots in the Russian empire, local Ukrainians (Ruthenians) were never offered the status of partners — neither in Vienna nor in their respective provinces" (ibid: 15). This claim is not to deny, however, that the Ukrainians of the Austro-Hungarian empire possessed more extensive political freedoms than those under the Russian rule. It is particularly this — extensive political rights of Western Ukrainians that, Hrystak estimates further, "turned Galicia into a hothouse of the Ukrainian nationalism." Already in 1914, "Galicia obtained the status of casus belli between the Habsburg and Romanov monarchies, turning into a citadel of 'Ukrainianess' for the years to come" (ibid: 16). He ends his discussion of the engagement of empires in the socio-political course of Ukraine with a statement that it was a "bitter irony" that Ukrainians of the Habsburg lands were fighting to liberate Ukrainians from the Russian Ukraine, which, he claims, "was hard to call a colony in a strict sense" (ibid: 17).

While academic discussion of the relations between Russia and Central Asian countries (those of distinct ethnic and religious variance) provokes fewer doubts in regard to their colonial character (Kuzio 2015; Shevel 2016; Szeptycki 2011), a number of objections appear when addressing states like Ukraine. Both lingering and acute is the debate on the colonial status of Ukraine within the union of 'Slavic brotherly countries' — Russia, Ukraine, and Belarus. In their study of the effects of consumer ethnocentrism and trade between Ukraine and Russia, Alexander Jakubanecs, Magne Shupphellen and Helge Thorbjørnsen (2005) argue that, among the three, Ukraine comprises an intricate case as the only state that has been resisting classification of 'Slavic brotherhood' in vigorous terms and, for centuries, has been making the socio-political turns toward the west.

The common Slavic background of Belarus, Russia and Ukraine is another claim used widely in both academic and political circles by the opponents of the 'colonial' definition of the post-Soviet states (e.g. Dugin 2014). "The three East Slavic nations are derived from the same stem (Kyivan Rus'), they are united *voluntarily* in pursuit of common interest (Union of Pereyaslav, 1654), and [thus] such community of religion and linguistic similarity rules out any talk about colonization" (Szeptycki 2011: 4). As being reflected in the Valuev Circular of 1863[9], which states that "no separate Little Russian (Ukrainian) language ever existed, does not exist, and could not exist," the Russians of the Tsarist era were politically cynical. Szepycki proposes further that the content of the Valuev Circular "must have also reflected a genuine belief of the tsarist Russia's political elites of the time in a missionary role of Russia in education and patronage of its Slavic neighbouring territories" (ibid: 7).

Finally, Khmelnytsky's meeting of the Cossack elite and the voluntary decision to accept the tsar's rule over Ukraine, historians argue, has elevated Moscovy as a great power (Danylenko 2016; Remy 2007; Yakovenko 2008). And thus, for better or for worse, "the fate of Ukraine became inextricably linked with that of Russia" (Subtelny 2000: 52). According to the Russian historian Vasilii Sergeevich, the 1654 agreement was a voluntary union between Muscovy and Ukraine, "where the two parties shared the same sover-

---

9   The *Valuev Circular* of 18 July 1863 was a secret decree of the Minister of Internal Affairs of the Russian Empire Pyotr Valuev (Valuyev) that incorporated an act of limiting Ukrainian language publishing. It included prohibition of publications of educational and religious content in Ukrainian within the Russian Empire. Accessed July 18, 2018. Source: https://www.academia.edu/3879076/Valuev_Circular_of_1863.

eign but maintained separate governments." In what became classics—*Ukraine: A History*, Subtelny refers to a specialist in Russian law, Nikolai Diakonov, who assures that "by accepting personal subjugation to the tsar, the Ukrainians unconditionally agreed to the incorporation of their land in the Muscovite state and the agreement was therefore a real union" (ibid: 55). On the other hand, historians such as Russian Venedikt Miakotin and the Ukrainian Mykhailo Hrushevsky, insist on the Pereiaslav Agreement being a form of vassalage in which the more powerful party (the tsar) agreed to protect the weaker party (the Ukrainians) on condition that he would not interfere in their internal affairs. Already in 1926, another Ukrainian historian Viacheslav Lypynsky proposed that "the 1654 agreement was but a temporary military alliance between Moscow and the Ukrainians." The Communist Party of the Soviet Union, on the other hand, interpreted the Pereyaslav Agreement as a natural culmination of the age-old desire of the Ukrainians and Russians to be united, with the union of the two peoples being the primary goal of the 1648 uprising (Subtelny 2000; Arkas 2012). In practice, Ukrainian hetmans became free to exercise their socio-political and cultural authority, and were considered to be the de facto rulers of Ukraine. By 1686, however, all of Ukraine was divided up among the powers that surrounded it.

In his analysis of the Russian-Ukrainian relations through the prism of the post-colonial theory, Myroslav Shkandrii affirms that "Russia had to reduce Ukrainians to colonial subjects in order to legitimize the Russian imperial project during the 19th and 20th centuries" (Shkandrii 2001: 8) As such, "as Ukraine stands as the egress of civilizational or cultural (e.g. religious) advancement of Russia (e.g. Kievan Rus'), most of the positive characteristics of the Ukrainian culture are attributed to Russian influence, while all negative ones (anti-Russian), to malign foreign (Western) influence" (Ryabchuk 2010: 11). Particularly after the Euromaidan revolution, however, in my view, such argument has virtually lost its validity within Ukraine, with the notion of 'Russian influence' obtaining a consensually negative connotation.

Debating Decommunization

In her work on "concept models of the society of Ukraine twenty years after independence," Karina Korostelina presents prevailing conceptual narrative models of the post-Soviet space employed by Ukrainian and international experts working on the post-communist domain. Her study reveals the following narrative categories: (1) a state without a national idea and common identity; (2) a country in an unfinished transition and degradation; (3) a divided society; and (4) the state as a colony of "wild capitalism" (Korostelina 2013: 15). Already in January 2013, months prior to the Euromaidan Revolution, the author argues, "analysis of these categories helped to assess conflict potential in the post-Soviet space," which, being forecasted by prominent analysts of socio-political, cultural and economic developments of the disintegrated USSR, was "highly plausible." The first three of Korostelina's models are directly relevant as they re-emerge as primary narratives articulated in the empirical materials that I address. Within the fourth category, "a state as a colony of wild capitalism," however, as I show in the discussion of the collected data, the emphasis is changed towards Ukraine being a colony of Russia. Triggered by losses of lives of the participants of the Euromaidan Revolution, the occupation of Crimea, and presence of the Russian Federation military formations in Donbas, the phenomenon of 'decolonization' evolved as the dominant discursive and legislative umbrella of post-Euromaidan Ukraine.

First to commence as early as in 1991, massive destruction of objects of the Soviet heritage took place in western, central and most of the southern parts of the country after the Euromaidan revolution. According to Zhurzhenko, in eastern regions, such as Kharkiv, Luhansk, or Donetsk, as well as dozens of smaller towns in Donbas, however, communist statues "were not only left standing, but received a new lease of life as sites of pro-Russian mobilization and symbols of discontent with the Kyiv government" (Zhurzhenko 2014: 4). Originally defined by Pirie (2007) as a manifestation of the "clash of values," decommunization evolved into the multifaceted phenomenon of national identity-making that

THE POSTCOLONIAL SOVIET   53

runs as both the discursive and legislative framework of the post-Soviet states.

Once again, the reasons for the resurrection of antagonism toward the Soviet heritage in Ukraine are apparent: the Euromaidan Revolution, the occupation of Crimea and war in Donbas. At the institutional level, physical or spatial markers of the Soviet identity, Lenin statues (and the communist insignia as such) became legislatively defined as the symbols of communist *and* modern oppression. Since 2015, that time drafter and proponent of what became known as decommunization laws, Volodymyr Viatrovych[10], made multiple public statements where he announced that "[the communist insignia] had to be cleared from the physical space of the streets to provide ideological domain for Europeanization of Ukraine."

Already at an early stage of its implementation, however, critical stands on extensive decommunization of Ukraine have been expressed by the Ukrainian and international scholars, as well as political figures. Both the Ukrainian and international community addressed decommunization as 'the primary socio-political and cultural objective of post-Euromaidan transformations [that were] missing the target' (Marples 2015; Shevel 2015; Zhurzhenko 2014). For scholars like Lev Gudkov, the confrontation of the Kyivan government with the Soviet cultural heritage has little to do with the eradication of an actual Soviet ideology or values (Gudkov 2015: 8). Instead, an overall phenomenon of de-communization of the post-Soviet space, Gudkov argues, could be defined as construction of

---

10 Volodymyr Viatrovych is a Ukrainian historian, publicist, professor of history and civic activist. He was the head of the Ukrainian Institute of National Memory from March 2014 until September 2019. A major lobbyist and leader of decommunization of post-Euromaidan Ukraine, Viatrovych is an author of multiple works on the Organization of Ukrainian Nationalists (OUN) and the Ukrainian Insurgent Army (UPA). Seen as a controversial figure in Ukraine and abroad, Viatrovych is criticized for his refusal to recognize crimes of the UPA committed against the Polish population in Volhynia and Eastern Galicia (1943-1945), and is accused of whitewashing the history of Ukraine. In 2010-2011, he was a visiting scholar at the Ukrainian Research Institute at Harvard University and was in the election list of European Solidarity in 2019. Accessed May 2, 2019. Source: https://www.Unian.ua/politics/10690008-hto-takiy-volodimir-v-yatrovich-ta-chim-vidomiy-skandalniy-dekomunizator.html.

"negative identity," which operates primarily within the category of the "enemy." According to Zhurzhenko, the basic consequences of such reformative practices is that "from the perspective of the pro-Russian protesters, [proponents of decommunization] are the "Banderists" and "nationalists" from Kyiv and western Ukraine, who want to destroy "[the pro-Russian population's] monuments" and "steal [their country's] past" (Zhurzhenko 2014: 252). She argues further that monuments of Lenin are "floating signifiers that carry no ideological value, but mark local identity as being 'anti-Kyiv," or in the case of the Lenin monument being located in western parts of the country, for instance, include an 'anti-Soviet' or 'anti-Russian' premise.

The broader phenomenon of 'de-Sovietization' or 'de-Russification,' however, is an occurrence of the socio-political and cultural changes that take place through destruction of physical remnants of the communist past. The process of values-replacement derives through distancing from the Soviet legacy via reformation of the state apparatus, or changing the value system within both private and public space. Following Dudek, the dominant procedural elements of post-Euromaidan decommunization include the following: "lustration, education (official changes of state policies regarding the Communist era), and demolition of the symbolic — physical and discursive elimination of the Soviet past via destruction of the communist monuments or renaming of the streets, squares or public places" (Dudek 2016: 4). As was stated earlier, the study of the physical aspects of de-Sovietization, such as decommunization of public space, has been the primary focus of the academic, as well as media and political research on Ukraine's post-2013 decommunization. Compared to cultural or mental transformations that do require time, physical toppling of a symbol is often the more agile, as well as simple to detect.

In practical terms, Antonina Kozyrska argues, "the policy of decommunization of public space was conducted inconsistently and superficially, [where] two models of Ukrainian identity emerged as the primary ones: the inclusive and the exclusive one [dominated] the discussions of the Ukrainian and international intellectuals" (Kozyrska 2016: 2) The former one accepted multiple cultural forms of the Ukrainian identity—Ukrainian, Russian, as well as the Soviet, with an objective of celebrating holidays and commemorating identities that were indicative of national heroes. The compromise and the freedom of opinions was the goal of such models, where co-existence of statutes of Stepan Bandera, Vladimir Lenin, or Taras Shevchenko[11] was to be regulated at the institutional level. However, the possibility of having communist symbols as part of a new, 'pro-European' Ukraine raised the question on limits of tolerance—that is whether Stalin, for instance, as a figure of the communist decade, could be considered a hero as well. The exclusive model, on the other hand, is based on the ethnic identity of Ukrainians "being shaped by Ukrainian history and collective memory" (ibid: 2). Already in 2002, Kuzio stated that the exclusive or 'ethnic' model "carries potential of a serious domestic crisis, [as well as] threatens an overall process of nation-building" particularly in the areas of Ukraine where national consciousness is weak. At that time, the region of Donbas, and eastern Ukraine as such were major reference points.

Commencing as early as in 1991, both the 'inclusive' and 'exclusive' models have found their implementation in the socio-political and cultural apparatus of Ukraine. The process of the official removal of the communist symbols started from Western regions of Ukraine. Particularly under the presidency of Leonid Kravchuk (presidential term: 1991-1994), dozens of Soviet monuments were toppled, with streets of the smaller cities and villages being renamed to eliminate both the discursive and architectural evidence of the communist past. However, upon the reign of Presidents Leonid Kuchma (presidential term: 1994-2005) and Viktor Yanukovych (presidential term: 2010-2014), official 'decommunization'

---

11 Taras Hryhorovych Shevchenko (March 9, 1814 —March 10, 1861) was a foremost Ukrainian poet of the 19th century. A writer and artist, he was also a folklorist and ethnographer and a major figure of the Ukrainian national revival of the time. His literary heritage is regarded to be the foundation of the Ukrainian literature, as well as modern Ukrainian language. He is also known for many masterpieces as a painter and illustrator, as well as for his open articulation of the ideas on Ukraine's political and cultural independence. Accessed May 2, 2018. Source: http://www.encyclopediaofukraine.com/display.asp?linkpath= pages%5CS %5CH%5CShevchenkoTaras.htm.

was replaced with the legislative measures of conciliatory nature. An attempt to legalize Russian as the second official language is one example of such operations. Starting in 2004, the exclusive model of politics of memory was once again promoted by President Viktor Yushchenko (presidential term: 2005-2010). Major criticism of Yushchenko's reforms was about cultural suppression of the Russian-speaking Ukrainians through the 'imposition' of Ukrainian language on the Russian-speakers of Ukraine. This claim was particularly popular in the country's central and eastern regions. Another criticism of Yushchenko's reforms, which often came from the Russian-speaking population of eastern oblasts, was on 'rewriting history' via the prism of Western Ukrainian narratives. At the same time, however, particularly under the rule of President Yushchenko, the regional authorities possessed extensive power to both demolish and raise symbols that were reflective of the socio-political and cultural loyalties of the population. The so-called "local politics of memory, tolerated by the government, provided an opportunity for erecting the statue of Bandera in Lviv, and that of Catherine the Great as the co-founder of the city of Odessa" (Osadchy 2014: 317).

Nevertheless, unlike in Poland or Czech Republic, since the official collapse of the Soviet Union, no open or national public debate regarding communism in Ukraine has been taking place. As early as in 2001, historian Yury Shapoval detected diversity in views on assessment of the communist past, while literary critic, scholar and politician, Mykola Zhulynsky, acknowledged "the condemnation of Communism and the purification of individual and collective memory from its effects as a necessary condition for democratization of the society" (Zhulynsky 2009: 8) At the same time, analysis of literature on de-Sovietization of pre-Euromaidan Ukraine demonstrates the discussions on impossibility of lustration without bridging of the generational divergences, as well as the necessity of public dialogue between left and right (e.g. the *Communist Party of Ukraine*[12] or the *Svoboda*[13] party, for instance).

Both the Ukrainian and international scholars working on socio-political developments of post-2013 Ukraine acknowledge rapid changes in the country's regional and national identity (Himka 2015; Kuzio 2017; Marpels 2016; Motyl 2015; Shevel 2016). The new wave of decommunization, which, symbolically speaking, began with toppling of the Lenin statue in Kyiv in December of 2013, and was followed by over 500 communist symbols being destroyed within 2014 alone, emerged into what Kozyrska claims to be the "radical decommunization of the Ukrainian society" (Kozyrska 2016: 5). As was stated by the President Petro Poroshenko, "it is not the communist statues that must be abolished. Communism should be gotten rid of mainly from people's heads" (Shorichne 2015). Treated as an integral part of 'Europeanization,' decommunization of post-Euromaidan Ukraine is also an "element of the humanitarian dimension of national safety" (ibid 2016: 7). In practice, the Institute of National Remembrance (UINR) became the official body that drafted the 'decommunization laws.' From March 2014 until September 2019, it was directed by the already mentioned historian, the reformist Volodymyr Viatrovych. The laws of the following content came into force May 21 2015:

---

12 The *Communist Party of Ukraine* is a Ukrainian political party that was known until 1952 as the Communist Party (Bolshevyk Party) of Ukraine. Within the political framework of the post-Soviet Ukraine, it was founded in 1993, after being banned in 1991. The Communist Party was the successor to the Soviet-era Communist Party of Ukraine. The Ministry of Justice is officially allowed to ban the Communist Party from participation in elections since implementation of the 2015 Ukrainian decommunization laws. Accessed September 12, 2018. Source: http://www.ucrdc.org/HA-UKRAINIAN _COMMUNIST _PARTY.html.

13 The "Svoboda" Party (translated as "Freedom" party) is the All-Ukrainian Union party. It was founded in 1991 as the Social-National Party of Ukraine and acts as a proponent of nationalism. It is positioned between the right-wing and the far-right of the political spectrum. The party was particularly popular during the 2009-2010 regional elections in western Ukraine. It won seats in the Ukrainian Parliamentary elections in 2012. Accessed September 19, 2018. Source: https://www.britannica.com/ topic/Svoboda-Party.

- Law No. 2558: "On the condemnation of the communist and national socialist (Nazi) regimes, and prohibition of propaganda of their symbols."
- Law No.2538-1: "On the legal status and honoring of fighters of Ukraine's independence in the 20th century."
- Law No.2539: "On remembering the victory over Nazism in the Second World War."
- Law No. 2540: "On access to the archives of repressive bodies of the communist totalitarian regime from 1917-1991."

Both the Ukrainian and international scholars who examine the aftermath of the laws have argued that the 2015 decommunization policies may cause expansion of the domestic socio-political and cultural polarity, particularly within the context of the ongoing war in Donbas. According to the Ukrainian Institute of National Memory, 877 localities had to be renamed by November 21 2015. The cities of Donets'k (with 10 cities, 27 towns, and 62 villages), Dnipropetrovs'k (3 cities, 10 towns and 71 villages) and Kharkiv (27 towns and 70 villages) were the first to be affected in eastern parts of the country. The banning of public expression of "wrong" opinions about the communist era, communist leaders, or "fighters for Ukraine's independence," such as Organization of Ukrainian Nationalists (OUN) and the Ukrainian Insurgent Army (UPA) has also provoked academic and public debates on the validity of 'pro-European' or democratic transitioning of post-Euromaidan Ukraine" (Shevel 2016: 259). Finally, considering Ukraine's economic stagnation, urgency in renaming of the streets and the removal of hundreds of Soviet monuments has been questioned by both international and Ukrainian scholars (Hitrova 2016; Motyl 2015; Shevel 2016).

In her analysis of Ukraine's infamous decommunization legislation, Oxana Shevel addresses two primary stands on the policies of de-Sovietization. As of 2016, she argues, "the process has not led to any form of seizable protests, [with] parties that vocally opposed the laws being unable to convert their stance into any actual mobilization." At the same time, "there is no evidence of the widespread support of decommunization within the society, with the reasoning being more economical than ideological" (Shevel 2016: 260). The available polling data also recorded the majority of Ukrainians being opposed to decommunization: according to the Kyiv International Institute of Sociology (2017), "10.5 percent only support decommunization and 89 percent do not (with 34.5 percent [being] strongly opposed to it and 54.6 percent [being] moderately opposed."

The academic research on post-Euromaidan 'Europeanization' addresses the following three reasons on why, despite salient lack of support of decommunization laws in Ukraine, the protest against the laws is not publicly visible. According to Kozyrska, Motyl, and Shevel, the occupation of Crimea and military support of the separatist movement in Donbas by the Russian Federation have lowered loyalty for the Soviet era and increased support for Ukraine's independence. In her analysis of the nature of historical memory in post-Euromaidan Ukraine, Shevel shows deliberately that "an overall rise of pro-Ukrainian patriotic sentiments has made the Ukrainian society more receptive to cutting ties with the communist era" (ibid: 261). The second prevailing factor that made decommunization less disputable is that many of the towns that were to be renamed by the Ukrainian government came under the control of the Russian (Crimea) or separatist (Donbas) territories. For instance, as of 2016, out of 54 localities that were to be renamed in the city of Luhans'k, only 19 were of the Ukrainian-controlled territory. In other words, as the region of potentially highest objection to decommunization policies – Donbas, remained outside the control of the Ukrainian government, the decommunization laws could not be fully installed.

Finally, according to Shevel, the studies of post-Euromaidan decommunization also reveal "the non-ideological nature of the opposition to decommunization [being] one of the primary reasons why the official legislative policies of 2015 have not sparked open ideological or physical resistance" (ibid: 261). The polls, interviews, and records of the town hall meetings of French journalist Sébastien

Gobert, and Swiss photographer Niels Ackermann illustrate that the inability of ordinary Ukrainians to have a say in both drafting and passing of the laws "led to a certain public passivity rather than physical protest" (Gobert and Ackermann 2017: 4). Another reason why implementation of decommunization policies did not cause the expected strife is because of an overall 'pro-Ukrainian' transformation of the civic strata (caused by the occupation of Crimea and war in Donbas), and geographic exclusion of the most "pro-Soviet" regions (Crimea and Donbas) from the national campaign (Shevel 2016: 261). At the same time, Shevel claims that despite the inability of the laws to increase pro-Ukrainian feelings and decrease support for separatism, the reform "gave citizens and activists a say in the process." The laws carried potential "of strengthening civic society in Ukraine, while helping it shed wide swathes of its monumental and Soviet legacies" (ibid: 261).

At this point, I will abstain from analysis of the claims above to leave the reader with a range of diverse viewpoints. Though, as was previously stated, I align with the idea of 'decolonization' or 'decommunization' being the primary legislative and discursive framework of post-Euromaidan Ukraine, I object to the assertion of decommunization laws being the mechanism for strengthening the country's civic society. As I discuss further in the following chapters, in-depth study of the grassroots, ordinary citizens' stands, as well as the governmental modes of their arituation, is the obligatory component for evaluation of effectiveness of the country's civil society, both within the historic and modern terms.

3. 'Researching' Methods

> "I sing out in dread at the movements of a hand with short fingers
> unexplained or unknown-
> an iron metal hand
> day begins its descent, uncovering a stone bed-
> searching the perimeter...Searching."
> — Taras Fedirko, "Hand"

In his study on how people experience their culture and how those experiences are expressed in forms such as narratives, ritual, or life review, Edward Bruner (1984) defines ethnography as "the study of continuity between the story and the experience." He eliminates the differences between what he calls a *life-as-lived* (what actually happened) and a life-as-experienced (the images, feelings, thoughts, and meanings known to the person whose life it is), and a *life-as-told* (the narrative). During data-collection process, I intended to answer similar questions: to address what has actually happened (*life-as-lived*), what the images, thoughts or feelings of the participants of socio-political transformations of (post)Euromaidan Ukraine were (*life-as-experienced*), and what broader narratives (*life-as-told*), or hegemonic formations, were being articulated by the discursive and physical meaning-making. The intention in this chapter is to provide an overview of the methods that were used for data collection, and hopefully, to bring the reader one step closer to understanding of the geographic and cultural particularities of Ukraine. After all, to fully grasp the subject, we need to know the ground it sprouts from.

The following map (Figure A) illustrates the geographic framework of the conducted fieldwork and indicates major cities where it was conducted, an approximate measure of the time spent in each location, and the amount of data collected.

Figure A: Map of Ukraine: visual presentation of the collected data

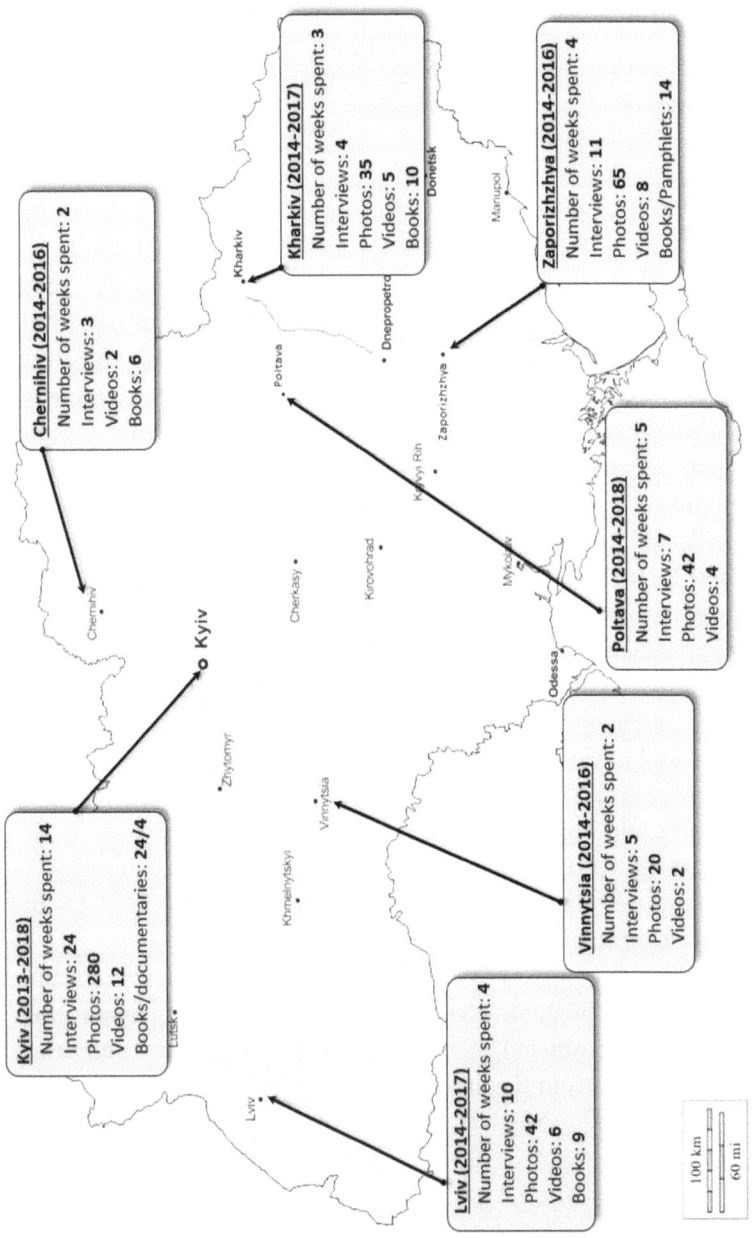

In their survey on International migration and assessment of selection biases in destination countries, Beauchemin and González-Ferrer (2011) define the snowballing sampling method as "the primary data sources nominating other potential primary data sources to be used further in the research." For my data gathering, I used the "exponential non-discriminative snowballing sampling method" (Dudovskiy 2012), where the first subject involved in the sampling provided multiple referrals. Each new referral was then explored until primary data formed a sufficient amount of samples—for the video, interview and photo analysis, it was usually three to four rounds of samples-collection (Figure B).

Figure B: Exponential non-discriminative snowballing sampling (Dudovskiy 2012)

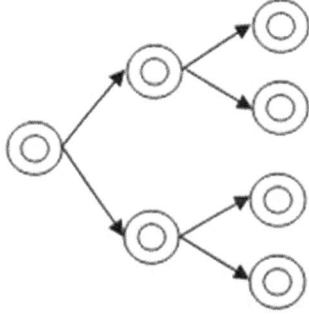

On a broader scale, besides the interviews, where the snowballing sampling was employed, I also used snowballing in other aspects of the material collection. The Euromaidan revolution, the exhibition of the political posters or the toppling of communist symbols, for instance, served as points of referral in themselves that, upon my arrival to the location of the event, provided physical (and discursive) references for further research. The snowballing technique was also applied to the acquisition of images, videos, and written texts or e-texts, with the primary objective being to obtain data that reflected modes of ordinary activities, as well as the sociopolitical transformations of the discursive and physical space of Ukraine.

Following the traditional framework of ethnographic research (Burns 1992; Geertz 1973; Lassiter 2005; Dewan 2015), upon my arrival in the field, the emphasis was made on, first, exploring the social phenomena rather than testing a particular hypothesis. In other words, the goal was *not* to look for generalization of the findings, but rather to consider them in reference to the context of the situation. In other words, I applied ethnography as a qualitative technique to uncover the process of articulation, and then used the theoretical framework to interpret hegemonic meaning-making in the data.

Throughout my fieldwork, I was both an insider and outsider in the field. As Mikheshin argues (2016: 25), "such dichotomy may be outdated as a simplistic understanding of the participant observation...There are numerous examples of the field research, starting from Malinowski, where the investigator is an obvious other, and finding similarities in the cultural context is encouragingly challenging." In other cases, "where the ethnographer belongs to the group she or he studies, the dissimilarities are constructed by the fact of the research itself" (Mikheshin 2016: 26). As a native Ukrainian residing outside of Ukraine for over 15 years, prospecting for Ukraine for a foreign university brought certain expectations in terms of production of the research that was both 'sensitive' and 'detached' from the subject of the analysis—native Ukrainians and their particular socio-political stands. Such context was both pragmatic and beneficial, "since a certain amount of expertise and linguistic fluency [was] expected" (Mikheshin 2016), and, at the same time, could also limit the possibilities of the researcher at any stage of the data collection process.

Inherently, a turbulent period of the Euromaidan and later war in Donbas placed a number of challenges on the data-gathering process. The revolutionary and further military context set physical limitations on my stay in different regions of Ukraine and, at the same time, promoted navigation between two modes of operation—what Bate (1997: 12) defines as "thick and quick description." A term introduced by Clifford Geertz (1973), "thick description involves long-term immersion in the field setting, development of incredibly rich, detailed and (con)textured observations, establishment of close relations with those studied, and incorporation into the ethnographic text of numerous reference points (from myths to historical texts and works of art)" (Neyland 2008: 34). A 'quick description,' on the other hand, "[is a] brief immersion in the field, often directed towards achieving a specific and sometimes quite narrow goal" (ibid: 34). Nayland suggests further that quick description often involves visits to several locations and presentation of the findings. Two of my research trips to Maidan (three weeks and one month each) in winter 2013/2014-spring 2014, respectively, were my long-term immersion in the field, where I was able to dwell in the revolutionary context and observe, interview, and make photo and video recordings. My stay at the war/borderline regions of Donbas was shorter, yet equally intense. In Bate's terms, 'thick description is more genuinely ethnographic,' while Hammersley and Atkinson (1998: 58) also suggest that "[spending] maximum time in the field to understand what is going on." In such a context, the benefits were driven from both 'thick' and 'quick' fieldwork, where I gathered diverse data such as pictures, documents and interviews, as well as collected books and videos that added grassroots, personalized interpretation of the events.

A "selective intermittent time mode," defined by Jeffrey and Troman (2004: 542) as a method where "one devotes some time to doing research (two-three years), but only spends part of that time immersed in the field," is the technique that I used when it comes to time. Oftentimes, understanding what might be important or who should be seen as a reliable source of information is rather time-consuming. Because I had an opportunity to visit Ukraine numerous times within 4.5 years, the distance between the researcher (myself) and the researched (my interviewees, physical space of Maidan, the cities or villages, museums, squares or graffiti sides) was established. Such distance had the most effect on communication with my interviewees, since particularly close, daily interaction with the protestors of Euromaidan, for example, was difficult to maintain after the protestors left Kyiv. The unique atmosphere of 'brotherhood,' social and cultural equality that was one of the primary characteristics of Maidan, at times was challenging to revive upon the return for the follow-up meetings: often, the interviewees felt pressure from their family or friends, or felt uncomfortable expressing their stands in front of their loved ones.

Finally, when it comes to specifics of the data collection process, acknowledgement of the difference between 'time' elements — critical, subjective and substantive distance, was crucial. What struck a viewer, or the participant of the event as significant in one moment did not perform the same function a week or a month later. Equally, in ethical terms, what was appropriate to ask or discuss during instances like battles or the force majeure situations of the Euromaidan or war in Donbas, naturally, was socially inept within a peaceful context.

In practical terms, the geographic location of the fieldwork was determined both by means of the snowballing sampling and acuteness of the socio-political developments. Usually, I would arrive in Kyiv and then proceed to the location of the most salient events — the revolutionary clashes, toppling of the communist statues, viches[14], or the military activities in the east. Prevalently, as the capital city, Kyiv was the site where the most versatile data was collected. Both during and after the Maidan, citizens of different regions of Ukraine came to the capital to articulate their political stands, address the government, or simply observe and live through what was the biggest political transformation of the country. Oftentimes, the data collected in Kyiv could be easily examined as being reflective of both regional and national socio-political developments, since virtually 'all' of the country was represented

---

14 *Viche* is the term originated during times of the Kyivan Rus' (882 AD). It is used in Ukraine to address meetings of the country's ordinary citizens to discuss important socio-political or cultural matters faced by the community. The origins of the *viche* were in a tribal court system, which was a characteristic governing entity for all East Slavic peoples. In terms of its legal authority, the *viche* was a manifestation of popular rule, analogous to the popular meetings held in the cities of ancient Greece and in Western European cities during the Middle Ages. During the Euromaidan revolution (2013-2014), 'Viche' was a common political practice where the citizens of Kyiv and other large cities of western, southern, northern and eastern parts of the country gathered together to articulate their socio-political stands. Accessed May 17, 2015. Source: http://www.encyclopediaofukraine.com/display.asp?linkpath=pages%5CV%5CI%5CVicheIT.htm.

within the physical space of the protest. Further on, while in the field, I collected research material based on the subject or the location in question. This means that I either interviewed, attended places I was referred to by my interviewees, or did both. I also attended political poster exhibitions, art galleries, and all major sides of the toppling of the communist symbols.

In total, within the time-framework of over 4.5 years, 14 trips to different regions of Ukraine were made. In terms of intensity of the conducted fieldwork and volume of the collected material, the first two-and-half years (2013-2016) were the 'primary' period of the data-gathering. Overall, the duration of my stay in Ukraine varied from two weeks to three months. Since December of 2013 and until October of 2018, I took over 200 pictures of the Maidan Nezalezhnosti Square, conducted 64 interviews with the participants of the revolution, the state and media officials, soldiers, and the ordinary citizens, and recorded 28 videos of the revolution, the military activities and toppling of the Soviet statues in Kyiv and other regions of Ukraine (e.g. Lviv, Vinnytsia, Zaporizhzhya, Chernihiv, Odessa, or Kharkiv). During and shortly after the Maidan, my primary focus was to conduct interviews with the participants of the protests, artists, and media figures, as well as to take pictures of the political posters, buildings, graffiti and monuments' sides. I also came down to filming speeches and spontaneous events with the political, media, NGO, and religious figures. As the war in Donbas escalated and over two million of the internally displaced relocated to different regions of Ukraine, extensive interviews with the displaced population were also conducted. The primary objective of the interviews was to record the internally displaced citizens' stands on the socio-political and cultural developments of post-2013 Ukraine, examine modes of cultural and physical adaptation, and track their views on decommunization.

As an overall objective, my goal was to get involved in observation *and* participation. Carried on the snowballing basis, the interviewees, as well as multiple objects of the revolution (e.g. tents, posters, or different objects of art) provided both the discursive and physical (geographic) reference to further data. For instance, date and time of artistic installations was easily detectable through the signs at the Maidan Nezalezhnosti square. As such, from early 2014 and until summer 2017, at the *Pinchuk Art Center* only, I attended exhibitions on Maidan, de-Sovietization, and multiple installations on war in Donbas. All together, the collected photo, video and interview data can be divided into the following thematic categories:

1) The Euromaidan revolution (2013- summer 2014): pictures, videos, interviews, artistic exhibitions or posters that record diverse civic stands on the socio-political and cultural developments of post-2013 Ukraine.

2) War in Donbas (2014-2018): pictures, interviews, videos of the artistic installations that capture both ordinary citizens' and governmental stands on the military conflict in eastern Ukraine and its socio-political and cultural aftermath.

3) Spontaneous and institutionalized decommunization (2013-2018): toppling (or preservation) of monuments of Lenin, visual and discursive emergence of figures of the Ukrainian nationalist past (e.g. Bandera/members of the UPA), change of the street names and passing of the official decommunization laws.

Interviews, Visuals, Texts

As the interview data were being collected, distrust of politicians, anger, excitement, hope and despair were among the many narratives that dispersed into thousands of voices and, at the same time, articulated a common discursive denominator: a thematic umbrella of basic daily survival, collective mourning, and the pull of Ukraine between Europe and Russia.

I intentionally chose to examine interviews (and data such as photo or video material) that present a general view of the socio-political developments of post-Euromaidan Ukraine as diverse, and at times even fragmented. The implication of choosing otherwise — prospecting self-affirmative interviews that support popular stands on West-East division of Ukraine, oppression of Russian/Ukrainian-speaking population in eastern/western areas, or denote 'uniformity' of Maidan would suggest mere confirmation of popular clichés; it would add no particular value to neither academic nor political discussion (Westdal 2015; Oldfield 2014; Fedirko 2014; Vakhovska 2015; Zhurzhenko 2015).

When conducting the semi-structured interviews, the goal was to pose open-ended questions to allow space for diversity and further dialogue. During trips to Kyiv, Lviv, Kharkiv, Myrgorod, Poltava, Dnipro or Zaporizhzhya, general questions were posed to identify primary motives for one's involvement (or restraint) from the protest, military activities, toppling of the communist monuments, or the production and spread of political posters. Specifically, I was interested in inquiring as to one's stands on history, political positioning or ideology — in exploring views that seemed to be dominating at a particular moment or region, as well as analyzing the socio-political stands of the 'minorities' — voices that were suppressed throughout and after Maidan(s), both in Kyiv and in the regions.

In her reflections on the Euromaidan revolution, Lada Nakonechna (2014) argues that, considering "multitude of completely different people that would never cross paths ordinarily, precisely the intimate presence in one place causing to correlate one's views and interests with those of others," participation of people who relocated to the squares of Kyiv as early as in December of 2013, or traveled all the way to Donbas from western or central Ukraine in 2014 was expressed as an enormous sacrifice. At the same time, the majority of the protestors and activists I interviewed stated that participation in the revolution was "a fully conscious act." When a peaceful November 2013 protest began, the primary cost of involvement into the protest was homelessness.

The first day of my second major field trip to Maidan, May 24 2014, was a particularly distinct *visual* imprint. Already peaceful, yet still full of protesters, tents, posters, graffiti, both the Ukrainian and international political, media and social activists, the square of Maidan was a living embodiment of the physical complexity of the event: covered in ashes, burned and, at parts, completely destroyed, Khreschatyk street and the Independence Square were scarred. The faces, scenes, and narratives I recorded on video reflect struggle, obstruction and yet, immense unity and hope. The solidarity of ordinary citizens was apparent particularly within the framework of the daily reality that, at that time, was scarcely covered by both media and academic sources (Bikov 2017; Kakhidze 2015; Levytsky 2014). One of the most simple, yet intense experiences was to enter one of the tents. Owned by an engineer from Lviv, Stepan (as I came to know later on during the interview), the tent was designed to host approximately 15 people, and within the realities of Maidan, it accommodated over 50 protestors. The couches (or, in most cases, handmade sleeping space) were placed side-by-side to create a 'bed' that would hold as many protestors as possible. An overly long 'table' with varied types of canned food (all brought to the protesters mostly by the supporters of Maidan) was one of the most common objects of the 'household' surrounding. The amount of work that was invested into accommodation of such space into that of both activism and day-to-day residency was literally *colossal*.

As extreme as such living conditions on Madain could seem, especially during winter and then exceptionally hot late spring of 2014, the interviewees described the revolutionary life as "blessing rather than a curse." In May 2014, recalling his experiences of Maidan, the activist Petro Moholny addressed the challenge of such conditions as a "given that was neither rebutted nor questioned." According to the interviewees, the physical presence at Maidan was one of the primary modes of articulation of their political stands — at first, the government of President Yanukovych, and then the Russian Federation. Particularly during the Russian media-campaign, which portrayed Ukrainians as violent, savage transgressors, daily living conditions of the protestors exceeded the idea of basic physical needs being met. Maintenance of the tents, careful positioning of posters, and later on, attentive removal of debris from the Maidan Nezalezhnosti square, Khreschatyk, and the nearby streets on a purely voluntary basis was on its own a statement of civic awareness. Such acts, as a prominent writer, philosopher and public activist, Yurii Andrukhovych, argues in *Euromaidan: Chronicle of Feelings* (2014: 43), "is what constructs the basis for civilized, European identity." During and shortly after the Euromaidan revolution, the space of protest was both the domain of physical challenge and, at the same time, that of virtually unrestricted freedom. It evolved into a symbol of *personal choice* — to support, care or protect others at the expense of one's own physical comfort, safety and, at times, even life.

As such, the observation of protests in Kyiv, Chernihiv, Kharkiv, Zaporizhzhya, Dnipro, Poltava, Myrhorod, Odessa, Vinnytsia or Lviv, filming of the Automaidan demonstrations[15] or interviewing activists who were involved in demolition or preservation of the Soviet insignia, allowed access to data that was versatile in its contextual nature. I was able to interview people of diverse, oftentimes opposing socio-political and cultural backgrounds, and to document multiple forms of articulation of both similar *and* polar political stands. At both the regional and national level, the collected data revealed construction of hegemonic practices that carried "an attempt to establish particular relations and orders of meanings" (Palonen 2018).

In addition to interviews, the foremost research material collected is composed of over 400 photographs on graffiti, posters, toppled and preserved statues, the empty plinths, street signs, and the bookshelves. The data also includes videos of the protests, toppling of communist statues, spontaneous demonstrations, rallies of Automaidan, the presidential inauguration of Petro Poroshenko (Kyiv 2014), political poster exhibitions, and multiple spontaneous chats with the ordinary citizens recorded in different regions of Ukraine.

As I arrived in different cities, I collected pamphlets, books, printed collections of images and videos (documentaries) at the exhibitions, museums, spontaneous and themed meetings. With an *initial* objective of examining the grassroots narratives of the state undergoing the process of decommunization, I also collected documents, journals, and diaries of artists, writers, and philosophers. As

---

15   *Automaidan* was a political rally that began in Kiev during the Euromaidan Revolution and has spread to different cities of Ukraine. The original objective of the movement was to contribute to the overthrow of the corrupt regime of President Victor Yanukovych. After the Maidan, the movement became the springboard for the socio-politically active volunteers intending to fight corruption and standing for reformation of the legislative and executive branches of the government. Accessed July 5, 2015. Source: http://www.automaidan.org.ua/aboutus.html.

a rule, I would arrive with an attempt to follow major socio-political events and interview their participants. I would take photos and videos of the protests, public events, such as ordinary citizens' debates during the presidential inauguration (June 7, 2014, Kyiv), the *Viche* or the political poster exhibitions installed at central squares of the cities, for instance.

As the international center for contemporary art, the *Pinchuk Art Center* in Kyiv was one of the primary sources where I collected highly controversial, thought-provoking artistic data. An open platform for artists and ordinary Ukrainians, as well as the international audience, the center was a capital location for interactive critical exhibitions. It was also the key check-point for the politically-minded artists, civic activists and the public who were willing to share their knowledge and personal experiences of creating art as means for articulation of the political and cultural stands. In total, 18 books and 38 pamphlets and posters have been purchased in Kyiv since my arrival to Ukraine in December of 2013. This and other material offered both anonymous and personalized space for expression of what were often distinctively multivocal views. The above reference material also served as a means for the mobilization of the masses, from the revolutionary events to the military activities and toppling of monuments of Lenin or renaming of the streets.

In January 2015, while attending one of the exhibitions, I purchased exceptional work called "Плохой-Хороший Человек" ("Bad-Good Human") of the Ukrainian artist Alevtina Kakhidze. An active participant of the Euromaidan revolution, born only ten kilometers from Viktor Yanukovych's hometown—Enakievo, Kakhidze (2015) declared about her multi-level, Ukrainian, Georgian and West European identity, and touched upon the subjects of war, protest, and 'Soviet [cultural] incarnation.' In what seemed like a simple notebook, the perennial antithesis of meanings, construction and definition of 'good' and 'bad' was explored. One of the many objects of the Ukrainian political art, the book offered space for *individual* interpretation and implementation of the concepts such as construction (or the discursive articulation) of 'us' and 'them,' the 'local' or the 'other,' the 'colonized' and the 'colonizer.'

An insert of this book included a list of popular artists of the Ukrainian, post-Soviet and international domain who were directly involved in participation, analysis and further artistic re-creation of the post-revolutionary events. Grounded on the snowballing method of contacting artists and finding out about their work, I obtained actual samples of the artists' creation (books, pamphlets, posters, and paintings), and compiled the authors' name-list to then contact and meet prominent political artists in person. Broadly speaking, vast portion of the collected data provided a multidimensional view on the construction of the hegemonic formations and the process of meaning-making as a whole within the Ukrainian post-revolutionary space. It presented 'raw' records (e.g: pictures/graffiti/personal journals), gave space for interaction (participatory items of the exhibitions/e.g the "Strike Poster" project) and triggered critical thinking providing ground for analysis of the discursive authenticity, uncertainty and, at times, provocation.

During interaction with both the Ukrainian and international political artists, such as Kristina Norman and Meelis Muhu (Estonia) (February-March 2014), Alevtina Kakhidze (Ukraine, March 2014) or Egor Petrov (Ukraine, May 2016), I was also introduced to profound documentaries on the Euromaidan revolution, war in Donbas and the official decommunization. "What motivates the Ukrainians to place their own bodies against the police cordons?" or "where do opinions diverge and when does solidarity triumph?" (*One World*, 2015) are one of the many questions that were raised by the film of Roman Bondarchuk, *Euromaidan. Rough Cut* (2014). Ranging from a protest to the military activities in Donbas, multiple forms of decommunization also have been captured by the cameras of both the Ukrainian and international documentarians. The documentaries record the most vivid cases of "an explosion of revived dignity, the euphoria of freedom, pain of awareness of the cost, and [most importantly] birth of modern Ukrainian nation" (*The Institute of Documentary Film*, 2015). The following are the documentaries that have been reviewed and used as the supplementary data for deepening of the analysis:

- All Things Ablaze (2013) (Directors: Oleksandr Technynskyi, Aleksey Solodunov, Dmitry Stoykov)
- Euromaidan. Rough Cut (2014) (Director: Roman Bondarchuk)
- The Female Faces of the Revolution (2014) (Director: Nataliya Pyatygyna)
- The Winter That Changed Us (2014) (The joint project of "1 +1" Production and Creative Union of Babylon 130)
- Maidan (2014) (Director: Sergei Loznitsia)
- Maidan. The Art of Resistance (2014) (Director: Antin Mukharskiy).

Textual and Narrative Analysis

Grounded in the theoretical framework of discourse analysis (Laclau and Mouffe 1985) that addresses hegemony as the phenomena being mediated through discourse (Cox 2019; Modelski 1999; Thompson 2015), the data implied 'living,' 'experiencing' and 'telling' as methodological elements of articulation. The research material was collected on a snowballing basis, with the analysis illustrating the political and cultural multivocality of the Ukrainian population. Repeatedly, the collected data enabled examination of decommunization as both contextually and visually-diverse phenomenon that amalgamates demolition of the communist legacy at the governmental, cultural and mental level. The collected material also exposed diversity of the positions or modes of articulation of the same events and provided examples of what I argue to be the construction of the 'imagined communities' (Anderson 1983). In broader terms, the data illustrated multiple attempts of establishment of particular relations and order of meanings—construction of hegemonic formations that presuppose counter-hegemonic constructions because of the ultimately contested nature of the formations indicated first.

In examining the research material, I used the method of "layered textual analysis" (Covert 2014). Developed on Collier's (2001: 12) model of drawing analytical relationship between photos, narratives and physical objects of civic space to "produce a complete sequence of both the discursive and visual layers of the findings," layered textural analysis brings together images, texts and physical objects (e.g. statues) to provide comprehensive understanding of different types of data. This method consists of structural analysis of the narratives present in the interview text or visual analysis of the photos, and guiding questions related to the content and relationship of the photos, objects and narratives. As being illustrated by Figure C (Covert 2014), an outcome of the 'structural narrative analysis' (Layer 1), the 'visual analysis' (Layer 2) and the 'thematic analysis' (Layer 3) leads to construction of a broader framework that includes interpretations and findings of the data. Such findings, Covert and Koro-Ljungberg (2014: 310) argue, "consist of individual experiences, images, objects or texts that reflect complex connections between matter and thought." Further on, according to Covert and Koro-Ljungberg (2014: 311), "the multilayered analysis leads to understandings and representations of the participants' learning and interpretation of cultural differences, and allows us to examine photo-narrative events or the participants' individual meaning-making processes."

Figure C: Layered textual analysis (Covert 2014)

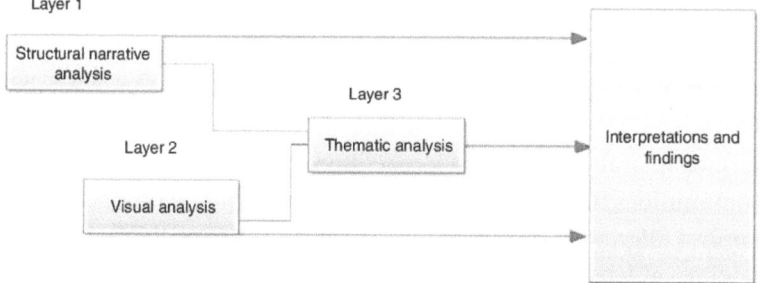

I kept the content of Covert's model since it matches the nature of the collected data: it sets the framework for simultaneous examination of the interview ('Layer 1') and visual ('Layer 2') data, and can be combined with a broader thematic analysis ('Layer 3'). However, I chose to change the numbering of the layers' — the 'structural narrative analysis' and the 'visual analysis' is made parallel (both labeled as 'Layer 1'), and the 'thematic analysis' is marked as 'Layer 2'. Such changes reflect the coequality of the narrative and visual data: within my research, both interviews and images (e.g. political posters, images of the toppled communist statues or graffiti) were of equal importance and were collected simultaneously. The 'thematic analysis,' thereon, is defined as 'Layer 2' to link the interview and visual data under the umbrella of common analytical themes. The 'interpretations and findings,' as shown by the original diagram of Covert (2014), would be left intact and provide space for presentation of the methodological and theoretical results.

Finally, I used the concept of *narrative* to create a broader framework for categorization of the collected data. If one thinks of normal, everyday storytelling, Hyvärinen (2008: 4) argues, "narrative must be looked at as a strategic performance within specific and multileveled context that orders embodiment, situation, and discourse." Since my research explored the implementation of political identity transformations that occurred via multiple forms of discursive and physical articulation, I examined the interviews, videos and images as means for construction of the discursive narratives. The toppled monuments of the Soviet era, political photo exhibitions or videos, such as documentaries, narrated the 'plot' of decommunization—they served as multiple modes of the political performance of the state eliminating ideological and physical remnants of its Soviet past.

In his analysis of the 'narrative form and narrative content,' Hyvärinen (2008: 5) argues further that "the storytelling is performed at multiple levels of local cultures and creates the imagined communities that are made real within the narrative process." Certainly, I align with this statement. I applied the narrative as a methodological lens that, I argue, allows us to detect particular experiences of the citizens' daily lives and address multiple means of articulation of their cultural and political stands. Here, 'articulation' stands for creation of popular visuals of the revolution (e.g. graffiti, slogans, or posters), as well as for dismantling of physical elements of the city landscape (e.g. the demolition of Lenin statues). In broader terms, I use contextual examination of such narratives to define mechanisms of establishment of multiple hegemonic formations that add to onset of the imagined communities.

In his proposal for "social narratology," David Herman (1999) suggests that "the distinction between *story* and *narrative* discourse is one of the most important elements that social scientists could and should adopt from the literary study of a narrative." 'Story,' in this language, refers to "the presumed 'sequence of events' — that is the 'what' or 'content' of narrative." Instead, a new concept of the 'narrative discourse,' or shortly 'narrative,' Herman (1999: 5) claims further, refers to "the how or way of narration — the order, mood, voice, distance, style in which the events are accounted for in the narrative." Within the context of some of the post-Soviet states such as Ukraine, distinct, at times opposing positions on the country's socio-political and cultural advent, the story or narrative has not been available as such. By using ethnography as the methodology that involves both observation and participation in the society, I approach the 'how,' or what I define as the examination of multiple modes of articulation of the discursive narratives.

In practical terms, all data were recorded and fully transcribed in original languages (Ukrainian and Russian). The transcripts were then thematically coded and analyzed in their original spoken languages. Due to the vast volume of the collected material, the images of the posters and graffiti are listed in the Appendix.

4. The Poster — Roots of the Lenin cult

"Beat the Whites with the Red Wedge"
— El Lissitzky

In his article entitled "Events: Visual Studies Today: the Power of Images," Kresimir Purgar defines the *pictorial turn* as a "set of symptoms which we can notice in the western postcapitalist societies, and which are characterized by the domination of the image and the visual communication in everyday life" (Purgar 2017: 10). As the discussion of multiple modes of visual culture — fine art, cinema, the internet, performance, photography or television evolves among the authors studying visuals (Dikovitskaya 2005; Mitchell 1994; Mirzoeff 1999), the general argument that these theoreticians present is the following: the old language paradigm is being replaced (or "has been replaced" already) by the new image paradigm. What that means is that within the framework of visual studies and beyond the image paradigm becomes the "new visual subjectivity" (Dikovitskaya 2005: 15). While the ordinary citizens, politicians or artists are constructing or looking at objects of art, they themselves are being observed or looked at. The objects are being created through different modes of viewing and multiple interrelation of visual and physical facts. Such process, the authors of the visual studies argue further, is a modern socio-political occurrence that "does not have a defined social programme, vocation or a higher goal except the one aiming for a better understanding of images and for the study of the mechanism of the visual construction of reality" (Purgar 2017: 12).

Not objecting to the claim that "visual studies remain focused on images, regardless of what historical, political, artistic, textual or extratextual context it is set in" (Purgar 2017: 12), I argue in favor of in-depth examination of how the construction of reality with images is a social, highly political act. The post-Euromaidan decommunization is an acute example of the meaning-making process, where multiple forms of political art (e.g. exhibition of the political posters, toppling or preservation of monuments or creative renaming of the streets) are one of the primary elements of the hegemonic formations. Prior to analyzing specific examples of the data I collected, I suggest looking at how the political poster of central and eastern Europe, as well as political art as a whole, was designed to patronize and, at the same time, give space to new social and political constructions. When examining images as the site for establishing politics, it is nearly impossible to avoid studying visuals being used by the state to control and define lives of the ordinary citizens. In this sense, the poster of central and eastern Europe is no exception: it emerged to articulate power and establish the political tradition of the government controlling the discursive, ideological and physical space of the state. I offer to examine what could be seen as both the cause and effect of state-control over the physical and ideological domain: the personality cult. Both the political and cultural link between the state and the people was set by romanticization of the communist leaders, specific socio-political events, and the ordinary public.

My stand on understanding 'roots' of decommunization is grounded on studying memory as both the collective and individual act that is used by the state to construct its ideological and socio-political framework. The de-Sovietization of Ukraine is a vivid example of memory being used as a social practice of the imagining that connects ideological and physical modes of civic existence through diverse interpretations of the past. The primary characteristic of (post)Euromaidan decommunization is *multivocality*. The images, statues or street-names are used as means for articulation of multiple stands on decommunization which, I argue, still carry elements of the old Soviet regime. In one respect, as means of the meaning-making, the political posters of post-2013 Ukraine serve as powerful space for articulation of messages of 'decommunization.' At the same time, they preserve substantial traces of the communist characteristics: the state continues to articulate its political narratives within the space of the posters; the enemy or the 'other' is being constructed by means of political posters and is being used to justify the armed conflict in Donbas.

As I examine further in more detail, despite dramatic violence and high mortality rates in the war zone, the citizens, both women and men, are portrayed in a manner similar to that of the Soviet Union. 'Happy,' 'patient' and 'freedom-loving,' they are proud citizens who are willing to sacrifice their lives for the territorial integrity of the state and bright future of their country. Finally, the explicit portrayal of individuals that are to 'represent' the nation is occurring within the visual space of modern Ukrainian posters. At the same time, at the grassroots level, political posters of post-2013 Ukraine construct a new narrative of diversity of the socio-political and cultural positions, and lead to the formation of the 'imagined communities' that juxtapose the homogenising narrative of the state.

Methodology of the Poster

Produced as affirmations or challenges of the communist ideology, political posters of central and eastern Europe articulate the discourse of power. According to Aulich and Sylvestrova, they acquire "manifold relations of power which permeate, characterize and constitute the social body...[which] cannot itself be established, consolidated nor implemented without the production, accumulation, circulation and functioning of a discourse" (Aulich and Sylvestrova 1999: 5). Formulated by both ordinary citizens and the government, the discourses articulated within the political posters carry potential of rendering citizens into the imaginary identities. It could be stated that the very essence of the political poster, therefore, lies in the production of official narratives as means for claiming legitimacy of the state or institutionalization of a particular value system for everyday life. The socialist poster, embracing specific messages or ideas of the state, became a powerful mechanism for 'defining' ordinary citizens. Operating at both the physical and discursive space of the state, it presented power as the primary tool of 'democratic governance,' multiculturalism and 'friendship of the peoples.' It addressed control as an integral part of democratization, "repression as a condition of freedom, privilege as necessary for equality, and the humanistic claims of Marxism-Leninism as the justification of human rights abuses" (Aulich and Sylvestrova 1999: 5).

Though to a lesser extent, the poster has been used by both the government and ordinary citizens of (post)Euromaidan Ukraine as a powerful tool of meaning-making; it provided space for articulation of multiple, at times contrasting hegemonic meanings. As both contradictory and analogous meanings are being formulated, both the ordinary citizens and the government are using political posters to communicate the transformation from the old to the new political regimes. Within such a process, heterogeneity of interpretations of the country's socio-political course is being articulated through diverse forms of the visuals. In the communist tradition of using posters one of the primary visual narratives was that of the 'new happy people.' This narrative is also found in multiple posters and graffiti of post-Euromaidan Ukraine, where images of soldiers of war in Donbas are also presented within a romanticized, 'happy individuals' framework.

Rooted in the context of decades of psychological trauma and wars, the political posters of the communist era articulated an image of how the party saw itself and the nation to be. Though rarely cited, the ground point of both early and mid-20th century Bolshevik posters was a "visual script" (Bonnel 1999: 14) — a visual, social space for a new citizen who was to appear a counterpart of his or her pre-revolutionary antithesis. Dedicated egalitarian workers of the new ruling class were to rise up out of social injustice, inequality and historical contradictions of capitalism. Dramatic social change would emerge to affect both the emotional and physical state of the Soviet citizens and transform the society into an army of happy and physically strong individuals.

Within the scope of socio-political and cultural rivalry of the Soviet Union and the West, the subjects of the Soviet posters were portrayed as virtuous and healthy. Produced as a response to political and social demands of the state, the poster was also used as the space for contextualization of power relations between the political elites and the ordinary citizens. All the way since the times of Lenin, the need to create and promote heroes has been one of the primary features of the communist poster. The dominant idea behind cultivation or the process of 'hero'-envisioning was that the figure to be praised was to be appealing and recognized by the Soviet public. It had to be strong and signify both care and protection. For these criteria to be met, one of the most popular symbols of the Soviet state was a figure of a soldier. Embracing both the urban masculinity of industrial life and the rural, more feminine qualities of the countryside, a soldier of the Red Army is one of the central figures of the Soviet poster. It signifies both the protection and omnipresence of the state. Viktor Koretsky's poster, *Our flag, victorious flag*, from 1945, for example, is a concise illustration of the matter.

Particularly during and after World War II, traditional characteristics of women being 'weak' and in need of protection or care were also blurred. The Soviet poster articulated women as equally powerful, strong individuals who were capable of performing factory, agricultural or military work while being mothers and educators of their children. In her discussion of construction of new gendered spaces through the means of state-sponsored propaganda, Bazylevych illustrates that, in contrast to the political posters of the 1920s, women of post-WWII USSR were depicted as those "surrounded by books rather than family or children...In the background [were] the socialist institutions that allowed for their emancipation, such as kindergartens, vocational schools, and factories" (Bazylevych 2010: 4). As such, the language of the political poster reflects both social and gender transformations that become politically visible through both the discursive and visual framework of political art.

Finally, within the process of unification of the nation around discursive segments of ideology, political posters were also used as visual points for creating psychological and moral standards that reinforced the socio-political policies of the communist block. In the light of the socio-political rivalry of the Soviet Union and the West, for instance, consolidation of the communist space was to occur around the figure of the common enemy. To justify the internal political repressions, the posters pictured the 'other' as the source of oppression. In such terms, the war on the 'other' was both the discursive and physical maneuver that was launched by the Soviet state to distract its citizens from the domestic disparities, both social and political. The enemy or the other could be found internally or externally — the bourgeois or noble-origin Soviet citizen, or the foreign, American 'imperialist.'

In their discussion of the socialist visual legacy, Aulich and Sylvestrova refer to Czechoslovakia as one of the places where the category of the 'enemy' included diverse social elements. The representatives of the Church, for example, "possessed a spiritual faith and institutional structure [that was] antipathetic to the communist atheist worldview being based on dialectical materialism" (Aulich and Sylvestrova 1999: 179). The Second World War, on the other hand, left extensive heritage of the international enemies who threatened the communist system with their liberal, bourgeois ideals. Particularly during the 1940s and 1950s, many of the so-called "internal enemies" of socialism were executed, sentenced to prolonged periods in prison or used as slave labor in excruciating labor camps. In this sense, the class and ideological struggle became the subject of a major propaganda campaign that was visualized in political posters of that time. The popular caricature of the Kukrinisky group, *Pest ridgeway in western Europe! Maximum vigilance and battle readiness protects our GDR* from 1952, is one of the many examples of prevailing on the European socialists-controlled space.

As the atmosphere of animosity and fear rooted within the Soviet society, the political poster also turned into a powerful tool for promotion of watchfulness and civic awareness. The militia man, or an ordinary factory worker, the Soviet citizen was portrayed as the one warning others of potential military or ideological aggression. Particularly after the World War II, amidst geopolitical transformations and forced population displacement, the figure of the "defender of the state" ("защитник родины") obtained the scale of both moral and physical perfection, where a holder of surpassing physical and ideological characteristics, the socialist citizen was a symbol of both physical strength and unquestionable political loyalty. As such, both physical and moral perfection, utter devotion to labor, and complete ideological obedience to the state were the primary narratives of the socialist political art that created a space of distinct order — "political mythology." Such process of meaning-making via political posters was an effective mechanism for constructing a discursive framework, where "the personal was virtually degraded to the level of public consumption" (Yurchak 2008: 5). I leave the discussion of the Soviet people's reaction to such political propaganda to other history-curious minds. As the bottom line, whether supporting or rejecting political art of such kind, citizens of the USSR were forced to operate within the boundaries of their state, and to construct their lives in accordance with its discursive scope.

In the following, the role of political poster within the Soviet or socialist context is summarized:

- Throughout the course of the late 19th and the entire 20th century, the poster has been used as a powerful tool for articulation and implementation of the state ideology and vision of the ordinary people's lives.
- Fundamentally, political posters have been widely used for visualization or articulation of the utopian ideas of the state.
- One of the general narratives articulated within the political posters was that consolidation of the state had to occur around the figure of the common enemy, or the 'other.' It is the 'other' that also justified intrastate violence, such as repressions of the internal 'enemies of the state.'
- Finally, the political poster of the communist times is the iconography of the social changes. Within the visual space of a poster, the 'personal' was articulated to become 'political,' where the martyr-like figures such as Pavlik Morozov[16] were used to embody devoted communist character.

---

16 Pavel Morozov (14 November 1918 – 3 September 1932), better known by the diminutive Pavlik, was the leader of the Young Pioneers' group at his village school and was a fanatical supporter of the Soviet government's collectivization drive in the countryside. In 1930, at age 12, he gained notoriety for denouncing his father to the Soviet authorities. Morozov also accused other peasants of hoarding their grain and withholding it from the authorities. As a consequence of his denunciations, Morozov was brutally murdered by several local kulaks, as historians claim, members of his family. Accessed October 16, 2018. Source: https://www.britannica.com/biography/Pavlik-Morozov.

The Leaders Cult

Historically, centrality and absolutism have been distinct features of the socio-political and cultural domain of eastern Europe. The personality cult is the practice emerging from this tradition. Commencing with Lenin and reaching its peak with Stalin, the cult is rooted in tsarist structures that were constructed around hierarchic relations between the elites or the state, and the ordinary public. Particularly after the revolutions that carry a tendency of being grounded in romantic nationalism, the ideology of cultivation of particular leaders comes into play. In his critical analysis of Eurocentric history, German philosopher Oswald Spengler defines the worship or cultivation of a specific personality as "a catalyst of national identity." According to Aulich and Sylvestrova, Stalinists, inspired by pan-Slavist thought "shared with the nationalisms of the area the irrationalist myth of spiritual greatness ultimately derived from Herder's definition of the *Volksgeist* (folk spirit)" (Aulich and Sylvestrova 1999: 86). If during the interwar period the cult of militarist heroic leaders was the dominant feature of central and east European state-narrative, the victory of the communist regime over fascism in the Second World War raised Stalin to the top of a personal cult. The figure of a leader became an embodiment of the party *and* the nation—a symbol that served as a discursive cementing between the public and the private, the state and the ordinary citizens.

Originally, the bust was the most common form of depiction or public glorification of the leader. Particularly during the Stalinist regime, collective portrayal of the founders of the revolution—Karl Marx, Frederick Engels, and the great founder of the Russian Revolution, Vladimir Lenin, became a popular mechanism that glorified Stalin by juxtaposing his figure to the rest. The presentation of the communist leaders (primarily those of the past) on a banner, poster, or in the form of a statue, for instance, was a demonstration of the conformity of the regional to the national. Theoretically, "the object and the demiurge of national adulation, the leader of the communist regime was a 'great architect' who was an 'expert' in everything, [knew] everything, [and ran] everything" (Fejto 1971: 10).

The architectural creation of Otakar Švec, *Stalin's Monument*, Prague 1959 (Figure 1) is an example of the distinct embodiment of such practice—the positioning of the figure of Stalin is affirmative of the ideological narrative of the state. The title of the monument and the creation itself address descriptive discrepancy—though set in the background, the Soviet people are the substantial part of the visual domain of the monument. However, the only name that the sculpture bears is "Stalin." The public image of the leader is both paternal and appeasing, and holds particular missionary value. The head of the state, Stalin, imposes meaning on the present, past and future, and leads the nation toward further victories, both over the external and internal foes. For decades, the mentality of the Soviet people was crafted along the narrative where, though serving as an integral part of the state's texture, the citizens were composed as an array of nameless-figures. An ordinary citizen was given a professional or ideological category—'a miner,' 'a worker,' or 'a collective farmer.' The *nameless*, general rank was juxtaposed to the specific leader—Lenin or Stalin. Such visual and narrative framework contributed to the formation of what is known as 'the Soviet mentality'—a particular path of socio-political thinking where an individual withholds political existence in the absence of an autocratic ruler. The personal is being displaced by the collective, with the statues of Stalin or Lenin becoming the dominant symbol of a particular historical context and serving as an embodiment of specific experiences of the Soviet generation. Not surprisingly, despite the official implementation of the decommunization laws of (post)Euromaidan Ukraine, the personality cult remains a deeply-rooted cultural phenomenon—the mentality-trade that is to be distinguished from a purely political or economic domain.

Public condemnation of the communist regime through artistic expressions, such as posters, paintings or pieces of critical literature, emerged already during the years of the communist rule. As early as 1982, "NSK in Yugoslavia juxtaposed the heads of Marx, Engels and Lenin with the heads of the victims of communism and a version of Malevich's black cross on a white ground to speak for the fate of the utopian hopes of the revolution" (Aulich and Sylvestrova 1999: 92). Further on, the 1988 Warsaw Biennale was one of the first denunciations of the regime outside the Soviet Union. In that manner, artistic protest established means of articulation of what could not be publicly spoken. The Leninfall[17] and other forms of removal of the symbols of communist oppression in Ukraine is but a mirror phenomenon of modern post-Soviet space where the discursive vacuum of silenced socio-political dominance is being filled with the active deposition of the political system and its symbols.

In historical terms, the socio-political realm of the post-Soviet space has been marked by numerous rounds of counter-idealization. Upon the death of Stalin in 1953, for instance, Khrushchev's "thaw" transformed memorialization of the past through the cult of mortality into celebration of a new existence. Thousands of busts, monuments or paintings of Stalin were replaced by posters and statues of Lenin who became a counter-repressive symbol of "humanization" of the communist regime. In an attempt to establish a connection between the Marxist-Leninist ideology, the party and the ordinary citizens, memory of Lenin became romanticized by discursive and visual construction of a symbol that was oriented toward the bright, serene future ("светлое будущее"). Monumental and cogent, his statues reached all corners of the Soviet Union, occupying central squares and parks of urban centers, smaller cities and villages. As a form of virtual denial of the personality cult, Lenin was placed within the daily space of ordinary people.

As such, the cult of Lenin is but a mere cult of personality. It is a declaration of the political (party) ideology and the state agenda. Depersonalized at the regional level, the figure of Lenin is

---

17 To remind the reader, *Leninfall* is the term used to describe the removal of the statues of Vladimir Lenin in modern Ukraine. The process of toppling of the Soviet statues in Ukraine started mainly in the western regions of the country in the early 1990s. During and after the Euromaidan revolution, the "Leninfall" became a widespread phenomenon and was followed by the official policies of "decommunization" (e.g. 2015 decommunization laws). Accessed July 7, 2018. Source: http://www.memory.gov.ua/news/leninopad-yak-proshchannya-z-radyanskim-minulim.

also typical in its 'implementation': the locations of Lenin statues reveal traditional methods of ideological indoctrination of the communist regime which occur via control over space and symbols. Dominating the most populated and socially symbolic centers, such as railway stations or frontlines of the governmental buildings, statues of Lenin are a clear embracement of the ideological objectives of the state — the immortality and omnipresence of the communist rule. Grandiose and monumental, monuments of Lenin reached over 100 meters in height, occasionally topping 320 meters tall buildings, such as the Palace of the Soviets in Moscow (1934). Both the political posters and statues of communist chiefs came into life to construct the reality where, both visually and discursively, the political leaders (or ideologies) become an integral part of the ordinary citizens' being.

Derived from the gesture of the Statue of Liberty, Michalski argues, the role the statue of Lenin played during the Soviet Union is comparable to the role the Statue of Liberty served in the United States: it "seems to entertain a kind of gestural dialogue — an idea prevalent in political cartoons that show personified countries acting on a small globe" (Michalski 1998: 119). The analyst of the political personifications, Marina Warner observes that "the female form [such as the Statue of Liberty] tends to be perceived as universal, while the male is shown as an individual" (Warner 1985: 12). The situation with Lenin, nevertheless, is different. Requiring no further symbolism such as red star or a torch, his figure in itself serves as a symbol of world-wide glaze and relevance of his ideas.

In the course of time, therefore, the era of the communist rule in eastern and central Europe evolved into a continuous manifestation of the leaders' cult, with the figure of Lenin being (re)articulated within multiple forms of the statues and political posters. Toppled, displaced or left on the ground, the statues constructed a powerful visual and discursive formation that served as the demarcation between the supporters and the opponents of the regime. The decommunization of post-Euromaidan Ukraine has not only revived dead symbols of a former political era as both objects and tools of administrative and political confrontation, but has also opened the conceptual space for objects, as well as means of further commemoration.

Historical Memory

As an integral act of both collective and individual meaning-making, remembering and memory as such are often used by the state to construct ideological formations. In the remaining part of this chapter, I suggest examining memory to understand the connection between the Soviet and modern Ukrainian practices of institutionalization of the selected aspects of the state's history.

In his extensive study of Russian-Ukrainian relations, "The Soviet Historical Imagination," the Ukrainian Canadian historian, Serhy Yekelchyk, argues that "nations are always imagined through the concrete social and cultural practices of their given societies" (Yekelchyk 2015: 5). According to the author, "states and intellectuals do not have a free hand to invent or manipulate national traditions and memories" because [as Arjuna Appadurai noted back in 1981], "history is not a limitless and plastic symbolic resource." The presence of the glorified Cossack past in the Ukrainian national context is one of the examples of narratives existing within the country's cultural space. Such 'stories' are to be mobilized during moments of the transitioning, be it a revolution or implementation of the official decommunization laws. Examining the construction of national identity, Yekelchyk provides an example of the 19th and 20th century intellectuals who operated within a densely limited space for social engineering: "they were evoking narratives, objects, and images that were already associated with certain inherited notions and emotions." Similar patterns of using history within the meaning-making process of modern political transitioning are observed in the post-Soviet space. In order to gain or sustain the support of the electorate, or construct 'new' political orders, political elites are using symbols derived from the past. Such symbols, however, have a tendency of being adjusted to retain qualities that resonate with the social demands of the time.

Even if granted freedom of implementation of the historical narratives, both the empire- and nation-builders may have difficulty explaining present use of historical symbols outside the country's public domain. In his first systematic account between the nation-state and the concept of linear history, Prasenjit Duara argues that "nationalism is rarely the nationalism of the nation, but rather marks the site where different representations of the nation contest and negotiate with each other" (Duara 1996: 18). In this sense, the Soviet regime has shown its ability to impose uniformity on public presentation of the past. The individual interpretations of those presentations, however, are diverse. Within the post-Soviet space, memory is equally tangible and hard to schematize. Broadly speaking, it should be noted that the obsession with interpreting the past is one of the primary characteristics of all nationalisms. According to Yekelchyk, it reflects "the nature of modern national identity which relies on the prescription of 'natural' continuity among the people's collective past, present, and future" (Yekelchyk 2015: 8). Such nationalist fixation is supported by the fact that remembering is also an individual act that, either voluntary or not, exists within the broader framework of the collective memory. The early twentieth-century sociologist Maurice Halbwachs suggests that individuals cannot preserve or invigorate mere personal memories unless they are created in particular social texture (such as family, religion, or nation) and sustained by such groups. Halbwachs's accentuation of social contextualization of individual memories is shown to influence prominent scholars working on social memory, such as Yosef Yerushalmi (2001) and Pierre Nora (2004), who assent to Halbwachs's distinction between the collective memory and history.

According to Halbwachs, "general history starts only when tradition ends and the social memory is fading or breaking up" (Halbwachs 1992: 24). Historical memory, therefore, represents a distant past, which no longer exists as a collective memory and with which living contact has been lost. In addition, "collective memory consists of the multiple voices of different groups, whereas historical narrative is unitary" (Yekelchyk 2015: 8). The analysis of the collected data allows me to align with Yekelchyk's claim—the interviews, videos, posters and photos reveal the multiplicity of opinions on both the past and the present of Ukraine. The 'voices' are articulated within multiple forms of citizens' interaction with objects of political art, memorials and acts of protests against (or in support of) the decommunization reforms. On a broader, national scale, the historical narrative is unitary in a sense of providing space for vocalization of multiple voices, as all the citizens have a point of reference within the historical context of their state. At the same time, as I show further, interpretation *and* presentation of the historical data are rather diverse. It is being articulated and contested within public space which offers room for articulation and construction of diverse hegemonic formations.

In his famous *Lieux de mémoire series*, Pierre Nora examines numerous French monuments, places and images as sites of memory, which were once a vivid collective recollection, but became institutionalized as historical memory (Nora 2004: 10). Similarly, Yerushalmi (2001) addresses the loss of living collective memory in the context of modern historical representations (e.g. production of scholarly history or preservationist discourse). In his interpretation of "the conflict in Ukraine," Yekelchyk argues that "present-day collective memory incorporates both historical memory as our knowledge of the past and social memory of our lived experience, [where] the latter is bound to disappear and be replaced in the next generations by the learned historical memory about our time" (Yekelchyk 2015: 14).

Finally, in an attempt to address the recovery of individual agency in the moment that seems to be missing from this scheme—the point of historical memory being internalized by the individual, Amos Funkenstein introduces the term 'historical consciousness' to comprise one's pursuit of understanding experiences historically. The editor of *Museums of Memory* and a researcher of historical consciousness, Susan A. Crane, further on, addresses the possibility of individuals "to internalize public historical memory as their collective memory through their lived experiences of learning about the past" (Crane 1997: 5). In other words, a person no longer has to witness the actions of his or her ancestors. Based on this theory, it is enough to simply read a history book to develop an understanding of a distant past, which does not have to concur with that of the book's interpretation or that of the majority. A reader can simply advocate devotedly based on his or her background of learning. Such theory is a rather perilous one, since, grounded on remote secondary sources that could be produced by an individual holding no first-hand experience or knowledge of the event, it can provoke misleading, hazardous action.

The communist project of memory is an example of such deceitful act. It is detrimental from its mere origins due the state's inability to control individual interpretations of the historical narratives. Even if individual conscious involvement in the process of remembering or forgetting is one of the base requirements of the formation of a society's 'historical consciousness,' incorporation of both the tsarist and Soviet leaders' mythology into the political narrative of the USSR created an ideology that often confused both intellectuals and common people. For instance, when in the 1930s the Stalinist regime became the self-conscious successor of the Russian Empire, "it had to incorporate into its narrative the story of tsarist conquests and territorial acquisitions, but has never quite reconciled it with the previous notion of 'class history' or with the separate mythologies of the non-Russian peoples" (Yekelchyk 2015: 15). In the post-Soviet states like Ukraine, established counter-memories of the pre-Bolshevik nationalist historical narratives, fueled by both the Nazi and Soviet intervention, survived long after the Second World War, which also brought nationalist ethos such as that of Western Ukrainians into the Soviet Union and later the independent Ukraine. "Friendship of the peoples" ("дружба народов") is one of the primary ideological terms of the USSR, which meant to acknowledge the manifold socio-cultural and ethnic composition of the communist empire, and at the same time, prescribe and homogenize social memory. Unable to address multiplicity of cultural and ethnic units of the state, however, the Soviet authorities could not assign collective meaning to the past from which the Soviet peoples supposedly obtained the sense of orientation for their future.

In the case of the USSR, the empire of memory was retained by means of careful filtering of the elements of commemoration.

When it comes to the socio-political context of the post-Soviet Ukraine, the national memory evolved into a living mosaic of regional narratives that were kept virtually 'silent' under the discursive umbrella of "independence" ("незалежність"). In this sense, the Euromaidan revolution was the turning point of the country's history. The casualties of Maidan, as well as the following hybrid war in Donbass, unraveled a similar scenario where, affected by rapid political developments, citizens of Ukraine became active participants of the colossal national transformations. Nevertheless, even though the eradication of an old regime has cleared discursive and topographic space for the creation of 'new' Ukraine, the process of intensive decommunization has shown similar tendencies to those of the Soviet times: when it comes to dealing with history, the state authorities are struggling with articulation of *national* narrative of the country's past.

The following chapter commences analysis of specific examples of versatile modes of (post)Euromaidan decommunization. Specifically, it looks at what I argue to be the explicitly diverse forms of decommunization being expressed through both the grassroots and state involvement with posters and different forms of political art. Examining images of the political art of the Euromaidan revolution, as well as the graffiti and interview data collected during fieldwork trips to different regions of Ukraine, it addresses creation of hegemonic formations at both the grassroots and state level. The analysis of the discursive and physical modes of articulation of the detachment of (post)Euromaidan Ukraine from its 'colonial,' communist past is also presented, where I draw the analytical parallel between the political art of the communist era and that of the (post)Euromaidan Ukraine. As any contemporary mythology, that of Maidan is strongly linked to art. Without wanting to give away too many spoilers for the content of the artistic expressions, I would give over by arguing that it is the 'Art of the Protest' that articulated unity and at the same time, resolved and presented diversity. And now, we are to see how.

5. Art of the Protest

> "Art is magic delivered from the lie of being truth."
> — Theodor W. Adorno

In her analysis of the public images and political art in Ukraine, Maryna Bazylevych asserts that "the Ukrainian nation-building project emphasizes historical events that are assumed to demonstrate the monstrosity of the Soviet state, and the crucial role of independence and cultural authenticity" (Bazylevych 2010: 12). Rubchak, on the other hand, views Ukraine as a post-colonial society that "strips away layer upon layer of accumulated colonial baggage...striving to reclaim its lost heritage — its cultural, linguistic and spiritual traditions" (Rubchak 1996: 315). By accepting communism as a burden of an authoritarian, colonial past, Ukrainians are not alone in such a stance. In her examination of "hopes and perils of the Euromaidan protests in Ukraine," Professor of Sociology Anastasiya Ryabchuk addresses the 2013 pro-EU protests in Bulgaria as one of the examples where the ruling elites are defined as 'communists' by the ordinary public due to the economic profit that the former have gained by "[taking] advantage of the 'transition' for their own private [good]" (Ryabchuk 2014: 128). Within the context of the Euromaidan revolution and its socio-political aftermath, the citizens' perception of the state carry characteristics of the following kind: at the beginning, a peaceful protest of the middle class expressing its desire to join Europe, the Euromaidan revolution turned into an autonomous body, a self-organized 'state within the state' that rebelled against an oligarchic regime. The articulation of the ordinary citizens' demands took various discursive and physical modes, within which a boarder common framework of 'Europeanization' of Ukraine became synonymous with decolonization or decommunization of the state through multiple forms of political art.

According to Bakhtin, who delineates the world as a 'polyglossic' or 'multivocal' formation, the discursive formation is being produced by means of a dialogue (or 'dialogism'), which in itself implies or originates social changes. The photo, graffiti and interview data that I collected in Ukraine as of 2013-2018 captures multiple forms of what I define as 'dialogical artistic decommunization.' The political posters, graffiti or toppling (or preservation) of the communist statues serve as discursive and physical space, where the mixing of elements of both present and past is an ongoing political phenomenon. Originated as both the discursive and physical attempt to construct 'new,' democratic or 'pro-European' Ukraine, Maidan Nezalezhnosti square in Kyiv, as well as central squares of cities such as Lviv, Poltava, Odessa, Zaporizhzhya or Kharkiv, became the domain for presentation of multivocal, at times contesting meanings. To understand decommunization as a complex, multilayered process of cultural and socio-political transitioning, I examine the evolution of both the ordinary citizens' and the governmental narratives, and trace their operation within the newly negotiated spaces.

In June of 2014, the article of Jacek Sacek Saryusz-Wolski was published under the title "Euromaidan: Time to draw conclusions." In an attempt to assess the scale of the socio-political and cultural effect that the Euromaidan revolution had on Ukraine, the author argued that it had two major impacts. The first is that, as a movement that emerged to represent citizens of diverse political, economic or educational backgrounds, the Madain "consolidated the Ukrainian society" by means of articulation of what could be seen as a national objective: an overthrow of an oligarchic system and obtainment of the right to live in a democratic state. The former — the toppling of the corrupt regime, is the demand that has been shared at both ends of the political spectrum of Ukraine, both western ('pro-European') and eastern ('pro-Russian') regions of the country (Krasko 2017: 25). Another component of the revolutionary narrative, that of "allowing Ukrainians to bring about desired political changes in governance, as well as making changes to the political system by bringing back the previous Constitution" (Saryusz-Wolski 2014: 12), is both the objective and an outcome of the Euromaidan revolution. It was articulated by the protestors and was among the many demands of 'pro-European' Ukrainians.

In his analysis of the Euromaidan revolution as "art embedded into protest," senior research scholar of Ivan Franko Lviv National University, Nazar Kozak, divides multiple forms of artistic work that evolved during revolution into the exhibit that "embedded through two protest modes: nonviolent resistance and the riot" (Kozak 2017: 3). At its early stage, the Euromaidan revolution came to embrace peaceful articulation of political demands—the artistic creations such as political posters, symbols (e.g. the Christmas tree) or slogans that were similar in their stylistic and visual texture to those of the Orange revolution (2004) (e.g. political posters or songs that aimed at unification of the public around the common goal of democratic transitioning, and as in 2004, the protest against the same political figure—Viktor Yanukovych). However, as the protesters' objection to the President Yanukovych's refusal to sign the Association agreement with the EU was addressed with state violence, there occurred a fundamental transformation of the protestors identity. In his essay, Kozak defines such transitioning as the "aesthetic redefinition of the preexisting public space informing the occupation's identity with the spirit of militancy, [where] eventually, artworks anticipated the tragic outcomes and reflected on the violent events" (Kozak 2017: 4).

The proposed mode of classification of the artistic expressions of Euromaidan into the categories of the 'nonviolent' and 'violent' resistance is an accurate framework for addressing both nature and outcome(s) of the protest. However, what is also necessary is to expand the framework of analysis of the artistic creations of (post)Euromaidan Ukraine by examining both 'how' and 'what' has been articulated via multiple forms of political vocalization.

According to Kozak, in the Maidan's riot mode, "the artworks metamorphosed into weapons of those [participating] in battles...and have inspired and protected the protesters" (Kozak 2017: 4) Reading the posters, graffiti or videos as means for articulating political narratives allowed examining the collected data as both the discursive and physical space, where fixing of meanings was never fully completed (Cox 2019; Laclau 1985; Thompson 2015). It involved "the discursive competition as an intrinsic element of hegemonic formation" (Cox 2019: 366), where heterogeneity of the citizens' political and cultural stands was articulated and became visible within the discursive struggle.

Starting from the very first days of my arrival in Maidan (December 2013), diversity was the most vivid characteristic of both the discursive and visual articulation of the protest. On one hand, the ordinary citizens who supported the 'pro-European' choice were unified in their desire to detach from the geopolitical influence of the Russian Federation and to deviate from the 'colonial' print of the Soviet era. On the other hand, there existed explicit variety in the discursive and visual modes of articulation of the so-called 'Europeanization' or 'decommunization.' When I arrived at Maidan in spring of 2014, what stood out as one of the largest visual statements was a massive poster "Unified Ukraine" (Figure 2). The slogan was written in both Ukrainian and Russian on what looked like a giant Ukrainian flag stretched across the central department store of Kyiv, TSUM. At that time, when examined as part of a broader visual narrative of the protest-space, however, the central image of "unified Ukraine" was juxtaposed with dozens of slogans and symbols of the distinctively different nature.

In the interview that I held with one of the participants of the Euromaidan revolution, Ivan Demianenko described the graffiti "Zaporizhzhya Kyiv" ("Запоріжжя Київ") (Figure 2) as the "visual gate to the space of the protest." Discursively, it echoed the poster "Unified Ukraine" by articulating the narrative of unity of eastern oblasts, such as the city of Zaporizhzhya, and the country's capital. Within the context of occupation of Crimea by the Russian Federation and the beginning of the military conflict in Donbas, the graffiti also symbolized national unity of all Ukrainians. At the same time, as being shown by Figure 2, already during and shortly after the Euromaidan revolution (May 2014), articulation of a 'common' pro-European or anti-Russian course of Ukraine has taken place through highly multivocal political language: the flag of the EU was surrounded by that of Ukraine and the official red-and-black emblem of the controversial nationalist formation, such as the Ukrainian Insurgent Army (UPA)[18] (Figure 2).

In *Art and Answerability: Early Philosophical Essays*, Mikhail Bakhtin asserts that "every worldview conditions one another as to turn into production of different, at times opposing meanings" (Bakhtin 1990: 12). The simultaneous presence of opposing symbols such as the flags of the EU and UPA within a common space of Maidan is an example of such occurrence—the original meanings of these symbols being re-articulated and eventually changed. Placement of the flag of UPA next to the insignia of the EU and Ukraine illustrates what Patrick Mackie argues to be one of the primary effects of the 2013-2014 revolution: "Maidan makes liberalism sound more radical than it deserves, also makes radicalism sound more liberal than it has wanted to claim to be" (Mackie, 2014: 15). As I expand further, within the context of the Euromaidan revolution, simultaneous positioning of nationalist and democratic insignia is an example of nationalism acquiring its *new*, 'democratic' meaning. Within such a process, there occurs a construction of fundamentally different modes of communication and the socio-political perception of the citizens by each other. In one respect, those who support the pro-Russian or anti-European geopolitical, cultural or religious developments find the existence of nationalist symbols such as flags of the UPA "openly threatening" (Interviews. By Anna Kutkina. Kyiv, Poltava, Chernihiv, 2014-2015). On the other hand, ignorance of questionable elements such as nationalist symbols or rhetoric being the attribute of the democratic transition-

---

18   The Ukrainian Insurgent Army (UPA) was a Ukrainian nationalist paramilitary and later partisan formation. During World War II, it was engaged in guerrilla warfare against Nazi Germany, the Soviet Union, the Polish Underground State and Communist Poland. Its ultimate purpose was an independent and unified Ukrainian state. In 1943, the UPA adopted a policy of massacring and expelling the Polish population. The Ukrainian Insurgent Army was also responsible for massacring the Jewish population of Ukraine. Accessed November 25, 2017. Source: http://www.encyclopediaofukraine.com/display.asp?linkpath=pages %5CU %5CK%5C UkrainianInsurgentArmy.htm.

ing of the post-communist state also calls credibility of democratization into question, be it within the Ukrainian or European domain.

Messages of the Revolution

In their discussion of the 1989 Tiananmen Square protest in Beijing, Joseph Esherick and Jeffrey Wasserstrom argue that absence of civil society serves as the foundation for art being "the only possible mode of political expression" (Esherick and Wasserstrom 1990: 836). Examining the graffiti of the Egyptian Tahrir revolution (2011), Elias Chad defines visual art of such kind as a "playful and self-reflexive set of semiotic strategies [that aim at raising] the consciousness of the society" (Chad 2018: 5). The graffiti and posters of Euromaidan are examples of such potent mechanisms of socio-political expression taking place via multiple forms of political art. In particular, the posters and graffiti of Maidan constructed a net of multiple meanings that varied from the ordinary citizens' confession of love towards Ukraine (e.g. Figure 3: "I love Ukraine" ("Я люблю Україну"—a graffiti painted in Ukrainian by the protestor(s) of the Euromaidan) to those of the openly anti-Putin or anti-military statements (Figures 7 and 8, respectively). According to one of my interviewees, Maksym Onichkin, "the primary objective of placement of the poster "Love Russians despise Putin" ("Любим русских презираем Путина") (Figure 11) on the central symbol of the Euromaidan revolution—the Christmas tree, was to send a broader message to both the Ukrainian and international opponents of the protest." The poster meant "to illustrate the ability of Ukrainians to distinguish politics from the people, and to show that the Euromaidan is a protest against the deadly Russian propaganda machine, not the innocent Russian or Ukrainian people" (Onichkin, Maksym. Interview. By Anna Kutkina. 28 April 2014).

Another dominant characteristic that was apparent within posters and graffiti of Maidan was playfulness and consciousness-raising. At the same time, articulation of similar (at times identical) messages has also taken place via both aggressive and peaceful images. The graffiti that pictures Putin having a moustache in the shape of a rocket (Figure 7), or a poster of Russian matryoshka doll holding a gun (Figure 6), for instance, carry identical messages of stopping the military aggression of the Russian Federation in Ukraine. The poster "No to War!" ("Нет войне!"), is a medium-size 'note' which has its message printed as part of the Ukrainian flag, and is placed on a gigantic bowl for making food as to feed anyone who is hungry (Figure 8). The 'Putin' graffiti and the 'matryoshka' poster, on the other hand, are both playful and yet already hostile reflections of the citizens' socio-political stands. The process of 'de-Russification,' therefore, is the phenomenon that emerged during early stages of (post)Euromaidan political transitioning. As I observed both in Kyiv and other regions of Ukraine, it was political posters and graffiti that served as the primary space for articulation of the discursively and stylistically diverse meanings.

The political posters and street art also offer the point of identification, where contestation is an integral part of the meaning-making process (Laclau 1985; Gills 1994; Kuhn and Weidemann 2010), and takes place through articulation or picturing of the 'enemy' or the 'other.' For some, the 'other' is addressed by a general slogan or call such as "no war!". Within the context of socio-political and cultural plurality of (post)Euromaidan Ukraine, and, in particular, war in Donbass, such mode of representation of anti-military narrative (Figure 8) was being directed not only towards the Russian aggressor, but also the Ukrainians themselves (e.g. the citizens who support the 'pro-Russian' and 'pro-European' stands). The poster "Brother?" (Figure 9), on the contrary, illustrates an instance of cutting one finger and attaching it to another hand as the sixth one. It is a direct accusation of Russia of its political cynicism: while calling Ukraine a younger brother, the Russian state 'cuts off' and illegally attaches Crimea to its territory.

At the early stage of the Euromaidan revolution and shortly after its official termination in June of 2014 I witnessed manifold, yet peaceful articulations of the 'other' at the grassroots level. Each of the graffiti or posters were used to narrate one or multiple interpretations of the occurring events. According to Laclau (1985), the cycle of overlapping and contestation of different elements of the culture, economy, class or ideology is inherent in hegemony. Likewise, posters and graffiti of the Euromaidan revolution represented multiple forms of cultural dialogue, where 'dialogism' (Bakhtin 1981) is the process that produces discursive and legislative response as to originate social changes.

In his examination of the relationship between practice of radical politics and art, Yates McKee explores the phenomenon of an artist being an "organizer" and the creator of the "movement building practices" (McKee 2011: 8). In particular, he focuses on the professional artists redirecting their talent "from the expansion of the artworld to the construction of new political imaginary set off against the common enemy" (ibid: 14). Here, professional artists themselves become generators of nationalist, radicalized stands. Even within the framework of the most radical, violent political clashes that involve physical trauma and even death of the participants on both sides of the protest, not only professional artists, but also the ordinary citizens are 'organizing' and 'creating' the "movement building practices" through art. As within McKee's study of the Occupy (Strike Art, 2011), articulation of the ongoing struggles around corruption, debt, or broader civic justice is taking place by means of discursive or physical (e.g. graffiti) integration of political discourses within the country's or city's topoi. Such process could be performed by "powerful social actors and groups with relational ties to past and future eras," (Palonen 2009: 4), as well as politically active citizens of the grassroots level (Fieldwork notes. By Anna Kutkina. Chernihiv, Kyiv, Dnipro, Kharkiv, Lviv, Odessa, Poltava, Myrhorod, Vinnytsia, Zaporizhzhya. 2013-2018).

In case of the Euromaidan revolution, the graffiti painted on the protestors' shields, helmets, or walls of the buildings are both the organizing and movement-building practices. Figures 11 and 12 illustrate further heterogeneity of the narratives articulated by the protestors of the revolution. What makes them particularly engaging is that they vary in their objectives and ideological context. Painted on the debris, the graffiti "People think" (Figure 12) and "We need a Ukrainian President" (Figure 13), for instance, articulate a call for political awareness. They target not only the participants of the revolution in Kyiv, but also the entire Ukrainian population. Containing irony as to point at the intensive Russian media-propaganda campaign of 2013-2014 that presented all the participants and the supporters of Euromaidan as "nationalists" or "Banderavites," the graffiti "We need a Ukrainian President" is 'signed' "A Banderovite" (or as being written by nationalists). The graffiti (Figure 13) is an example of what I argue to be a broader phenomenon of (post)Euromaidan Ukraine: creative articulation of the ordinary citizens' socio-political stands becoming the primary component of the meaning-making process (Cox 2019; Laclau 1985; Torfing 1999). Within such a process, detachment from the political and cultural patronage of Russia involves engagement of multiple voices, positions and socio-political subjects.

The maquette of the president Yanukovych made out of the fire extinguisher, glasses and a tie (Figure 14) or a red hanged doll (Figure 15) is a clear articulation of the primary objective of the Euromaidan revolution — the socio-political transition of Ukraine from 'communism' to 'democracy.' The elements of articulation of the Ukrainians' 'pro-European' choice within the physical space of Maidan, however, are rather diverse. They vary in both the content and means of their expression. In the case of the Yanukovych maquette (Figure 14), for instance, multiple narratives are being articulated within the space of a table, a sticker and objects of daily domain such as a tie, a hat or a fire distinguisher. The message of the blue sticker on the red table is a humorous mode of detachment from the pro-Russian political course — "to Europe without Yalynkovych[19]". A fire distinguisher in a hat, a tie and a pair of glasses (Figure 14), the handmade poster at the back of the 'Yanukovych' puppet, "First hat of Yanukovych" ("Первая шапка Януковича")

---

19 The last name of the President Yanukovych is changed into 'Yalynkovych' to remind of an ironic episode that took place in one of the cities of eastern Ukraine: when asked about whom they would vote for at the forthcoming presidential elections, the supporters of Viktor Yanukovych could not pronounce his last name correctly. CarambaTV. "Yanukovych, Yanukevych, Yakubovych." Carambavision. January 3, 2018. YouTube video, 2:34. https://www.youtube.com/watch?v=5gkpJMYzUmg.

is also a statement of ordinary Ukrainians who are making their awareness of the crimes of the Yanukovych's regime public.

Both the Khreshchatyk street and Maidan Nezalezhnosti square were used by the protesters as a discursive and physical space, where the narratives of 'pro-European' alternative, fighting of the corruption, or objection to the military conflict in Donbas were intertwined with the anti-communist affirmations. Figure 15 illustrates the desire to free Ukraine from its communist past being articulated as early as during the first weeks of the Euromaidan revolution, when the central monument of Lenin in Kyiv was toppled by a group of radical activists. At the same time, the phenomenon of massive, national decommunization emerged as one of the many narratives of the Euromaidan revolution. Similar to specific demands of the ordinary Ukrainians, explicit desire of detachment from the communist past was expressed by multiple forms of grassroots political art.

The "Strike Poster" — "Страйк Плакат"

In the beginning of December 2013, a renowned artist, civic activist and head of the art Banda Agency in Kyiv, Egor Petrov, created an open community project called the "Strike Poster" ("Страйк Плакат"). The project started with Petrov's idea of "participating in the Euromaidan revolution by doing what [he] was best at-- creating art" (Petrov, Egor. Interview. By Anna Kutkina. 27 May 2016). In what ended up being an over two hours long conversation, Petrov told me that since "it was impossible for [him] to stay home when people on the streets were protesting, [he] joined the protest by creating posters that would speak for the people." The idea was to use the discursive and physical space of the poster so that "the image would both plant the ideas and resonate with the people, as well as trigger thoughts that already existed or were yet to emerge" (ibid). Petrov said that originally the "Strike Poster" was to become the "spontaneous voice of the people, which was to be heard not only in Kyiv, but also across all regions of Ukraine."

Posted anonymously on Facebook by Petrov and his team of artists, the posters were free for download. The dominant technique of the "Strike Poster" (or the "Strike") was to unite the participants of the Euromaidan revolution by providing space for articulation of the socio-political, cultural or economic views with images (or slogans) being written (or printed) in the poster. The creativity, irony and humor became the distinct features of the images. At first, the online community was supported by several dozens of artists and advertisers; however, within a few weeks, the number of users increased to thousands. Originally, the creators of the "Strike Poster" avoided using typical political slogans or symbols. According to Petrov, the primary objective was "to restrain from potential aggravation of the socio-political division of the Ukrainian population, as well as to bring like-minded Ukrainians together." Particular efficiency of the "Strike Poster" images is that at the time when the majority of the opposition was lacking a clear conceptual image, posters of the "Strike" served as the discursive and visual space of its own universal language. It carried the ability of reacting to most urgent events of the Euromaidan revolution by being a live project of the ordinary Ukrainians: the "Strike" gave space for both anonymous and identified voices[20]. During my fieldwork, I spotted images of the "Strike" at Maidan Nezalezhnosti square in Kyiv, Zaporizhzhya, Vinnytsia, Lviv and other cities of Ukraine. Being the first artistic phenomenon of such amplitude, the "Strike Poster" not only provided space for ordinary Ukrainians willing to articulate their political stands. It also served as a bridge between the people and the government: by means of artistic expression, specific claims of the ordinary Ukrainians were made public and later addressed, surpassing direct contact of people and state officials who, both at the time of the revolution and thereafter, were often seen as hostile and aloof.

As the regimes fashion their iconographies of power, Aulich and Sylvestrova argue, "old national and state emblems are appropriated or discarded according to their worth within political or

---

20 During our interview in May 2016, Egor Petrov gave a permission to discuss and publish the images of the project. Petrov, Egor. "Strike Poster project." Strikeposter. May 30, 2016. https://www.facebook.com/strikeposter/.

revolutionary history" (Aulich and Sylvestrova 1999: 105). The Soviet Union is an example of a state where the stylistic 'communist' components such as the red color, the stars or sickles, for instance, were used for development of the national coat of arms. The Euromaidan revolution introduced particular figures and emblems that became symbols of stateless, wider categories such as 'democracy,' 'freedom,' 'liberation' or 'peace.' It also exposed an integral characteristic of Ukraine's evolution—despite Russia's and Ukraine's cultural affinity, many Ukrainians have chosen values that signify self-expression over those of survival. As Inglehart claims, once a shift from survival to self-expression values occurs, democracy becomes increasingly likely to prevail over authoritarian regimes.

Designed by ordinary citizens of different regions of Ukraine, the posters of the "Strike Poster" were shared on the project's official Facebook page both during and after the revolution. They were then printed by the Banda Agency of Egor Petrov, as well as on ordinary citizens' home printers, and placed on the billboards, walls of the buildings, street columns or trees. As Petrov shared, the posters "I am a drop in the Ocean" ("Я крапля в океані") (Figure 17) and the "Yanukovych's nose" ("Ніс Януковича") (Figure 19) were the first two visuals produced by Petrov and his team. These posters were placed on the billboards of Kyiv as a secret night action in early December of 2013. As Petro shared during our interview, both of these images "were very well perceived and immediately picked up by the people." The message of the poster "I am a drop in the Ocean" became a powerful tool for articulation of one of the core transformations that took place during the Euromaidan—articulation of the concept of unity as the basis of national integrity. The "Drop" came to symbolize the importance of every citizen's voice that, when unified with that of another Ukrainian, creates an 'ocean' of national cohesion. The unity, however, is that of the multivocal rather than homogeneous nature: it consists of diverse political and social demands of ordinary Ukrainians amalgamated by a common desire of the reformation of the state.

The "Yanukovych nose" ("Ніс Януковича") (Figure 19) poster became another distinct tool of vocalization of one's political stands that was adopted by thousands of Ukrainians across the country. Quoting Petrov, an image of President Viktor Yanukovych portrayed as a clown "emerged as an embodiment of the citizens' dissatisfaction and explicit frustration about the Yanukovych regime." By putting up posters such as "I am a drop in the Ocean" (Figures 31, 32 and 33) or the "Yanukovych nose," Ukrainians of western, central, southern, northern and eastern parts of the country created a community of the politically-like-minded citizens: they constructed a powerful hegemonic formation that objected to that time criminal government. At the same time, the posters provided space for articulation of independent voices into a common horizon of 'new' national identity — diversity and freedom of political self-expression.

In his analysis of the art of the Euromaidan revolution, Kozak argues that "taken as a whole, the artistic practices and objects in the first weeks of the Maidan both reflected its dominant nonviolent ethos and established that ethos as dominant" (Kozak 2017: 12). The 'father' of the "Strike Poster" project, Petrov, has also stated that "in general terms, peace and kindness were the primary messages of the "Strike" images and the art of the protest as such." Both during and after the Euromaidan revolution, the visuals of the "Strike Poster" project served as discursive and physical markers of peace. Produced as personal, visual statements of citizens of different regions of the country, they unified the population by offering space for nationally-shared values such as the fight against corruption, the reformation of the judicial system, freedom of speech or improvement of the economy.

Already in winter-spring of 2014, images of the "Strike Poster" project became the national phenomena, and were exhibited across Ukraine, from Lviv to Zaporizhzhya (e.g. Figures 31 and 32). When placed next to each other, posters of the "Strike" constructed a collection of manifold narratives that became part of both the physical and discursive domain of the cities. One year after the Euromaidan revolution and onwards, the posters "continued to serve as living reminders of values and civic stands that hundreds of Ukrainians have sacrificed their lives for in the year of 2013-2014." (Petrov, Egor. Interview. By Anna Kutkina. 27 May 2016). As such, over 30 images were put together into one exhibition by the artists of the

Banda Agency. Placed at the central squares of different cities of Ukraine (e.g. Figure 16), political, economic and cultural messages of the "Strike Poster" project traveled across the country, serving as visual reminders of the goals of the Euromaidan revolution.

In broader terms, the affirmation of Petrov on the immortality and social relevance of the posters found its proof during three-and-a-half years of my data-collection process. Terminated in physical terms as the tents, shields and other objects of the revolution were removed from Maidan Nezalezhnosti Square in Kyiv in June 2014, the revolution continued its course through articulation, representation and contestation of meanings within the physical space of the posters. The posters of the "Strike" are an example of hegemony never being complete. While during the Euromaidan revolution the posters were used for articulation of the ordinary citizens' socio-political stands, within the time-span of over one year and onwards the posters started to serve as both objects of memory and pointers at existence (or absence) of the promised political transformations.

Figure 16 is an example of such a kind, where posters serve as living barometers of the continuation of the revolution: it captures the ordinary citizens—the soldiers of war in Donbas, walking next to the images—one of the primary visual and discursive symbols of Maidan. A collection of multi-colored stickers with diverse personal messages, one of the posters of the "Strike" (Figure 27) is a vivid example of *personal* definitions of (post)Euromaidan transformations. It exposes the multivocality of the ordinary citizens' political demands and visions on democratic reformation of Ukraine. Juxtaposed to most popular cliché of the revolution—the choice of Ukraine to join the European Union, multiple meanings of what the Euromaidan and its outcome are about are being articulated: "This is not for Europe, but: for the future of our kids…for roads without pits…This is not for Europe, but for the medicine in the hospitals; this is not for Europe but for courts without bribes; this is not for

Europe but against bribes in the kindergartens; this is not for Europe, but for police without bribes; this is not against Russia but against the corrupt state authorities[21]".

The grassroots demands for an urgent reformation of the state apparatus are also expressed by means of explicit articulation of public awareness of the state-committed crimes. The visuals and narratives of Figures 20 and 21, for instance, hold the state responsible for physical violence against the peaceful protestors of Maidan: "We are being beaten at our own expense," "We do not need such hockey," respectively. The Figure 24, "Shame for the entire world," on the other hand, is the depiction of Lady Justice who carries handcuffs and a stick instead of a traditional balance and sword.

Further analysis of the images of the "Strike Poster" project exposes discursive and visual articulation of Russia and the Soviet legacy as an external 'other.' Produced within the time-frame of the revolution (December 2013-March 2014), the posters of the "Strike" are explicit of the Ukrainians' socio-political stands who view the political course of Russia as that of an aggressor. The posters "Imagine—there is no Putin" (Figure 22), or "The Ukrainian Nightmare" (Figure 26—depiction of Ukraine as a woman crying with blood) narrate the necessity for liberation of Ukraine from the political and cultural patronage of Russia. The Russian aggression is defined by Ukrainians as not only modern, but also a historic phenomenon. The poster entitled "March 2014" (Figure 29) presents the events of the Maidan as the process where both the protestors and the police are being watched, and are potentially overtaken by a monstrous myriapod figure. Emerging from the smoke of the protest, the figure intends to dominate Ukraine and, if being examined in more detail, has a hammer and sickle on its back—the symbol of the Soviet Union.

The "March 2014" poster (Figure 29) is not only about externalization and demonization of the Soviet past within the political context of (post)2013 Ukraine. During the "Strike Poster" exhibition

---

21 The "Strike Poster" exhibition was installed at Maidan Nezalezhnosti square in November of 2015 upon the permission of the city authorities.

in Kyiv (November 5-25, 2015), the image that presented toppling of the Lenin statues (Figure 30, "The Leninfall" ("Ленінопад") was placed directly next to the poster depicting the Soviet occupation of Ukraine (Figure 29). Linguistically analogous to the rainfall, "The Leninfall" is about the statues of Lenin falling as colorful drops next to grey communist buildings: detachment from the communist past obtains both regional and national scale, where a sense of a unified community is created under the common goal of democratization as decommunization.

Further analysis of the "Strike" posters illustrates that "reformation [of] the country" (Figure 28) has been an overall objective of the ordinary citizens of (post)Euromaidan Ukraine. In methodological terms, the process of production of the images of the "Strike Poster" exposes construction of the discursive and physical space that encourages personal contribution of Ukrainians to common, peaceful objectives of the revolution — what Kozak argues to be "the protest's ability to embrace everyone" (Kozak 2017: 12) In practical terms, besides becoming an essential part of the urban space of the Ukrainian cities, the images of the "Strike Poster" were also popularized online. The objective of online installations was to provide space for political activism for every citizen of Ukraine willing to become both the creator and the presenter of his or her civic stands. Printing and spreading of images of the "Strike" in different cities constructed a powerful hegemony of unity and yet multivocality of the citizens' vision of the country's democratization: articulated within a common space of political posters, the grassroots stands on means of 'Europeanization' of Ukraine were exceptionally versatile. (Fieldnotes. By Anna Kutkina. Kyiv, Zaporizhzhya, Kryvyi Rih, Lviv, Chernihiv, 2014-2017).

Despite the diversity of the grassroots demands, a common message of the necessity of urgent reforms emerged as both nationally and internationally appealing. Acknowledged at the national and international level as "art making the revolution" (Figure 35: the online article published on the official website of the Ministry of Foreign Affairs of Ukraine), meanings generated by the "Strike" 'left' the physical boundaries of the poster. The central symbol of the project, the drop of the ocean, was installed as an image of computer and phone desktops both in Ukraine and internationally, and was also widely printed as mobile phones cover (Figures 36 and 37). Both during and after the revolution, uploading, printing, publicizing, or downloading images and slogans of the "Strike Poster" project established a community of promoters of the democratic reformation of Ukraine. Without meeting each other in person (Anderson 1985), thousands of Ukrainians became involved in articulation of their personal definitions of what the post-2013 Ukraine was to be transformed into: "the country of unity, tolerance, equality or freedom from corruption" (Petrov, Egor. Interview. By Anna Kutkina. 27 May 2016).

Artistic practices such as the political posters of the Euromaidan revolution illustrate an important transition that is a new phenomenon in the political space of Ukraine. As a successor of socialist legacy of visual political propaganda of the Soviet posters, Ukraine has witnessed a dramatic transformation in the pictorial political representation. It has moved from what is a traditionally public, state-imposed imaging to a private, ordinary citizens' articulation of the socio-political space: a large number of posters are both made by the people *and* are about the people. Fictional, unnatural images of a citizen of the Soviet posters are being replaced by the visuals produced by real individuals who are ready to vocalize their political stands and reveal both their faces and names. As such, the poster also becomes a means for reciprocal action: the mechanism of political art that articulates the exchange of values, ideas and socio-political stands between the producer of the artistic object, the object and the viewer who, at times, is the same individual—an ordinary citizen.

Reading the posters politically, it could be argued that such transformation is also an indicator of the in-depth changes taking place as a result of both similarities and contradictions exposed within the process of hegemonic articulation (Cox 2019). The act of placing an image or a poster of him or herself (e.g. the protestor, Figure 10, "Human Rights"), or a poster with specific political messages such as those of the "Strike Poster" project in different cities of Ukraine is an example of a heterogeneous hegemonic formation:

amalgamated by a common goal of democratization, the citizens of Ukraine articulate manifold means of its implementation. As a next step for realization of the democratic transition of the post-communist state, the grassroots-produced political posters carry potential for engagement of both the ordinary citizens and the government into the process of dialogism (Bakhtin 1981)—peaceful exchange of the citizens-government vision on the potential reforms through political dialogue. Different images of the "Strike Poster" project are examples of the feasibility of such practice. They articulate multivocality of the grassroots political and social stands, and offer physical space of the poster as a domain for potential public dialogue.

Posters and the State

The comparative analysis of data that I collected during and after the revolutionary events of 2013-2014 shows re-activation of the state in the discursive and physical space of the country upon the official termination of the protests. Similar to the modes of grassroots political self-expression (e.g. the political posters), the state appealed to the poster as a powerful means of articulation of the political and cultural course of Ukraine. In their analysis of the country's elites and the state implemented policies of 'democratization,' scholars argue that the process of the government coinciding with popular narratives of the grassroots level—concepts of 'freedom,' 'independence' or 'anti-corruption campaign,' emerged to please the potential electorate (Kulyk 2016; Shevel 2016; Soroka 2018). At the governmental level, what started as a potential implementation of the ordinary Ukrainians' demands—the restoration of the Ukrainian 2004 Constitution, for instance, or decentralization of the state power, turned into institutionalization of the official decommunization, and, I argue, both the discursive and legislative promotion of the war in Donbas.

Compared to the grassroots narratives of (post)Euromaidan, the following tendency of the state-level meaning-making was observed: similar to that of the ordinary citizens of (post)2013 Ukraine, the state-sponsored imagery of *early* 2014 also restrained from explicitly denoting the 'other.' Yet, particularly after the occupation of Crimea and the beginning of war in Donbas, the Russian Federation or any form of its historical legacy became the primary subject of public, artistic condemnation. The 'new' narrative of the state evolved into an idea of national unification of Ukrainians around ideological and physical involvement of Ukrainians in the "war in the east."

In her study of the socio-political aftermath of the Euromaidan revolution, Oksana Shevel insists that "the process of consolidation of the Ukrainian national identity [occurred via] pivoting more decisively away from Russian influence" (Shevel 2016: 268). Although a society's values can change, they only do so within the limits of certain norms that are formed by a country's history and present. No doubt Russia's explicit aggression towards Ukraine welded Ukrainians together. At the same time, photo, video and interview data that I collected capture *diversity* of the ordinary citizens' modes of conducting decommunization: they vary from unsanctioned toppling of the communist symbols to creative ways of their preservation, as well as *restraint* from any form of civic activism as a means of making a political statement.

As I arrived in the same cities during different periods of the Euromaidan revolution and onwards, I observed the substitution of peaceful narratives of Maidan with military-promoting discourses of the state. For example, the same poster boards of central streets in Kyiv that were used for articulation of diverse, yet mutually-accepting stands of the protestors – noted earlier posters "I am a drop in the ocean" or the "Yanukovych's nose", have turned into space for disclosure of the state militarization campaign. Importantly, the state promoted recruitment for the Ukrainian army as an act of "protection of the territorial integrity of Ukraine," using the grassroots narratives of Euromaidan such as 'unity' or 'freedom' to boost the conscription. Within this process, however, both opposition and dialogue were the ground elements of the political poster campaigns. An example of such practice is an image of the Khreshchatyk street (Figure 38): over one year after the termination of the Euromaidan revolution, in October 2015, the concept of 'dignity[22]' has been virtually substituted by or expanded to that of 'protection of the state.' Originally, in the context of Maidan, dignity was an example of *diverse*, oftentimes personal interpretation of democratization; it incorporated multiple meanings that varied from an explicit fight against corruption, or demands of having a free and effective medical care system to an open protest against the alliance with Russia. Upon the official termination of the revolution, however, value-'symbols' of the Maidan became re-narrated by the state to construct the homogeneous hegemonic formation. Presented as the dedication to "memory of the heroes of the heavenly hundred[23]" (Figure 38), the slogan "Obtained dignity—let us [now] protect the state!" is written in the image of burning barricades of Maidan (Figure 38). The discursive and visual overlayering of the symbols of the revolution and images of war in Donbas became a particularly popular state-campaign as the number of volunteers to fight in the east went down, and the conflict obtained characteristics of a frozen geopolitical affair.

Another popular slogan of the revolution, "Heroes do not die," which generated political resonance after the sniper shooting of over one hundred activists on Hrushevskoho street in Kyiv, was made part of the official state-installed poster campaign (Figure 40). Further tracing of the collected data based on the date of the posters' installation denotes the following tendency: placed at the stand-boards across the cities of Kyiv, Lviv, Kharkiv, Zaporizhzhya, Poltava, and other regions of the country, political posters were used by the state as primary space for articulation of the military narratives. Already in May of 2014, when war in Donbas started to take its active form, the stand-board posters in Kyiv narrated an open call to join the Ukrainian army: "Friend! Have you

---

22   The concept of 'dignity' was used by the masses during the Euromaidan revolution, when the protests of overthrowing of the corrupt government of President Viktor Yanukovych, demonstrations in favor of joining the European Union, and people's revolt against massive shooting of the protesters were named by ordinary Ukrainians as the "Revolution of Dignity."
23   The Heavenly Hundred, or "Nebesna Sotnya" is the term used to honor memory of the deceased activists of the Euromaidan Revolution whose deaths are connected to the protests on Maidan in Kyiv, from 21 January to 22 February 2014.

signed up for the National Guard of Ukraine?" (Figure 39). Two and a half years later, in February of 2017, similar posters (e.g. Figure 41) were installed on the stand-boards of not only Kyiv, but also Kharkiv, Zaporizhzhya, Poltava, Chernihiv and other cities of Ukraine. The poster placed on the stand-boards of the streets, as well as inside of major metro lines of Kyiv, said: "60 000 of the best patriots have already signed the contract. Become the best!" (Figure 41). Upon the review of such images, an ordinary Ukrainian who considered him or herself the 'best' (or 'the patriot') was expected to join the community of the "best" and become the country's 'elite.' Broadly speaking, conscription 'through' posters became grounded on three core elements: the presentation of the statistical data on how many Ukrainians have joined the army, the definition of soldiers as 'patriots,' and the construction of a logical chain of 'all patriots being the best.'

In April 2017, major change in the style of state-promoted nationalization and militarization of Ukraine took place: attraction of ordinary Ukrainians into the military operation in Donbas became *personalized*. The combination of both the slogans and photographs of acting (or former) soldiers of the Ukrainian army emerged as a primary discursive and visual narrative of the state-sponsored political poster campaigns. The photographs of specific soldiers were combined with the slogans that emphasized voluntary nature of the military service: "National Guard of Ukraine: The service by the contract and the call of the heart —Serhij Shkabadura, the Printer" (Figure 42). Similar to the Soviet poster, the state-installed visuals included professional specialization of the soldiers. Figure 42 is one of the many examples of such practice, where both the name and professional occupation of the soldier—Serhij Shkabadura, the Printer, are revealed. Potentially, "the process of 'personalization' of the poster intended to make joining the army more open and accessible to all Ukrainians," asserted one of my interviewees, former participant of the Euromaidan revolution, Ivan. It also implicated a provision of narrative and visual means that promoted establishment of the imagined communities: a viewer of the poster is given means for forming a connection with a soldier whom he or she will never meet personally. A viewer (e.g. an ordinary Ukrainian) may choose between the category of a 'soldier' or a 'printer,' and, thus, relate to a broader idea of patriots willing to fight for the integrity of their state.

In his explanation of reasoning behind the ordinary people's will to participate in the military activities that can potentially lead to one's death, Anderson argues that "imagined as a community, regardless of the actual inequality and exploitation that may prevail in such, the nation is always conceived as a deep, horizontal comradeship" (Anderson 1983: 7). Ultimately, according to Anderson, "it is this fraternity that makes it possible, over the past two centuries, for so many millions of people, not so much to kill, as willingly to die for such limited imaginings." He further asserts that it is the process of presentation of the "shrunken imaginings of recent history" that leads to massive human sacrifices. In other words, emerging from the past, "absurdity of salvation lies in the cultural roots of nationalism" (ibid: 10). Within such a process, fatality is being articulated into continuity of an old tradition, where, according to Anderson, "contingency is then transformed into meaning." "As we shall see [he continues], few things are better suited to this end than an idea of nation." While claiming to be 'new,' the nations also are always historical: grounded in the immortal past, they aim at articulating the present to construct the future.

Four years after the Euromaidan revolution, the visuals that I collected during my fieldwork trip to Kyiv in September 2018 illustrate the accuracy of Anderson's analysis. The stand-board poster (Figure 43), for instance, is an image of a soldier who died during one of the military operations in Donbas. The poster is a mix of the visual and the text—a photo of a soldier is followed by a quote—"Obtained eternal life in a fight." With neither the name of a soldier, nor the date of his death being identified, a specific human being is virtually made non-personal. If being compared to the personalized military posters promoted by the state shortly after the Euromaidan, posters of 2018 articulate an explicit glorification and nationalization of death. By means of discursive articulation of the "eternal life [being] obtained in a fight", the value of human (biological) life is substituted by virtue of "eternal" existence. In other words, not only the fight, but also the "eternity" (or potential death) is being articulated into meaning.

Analysis of the visuals collected in Kyiv in September of 2018, such as the poster "Army! Language! Faith! We are walking our own path! We are Ukraine—Petro Poroshenko" (Figure 44), demonstrates blending of different, yet discursively homogeneous elements into one visual, as well as ideological formation. Depicted over the background of the official coat of arms of Ukraine—the golden trident over a blue tint, the concepts of 'army,' 'language' and 'faith' are being articulated into a political manual of a country that follows its own, independent path. Presented within both physical and discursive space of the poster of the President Petro Poroshenko's presidential election campaign, the elements of the ideological agitation ("army," "language" and "faith") are connected into a dominant horizon of action. The army, language and faith are made the basis of the Ukrainian national course, which implies preservation, protection and development of these elements as primary means of moving forward or "being Ukraine."

And so, when collecting data, I tried to proceed with caution. To keep in mind, the objective of such national idea was to protect Ukraine against the 'other'—the Russian Federation. Interestingly, back then when the posters were part of the cities' landscape, neither the importance, nor the relevance of these state narratives was questioned by the ordinary public. However, comparative analysis of the political posters of the grassroots and state level did unravel ongoing contestation: the visual and discursive narratives of the grassroots political posters, graffiti or multiple hand-made images compiled a powerful counter-hegemonic formation that clearly *challenged* the state. It articulated the diversity of the political positions of ordinary Ukrainians' when it came to language, military activities in Donbas, or decommunization, and entailed dialogue as explicit means of the state-citizens interaction.

118   BETWEEN LENIN AND BANDERA

Romanticization + Realism

Explicitly, the official denouement of the Euromaidan revolution and the consecutive military activities in Donbas led to re-articulation of the political narratives from peaceful to a war-oriented course. This phenomenon was especially apparent in the visuals of the political poster exhibitions. Upon the termination of the Euromaidan revolution in Kyiv, the central squares of Kyiv, Lviv, Kharkiv, Zaporizhzhya, Poltava, Chernihiv, Lubny and other cities of Ukraine turned into a platform for numerous poster exhibitions.

As the military presence of the Russian Federation in Donbas skyrocketed in summer of 2014, the death-toll of Ukrainians sacrificing their lives for the territorial integrity of Ukraine has peaked. In May 2017, a poster that was placed at the Sofiivska square in Kyiv (Figure 50) reflected the following statistical data: while in March, April and May of 2014 the Ukrainian side lost 2, 7 and 69 soldiers, respectively, in June, July and August of the same year the losses of the Ukrainian army were already 137, 320 and 604 soldiers, respectively. In total, as of 2014, the Ukrainian side has lost 1,694 soldiers, while during 2015 and 2016 the casualties were 1,071 and 25, respectively. As such, within two calendar years after Maidan, 2,790 Ukrainian fighters have been killed in Donbas (Figure 50). Already in 2016, the conflict has escalated to a full-scale undeclared war, totaling in over 9,000 casualties on both sides (Cummings-Bruce 2016). Considering this context, the articulation of war and its negative socio-economic aftermath as one of the primary subjects of the Ukrainians' daily existence is an innate phenomenon. However, to avoid turning an everyday act of violence and, eventually, a complex and increasingly vicious confrontation into a blind spot, it is important to consider divergence in attitudes and overall evaluation (or definition) of war by the government and the ordinary citizens.

In March and June 2016 in Kyiv, as well as in June 2016, February and April 2017 in Kharkiv, the military activities in Donbas was the primary subject of the political poster exhibitions. Here, I will dwell into a discussion of the images of the exhibition in Kyiv (Figure 45) in more detail since they summarize what I argue to be the dominant element of the state-level hegemonic formation of post-2013 Ukraine: both the realistic and highly romanticized articulation of the events, people and objects of war. Manifold in their content when it comes to representation of both peaceful (Figures 46 or 47) and violent stages of the military activities in Donbas, all posters of the exhibition are unified by the narrative of the "army saving, protecting, helping [Ukraine]." The war in Donbas is presented by the posters as both a literal and symbolic act of liberation from the political and cultural influence of Russia and its communist legacy. To some extent, the cultivation of war and portrayal of soldiers as somewhat joyful is a virtual replica of the Soviet hegemony — the state depicting its citizens as happy and optimistic fighters. The broader horizon, in this sense, is the protection of the state being the objective of both personal and national level. Figures 46 and 49 are the examples of such visuals where the Ukrainian soldiers in Donbas are smiling, holding a child or shaking hands with local citizens.

Similar to the communist posters, the state uses children to 'soften' the military occurrence — children participating in a voluntary concert in the city of Kramatorsk to collect funds to support the Ukrainian army, July 27 2014 (Figure 47). The state-supported posters such as those of the June 2016 exhibition in Kyiv also present women as fighters and protectors of post-Euromaidan Ukraine (Figure 48). In terms of their social objective, these images are similar to the Soviet posters of WWII, where women are portrayed as equally important and powerful participants of war. The images of victims are blended with those of real military action, as well as the daily routine of the Ukrainian soldiers and the potentially pro-Russian citizens of Donbas, side by side (Figure 51).

Besides the installation of war images in the political poster exhibitions, I also observed romanticization of the Euromaidan revolution and, in particular, war in Donbas by international artists. The photo exhibition of the "Projection" project of Youry Bilak, a French photographer of Ukrainian origin, was an eminent example of such a kind (Matsuzato 2017). The exhibition was held by Bilak at *Boryspil International Airport* in Kyiv in April of 2017. Originally, the images of the exhibition were part of the second floor Art Center located at the Administration of the President Petro Poroshenko. According to Bilak, "the photos came to life through images of paintings by the greatest—Leonardo da Vinci, Rembrandt van Rijn, and Vincent van Gogh" (e.g. Figures 52-58). The official description of the project indicates that the objective of such images was "to create a historical axis with the viewer at its center...[where] the very canvas that artists of different ages try to create time and time again" (Figure 52).

Not to deny the creative possibility of the artists to use images of the revolution or war, I believe the potential political and social effects of the political poster exhibitions such as "Projection" are also to be considered. The space of exposition of the images—the central airport of the country, assumes extensive viewing of the photographs by both the Ukrainian and international audiences. For many, if not the majority of the travelers who witnessed this exhibition, as a number of my interviewees explained, "it was the only point of interaction with war in Donbas" (Malashenko, Stas. Ivashenko, Nadia. Zubko, Olexander. Interview. By Anna Kutkina. 24 April 2017). What existed as a personal intent of the artist who aimed at presenting "modernity [as] being a project of the past in our minds" (Figure 52), the images of the "Projection" contributed to the mitigation of war. In her study of "education and ambivalence in war exhibitions," Debbie Lisle asserts that "potentially destabilising encounters with horrific objects (e.g. guns, bombs, shrapnel) are neutralized by celebratory narratives of victory and war as a whole" (Lisle 2006: 4). She further states that the "war exhibitions reproduce a politics of consensus by carefully managing the experience of the sublime" (ibid: 5). The images of the "Projection" provided both the discursive and physical space that illustrates careful 'management' of war: real soldiers who are fighting and are potentially sacrificing their lives in Donbas are depicted as 'classics' of the world art. Broadly speaking, distinct in its mode of artistic presentation, the "Projection" continued articulation of the political narrative that "[implied] loss of cultural hegemony of the communist universe" (Stepanenko and Pylynskyi 2015: 32) and at the same time, fell short in including alternative narratives of the grassroots level.

Birth of Dialogism?

Irrespective of the region I went to, be it the western, central or eastern Ukraine, the grassroots images and graffiti that were installed or painted within the same physical space of the state-installed exhibitions narrated far more diverse, pessimistic *and* realistic views of the war and an overall aftermath of the Euromaidan revolution. The ordinary Ukrainians were unified with the state in their desire to fight the Russian aggressor, and at the same time, expressed a highly manifold evaluation of the objectives and the socio-political outcomes of the military activities in Donbass.

The major distinction in content of the posters and graffiti of the grassroots level is that the people used visulas as means of *chronology* of their personal experiences of war. What could be seen as a similar practice to that of the state-promoted poster exhibitions on Donbas, the handmade posters at the grassroots level were also placed at the central squares of the cities (e.g. Figure 59). By means of conducting fieldwork in the same cities during different periods of time, I was able to record both the emergence and development of what I call the 'dialogical political practice': by posting photographs and posters of soldiers who died in Donbas, friends or family members of perished heroes used posters to initiate dialogue with the state. The grassroots images *challenged* the joyful state narrative on war, and created space for both memorials *and* mourning. A vivid example of such 'dialogism' is Figure 60: juxtaposed to the state-promoted stand-board poster "Father, will you protect?," a collage of images of specific soldiers who died in Donbas is posted on the column of the Statue of Independence (Maidan Nezalezhnosti square). Compared to the war-glorifying narrative of the state, the posters and images that were recorded in February 2016 in Kyiv imply no romanticization of human sacrifice. The anonymous graffiti painted directly under the image of the Ukrainian, cossack-looking soldier who died in Donbas grants an all-encompassing meaning to death: "For each of us death has a bullet" (Figure 61).

A broader spectrum of meanings that both the soldiers and the civilians construct in their visual and discursive narrative of war in

Donbas is also reflected in other images that I collected. For instance, the graffiti drawn on one of the columns of the Independence Statue at Maidan Nezalezhnosti square presents the view on the necessity of "ATO [beginning] from Verkhovna Rada" — the ordinary public demands compulsory participation of the state-officials in the military activities in Donbas (Figure 62). Another articulation of the socio-political division between the ordinary citizens and the state is the graffiti that was painted in different areas of Kyiv, as well as other cities of Ukraine — "this political power emerged on the blood of the heroes" (Figure 64). Painted on the wall next to Lybidska metro station, the graffiti is a reminder of the heroic acts of the protestors of Euromaidan. It is also a moral appeal to the President Poroshenko's government to continue political transformations of decommunization of Ukraine in accordance with core demands of the Maidan — fight of corruption, the reformation of the judicial system, implementation of the socio-economic reforms, and strengthening of the pro-European political course.

The state-promoted narratives that idealize war in Donbas were not the only discursive formations contested by the ordinary Ukrainians. Posted on the columns of Maidan Nezalezhnosti square, fences or walls of the buildings of Kyiv, as well as other cities across the country, the hand-made posters and graffiti of the grassroots level were diverse in their critical notions on the state-implemented policies. Three years into the Euromaidan revolution, the ordinary citizens equated poor economic conditions with unwillingness of the Ukrainian government to disrupt ties with the imperial Russian regime. Hand-written with a thick black marker, one of the anonymous posters placed on a column in Kyiv illustrated the matter: it stated that "the shocking socio-economic therapy which [has been] uselessly taking place during 15-20 years [was] obtaining all signs of the genocide. The secret plan of zionistic-satanistic regime of Poroshenko and Putin [became] obvious" (Figure 63). Another graffiti that was painted next to the portrait of a famous Ukrainian actor Bohdan Stupka was an explicit articulation of lack of notable changes in the socio-political course of post-

Euromaidan Ukraine (Figure 65). The graffiti equaled President Poroshenko with former President of Ukraine Victor Yanukovych, and President Putin — "Death to Putin! Death to Yanukovych! Death to Poroshenko!" The statement of distrust both to the toppled regime of President Yanukovych and that of Poroshenko was also articulated in one of the hand-made posters placed on the column of the Independence Statue at Maidan Nezalezhnosti square (2017). The poster recounted: "The thief has stolen the mace from the thief" (Figure 68), meaning the replacement of the corrupt regime of Yanukovych with the equally corrupt regime of Poroshenko.

Finally, by the fall of 2018, evaluation of the military activities in Donbas at the ordinary citizens' level exceeded the romanticized conception of war promoted by the state. Analysis of the collected data shows that the visual and discursive forms of commemoration of the victims of the military activities in Donbas was the primary mode of the grassroots referral to war. The data also contain multiple instances of both regional and national vocalization of the socio-political demands of the ordinary public. The photos and posters with images of the soldiers, political activists, as well as politically active celebrity figures (e.g. Figure 67) were placed in the same physical space of central squares of different cities of Ukraine. Juxtaposed to the state-installed political poster exhibitions, images and graffiti of the grassroots level constructed a net of discursive meanings that implied the necessity of the socio-political dialogue and, at the same time, created visual and ideological space for imagined communities of both the supporters and opponents of war in Donbas.

The handmade poster exhibition that was installed on the columns of the Statue of Independence in Kyiv in February of 2015 was another exceptionally powerful grassroots statement. Diverse in their stylistic presentation (Figures 66 and 67), the posters contained images and quotes of a leader of a famous Ukrainian rock band Skryabin, Andriy Kuzmenko (publicly known as "Kuzma[24]").

---

24 Andriy Kuzmenko (or "Kuzma") (17 August 1968 — 2 February 2015) was a Ukrainian singer, writer, poet, producer and actor. He was best known as the lead singer of the Ukrainian rock band "Skryabin," founded in 1989. At the end

A popular singer, Kuzmenko died in a car accident on February 2 2015 after publicizing explicit statements and songs that criticized the Ukrainian government's methods of carrying out war in Donbas. It is known that prior to his tragic death, Kuzma had visited the pro-Ukrainian side of Donbas, and participated in the ATO. He had spoken to both soldiers and local population of Donbas and conducted numerous press conferences where he was audibly critical of modes and "rationale" of the Ukrainian government's war in the east[25].

Right after Kuzma's death, an exhibition of the grassroots posters of the singer was placed on the columns of the Independence Statue in Kyiv (Figure 66). The lyrics of his songs were printed directly on the posters that contained pictures of Kuzma. They included clear referral to the Ukrainian political elites as those "dumping" their nation — "we were simply dumped. Like mugs behind the backs, [they] did their thing, flushed us," lyrics of one of Kuzma's last songs, "Dumped Us" (Figure 67). Juxtaposed to the state-supported poster exhibitions on war in Donbas, the exhibitions on the Euromaidan Revolution or post-2015 decommunization campaign, images of Kuzma were reposted in different regions of the country. They contributed to the creation of a national narrative of critical evaluation of the military activities in Donbas, where, unified under a common objective of a fearless expression of one's political stands, the public engaged in a dialogue with the state. In broader terms, though it cannot be claimed that posters or graffiti partake of rational discursive thought (Aulich and Sylvestrova 1999: 204), it is certainly so that, in case of post-Euromaidan Ukraine, as street graphics, they helped to constitute discourses of

---

of January 2014, Kuzmenko recorded a song that was dedicated to the events of the Euromaidan revolution where he expressed his support of the people on the Maidan. Since 2014, he has been helping the Ukrainian army in Donbas and was wounded during the Anti-Terrorist Operation (ATO). Shortly before his death, Kuzma expressed explicit criticism of the post-Euromaidan government, accusing it of corruption. Accessed January 15, 2019. Source: https://www.5.ua/suspilstvo/zavzhdy-hovoryv-lyshe-pravdu-iaka-b-ne-bula-pamiati-kuzmy-skriabina-175720.html.

25 Kuzmenko, Andriy. Hromadske TV. February 5, 2015. Interview, 48:25. https://www.youtube.com/watch?v =26X3BlGgjvk.

dissidence, opposition and critique, and established grounds for future democratic transitioning such as decommunization.

To sum up, therefore, my research shows that there were three major discourses that dominated the space of political art of (post)2013 Ukraine and contributed to commencement of the country's nation-wide de-Sovietization. The first two — criticism of political leaders and romanticization (and grassroots criticism) of war in Donbas have been discussed. The third one — presentation of the USSR and the Russian Federation as the oppressive, 'colonial other,' and massive legislative decommunization of post-Euromaidan Ukraine will be analysed in the following chapters of this book. Together, both during and after the Euromaidan revolution, these discourses, articulated by means of political posters and photo exhibitions, structured the social practices that led to activation of civil society. They also contributed to the promotion of the voluntary involvement in the military activities in Donbas, as well as implementation of institutional changes such as the 2015 decommunization laws. As part of the socio-political and cultural transformations of Ukraine, articulation of multiple meanings in political posters of the grassroots and governmental level is what I assert to be the *first stage* of (post)Euromaidan decommunization.

Both at the cultural and legislative level, the citizens-state dialogism is a fundamental element of the Ukrainian post-2013 decommunization. The discourses articulated within the space of the posters reached the level of national relevance in that their origins and intrinsic contingency were forgotten. In theoretical terms, such process is indicative of the political meaning-making that narrates discourses successfully becoming hegemonic (Laclau and Mouffe 1985). Yet, as was discussed, the phenomenon of hegemonic meaning-making is never complete. The infinity of articulation of decommunization is an expansive area that, therefore, I suggest we tackle further.

6. Meanings of Lenin

> "What do you have against nostalgia?
> It is the only entertainment for those who have no clear vision of the future."
> — "The Great Beauty," Paolo Sorrentino

The toppling of the statue of Vladimir Lenin in Kyiv at the Taras Shevchenko Boulevard on December 8 2013 was one of the culminating moments of the Euromaidan Revolution. It was followed by hundreds of Lenin and other communist monuments being taken down by far-right extremists, politically active minority groups and state-coordinated officials. This potent purge of the communist symbols became known as *Leninopad* (or the 'Leninfall'), and was captured by various forms of media, photography and political art. It laid the foundation for an extensive policy of decommunization which seized Ukraine by renaming thousands of streets, squares or metro stations, and caused the eradication of visual signs of the Soviet heritage (Kutkina 2018).

According to the director of Triptych Global Arts Workshop and research associate of the University of Oxford, Myroslava Hartmond, at the policy level, "the questions that arise in the context of urban conservation are much like the wider framework of issues faced by post-Soviet administrations: the selectivity of memory, disconnectedness of the aesthetic level from the political, the absence of competent expert bodies whose decisions are respected by political powers and financially backed, as well as a weak culture of public dialogue" (Hartmond 2016: 8). Edmund Griffiths, on the other hand, traces decommunization in Ukraine as a phenomenon that "tries to recapture the 'Spirit of '91" (Griffiths 2016: 2). The comparison of Ukraine to other post-communist states undergoing de-Sovietization during the first months of the 1990s, Hartmond argues further, "is quite misleading." The post-Euromaidan decommunization is not as efficient and 'European' as that of the Memento Park in Hungary or Grūtas Park in Lithuania, for instance: performed both as a vandalism and sanctioned practice, the Ukrainian 'Leninfall' lacks a solid judicial framework that would provide a practical outline of not only toppling, but also further maintenance of objects of the Soviet heritage (Budryte 2018; Holmes 2004; Koronenko 2019).

When it comes to examining decommunization and evaluation of the 'Leninfall' as one of the primary modes of implementation of decommunization laws, I align with existing scholarly arguments on the alarming nature of toppling of Lenin statues being one-sided articulation of 'one correct' reading of the past. At the same time, I suggest taking a different approach to the *Leninopad* and exploring it as one of the elements of broader, *versatile narratives* articulated within decommunization. Here, it is important to restrain from narrowing the approach to removal of the communist statues as "the war on monuments, or the war on communism" (Vakhovska 2014: 12). Originated during the first months of Maidan, all-national toppling of Lenin statues emerged in parallel with multiple modes of artistic articulation of the grassroots level, where the narrative of 'de-Sovitization' was *one of the many* components of change.

This chapter examines the 'Leninfall,' as well as implementation of the official decommunization laws of 2015, as one of many forms (post)Euromaidan transitioning. Rooted within the primarily vandalistic acts of nationalist minority groups, the demolition of the communist statues and, in particular, the official decommunization laws, continue the articulation of the homogeneous hegemonic formation of the state: the definition of the communist past and its symbols as a potentially "threatening external other" (Viatrovych 2015: 6). At the same time, as we will see shortly, the grassroots response to the state policies of de-Sovietization is that of a distinctively *multivocal* nature. It implies both demolition *and* preservation of the communist symbols, and contests the division of Ukrainians into 'us' or 'them' — the 'pro-Ukrainian' or 'pro-Russian' population, respectively. Importantly, before proceeding with investigation of the data, it should be noted that the heteroglossia (Bakhtin 1981) or the diversity of the grassroots stands on eradication of the communist heritage in (post)Euromaidan Ukraine has gone largely unnoticed. To understand both political and cultural implications of de-Sovietization, analysis of the Ukrainians' stands on 'how much' and 'what parts' of the communist legacy the citizens wish to be gone is to be performed. At the end, we are to talk of the Leninfall as an engaging phenomenon of civic 'domino effect,' where the toppling of communist statues reveals the socio-political plurality, ranging from physical confrontation to discursive and institutional dissent over both physical and ideological legacy of the idols, as well as a potential opportunity for improvement of the state.

The 'Leninfall' — Original Multivocality

The toppling of monuments of Lenin and other symbols of the Soviet reign in Ukraine could not have gone unnoted. If being compared to similar processes of the post-communist states such as Hungary or Lithuania, the removal of the communist statues became "the prime visual symbol of the historic change of regimes" (Michalski 1998: 148). The multivocal interpretation of the toppling of communist symbols was observed as early as during the first overthrow of Lenin in Kyiv on December 8 2013 (Kutkina 2018).

Originally, the monument of the 'great leader' was raised at Taras Shevchenko boulevard in Kyiv: made of rare red granite, the 3.45 meters statue was erected on top of the 6.8 meters pedestal of select Karelian quartz, and was officially opened December 5 1946. The inauguration of the monument was led by Nikita Khrushchev, famous Ukrainian writer Pavlo Tychyna, and the sculptor himself, Sergei Merkurov. Right before being brought to Kyiv, the statue was one of the few Soviet objects of the World Exhibition in New York (1939), where it was exhibited in the "Soviet Pavilion" together with the monument of Stalin. Inscribed in the Ukrainian catalogue of monuments of national value, the statue of Lenin in Kyiv was the central sculpture of the 'leader' that held historic saliency and was officially recognized as one of "exceptional artistic value." During the Second World War, there was a gibbet set by the Nazi regime next to the monument of Lenin in Kyiv to conduct public executions of Ukrainians. Particularly for local Kievans residing around the area, the statue of Lenin held both civic and personal value. It was a composite symbol of grief, struggle, and adversity of both private and national scale (Bikov 2017: 14). According to Liubarets, as decommunization unraveled, similar sentiments toward demolition of the statue of Lenin in Kyiv, as well as in other cities and villages of Ukraine, were widely shared by thousands of Ukrainians (Liubarets 2016: 198).

On August 3 2009 the Cabinet of Ministers of Ukraine led by Yulia Tymoshenko excluded the statue of Lenin in Kyiv, as well as other monuments of the communist regime, from the official registry of the country. The statue has lost its status of 'monument' and was no longer protected by the state. Already in June 2009, the first act of vandalism was registered when the monument was severely damaged by a group of nationalists who smashed the arm and nose of the 'leader.' The activists' justification for the act was that "they followed Presidential decree № 856/2008." In 2013, the vandals were imprisoned for two years, with both the public and state officials having different stands on the event.

While most of the Kievans condemned the act of vandalism (Lytvin 2015), the great-grandson of the monument's sculptor, Anton Merkurov, explained attachment of the local Kievans to the statue of Lenin from the historic and sentimental perspective. He defined the demolition as "an act of vandalism" and yet, stood against restoration of the statue. "Most certainly, I object to acts of vandalism. And I am also against the reconstruction of Lenin. The harm is absolutely irretrievable. Now, all this is just part of history's will. However, may these fragments of the statue serve as a reminder for generations to come of how ruthless, uneducated and violent their ancestors truly were," Merkurov posted in his blog "Good-bye Lenin, hello mediocre people!" in 2013. After the demolition, the monument was taken into pieces that were then put up for auction. The price of the communist idol depended on the part and weight of his 'body.' The palm, for example, was worth 1,000 UAH, while the fragment of his hand was worth 750 UAH. Separate pieces of feet and torso were also sold depending on weight. The head, however, was tagged as "priceless," and was put up for live auction (Radchenko 2013).

The columnist of The New York Times blog, Maria Gessen (2013: 2), described euphoria, anger and sorrow around the statue where "people attacked the monument and started hitting it vigorously with a stone-hammer, passing pieces of the statue to each other." Open confrontations between the opponents to and the instigators of the dismantling were also recorded by both professional documentalists and ordinary citizens.

In February 2014, during the interview with Estonian documentalist, scholar and political activist, Kristina Norman, I was introduced to a film of Roman Bondarchuk, Yulia Gontaruk and Kateryna Gornostai, Euromaidan: Rough Cut (2014). The screening is a collection of short documentaries that record different episodes of the Euromaidan revolution, and include a video document on the historic moment of toppling of the Lenin statue in Kyiv. The episode titled "Lenin's Teeth" is a recording of the statue's toppling as it happened live—it captures interaction of the ordinary Ukrainians who both support and object to the demolition. In the following quotes both participants and observers of Lenin's overthrow embark into a polemic on the role, value, and meaning of the monument. The film commences with an episode where one of the observers of an overthrow raises the question on "what the fault of the monument is?" The answer that follows from the crowd is rather self-explanatory—'"his fault is in being Lenin." And so the dialogue unravels further:

> *Woman* (from the crowd, speaking Russian): -And what was the Berlin Wall guilty of then? Okay, wait. All right. Guys, wait!
>
> *Participant 1 (P1):* Why should a monument of the murderer of the Ukrainian people stand here?
>
> *Woman:* No, no. Wait!
>
> *P1:* We should have pulled him down in 1991.
>
> *Woman:* No, it's a symbol! Do you smash your symbols? No, you respect them. And I...You...we can criticize, but not smash them! Understand my position...Wait. My position is the following—I live in this place. I

used to walk past this monument of Lenin on my way to school. It's sad. Just so sad!

P1: There should be a monument to victims of genocide.

Woman: What?

Participant 2 (speaking Ukrainian)*:* There will be some figure on the top.

Participant 3: Maybe Bandera (in Ukrainian)

The crowd: Down with Lenin! Down with Commies! Down with oligarch Commies!

At first, this episode of the documentary provided what could be seen as a perfect justification of popular propaganda stands of the Russian media, where a native Kievan woman, a Russian speaker, entreats radically-set nationalists not to vandalize her monument. A clear 'us' versus 'them' distinction is established when she asks if "[they would] smash [their] symbols." Clearly, the destruction of Lenin invokes grief that is rooted in a loss of a personal symbol—the physical object that was part of the city's topography, an integral element of the woman's daily routine such as "going to school." Objection of the statue's demolition is also grounded on nostalgia and not necessarily the disagreement with political transformations of the Euromaidan Ukraine—a popular stand that was broadcasted by the vast majority of Russian media sources during and after the revolution. Another discussion of the video on the possibility of replacing Lenin with a statue of victims of genocide or Bandera is also the primary narrative that set the discursive horizon for ardent grassroots debates and controversial state policies.

Finally, as articulated by one of the participants of this video, destruction of Lenin monument is a symbolic act of not only toppling of the oppressive communist regime, but also an overthrow of an oligarchic clan rooted in the Soviet domain. The equalization of the 'lithic corps of the monument,' the 'commies,' and the 'oligarchs' is done by chanting 'Down with Lenin! Down with Commies! Down with oligarch Commies!'. As the statue of Lenin is being removed, the episode captures explicit de-personification of Lenin. Itself the symbol of the revolution and struggle against imperialism, the figure of Lenin articulates an empire. As a symbol of the oppressive communist past, however, toppling of the Lenin monument is an embracement of one of the primary goals of the Euromaidan revolution—'Europeanization' of the country by means of detachment from cultural and political remnants of the Soviet past.

As the camera of Gornostai slides across the crowd, multivocality of the grassroots population is apparent further—this time, it is the split of the generations—the youth are shown to be the more tolerant of political diversity, as well as open to contrasting opinions of the fellow citizens:

> *Girl from the crowd* (in Ukrainian): Why are you crying, grandpa? Have you remembered something, or what? Are you cold?
>
> *Grandpa* (in Ukrainian): No…
>
> *Girl:* Please tell me what happened?…Are you so worried about Lenin, grandpa?
>
> *Grandpa:* 'This is…this is…This is inhumane.
>
> *Girl:* You mean this event?
>
> *Grandpa:* This is inhumane…
>
> *Girl:* Grandpa, it's for the best. People want something better.
>
> *Grandpa:* This is inhumane. When my mother… (crying, unable to speak further)…

This video records the scale of trauma caused by the fall of Lenin as one that exceeds the physical ability of an elderly man to even talk. A Ukrainian speaker, he defines the process as "inhumane" and, as in the first dialogue, makes personal reference to "[his] mother." Even though no further details on where the dialogue might have gone are recorded, there is evidence of the contrasting stereotypes of linguistic preferences of the Ukrainian population being reciprocal to supporting or rejecting the communist past. A Ukrainian-speaking man is clearly expressing approval of preservation of the statue of Lenin. At the same time, the episode unravels divergence in interpretation of the toppling of the statue, where the younger generation perceives demolition of Lenin as a transformation "for the best." The question that persists, however, is on the content of new discursive formations, as well as visual modes of articulation of 'de-colonial' or anti-Soviet narratives, that would be inclusive rather than exclusive of the political and cultural diversity. When Lenin falls, what would the symbols that replace him be? Also, if we are to address decommunization as both the regional and national phenomenon, whom do we see as the principal architect(s) of decommunization — the ordinary citizens or the state? Back in December of 2013, the Leninfall was still in-the-making, and yet, already reflective of both dialogue and contestation.

The final scene of Gornostai's documentary captures people sharing pieces of Lenin and proclaiming that "that's way too much. [They] do not deserve that much Lenin." At the same time, explicit silencing of the proponent of the statue's preservation is apparent — a man (Participant 4) who stands up for the monument, is discouraged from expressing his stands, and is propelled into both physical and discursive exclusion.

> *Participant 4 (P4)* (in Ukrainian): So, how should we live this life, father?
>
> *Participant 5 (P5)* (in Ukrainian): You should live this life so that you do no harm to people. Right now these people want just one thing, and you are starting to stir up all kinds of different things (in Ukrainian)

P4: I am just asking!

P5: Don't ask, just stand and watch.

P4: Wait, wait…you are not listening to me at all! Wait!

P5: This is it, go away. Goodbye.

P4: Listen, I served for the Mediterranean fleet. I am for the Motherland!

P5: They did not teach you anything, those two tours of duty.

P4: It was in 1982-83.

P5: You could have done a hundred tours and you would still be the same.

P4: I came here to ask people!

P5: What are you interested in?

P4: That…I would say I'm interested (says with tears in his eyes)…What did you, or what did we get from this? (self-emphasized, referring to toppling of the Lenin statue).

P5: Those who wanted something, they got it.

P4: What?

P5: Just go away.

(Participant '4' goes away).

Participant 6 (P6) (in Ukrainian): Please, hold on strong!

P4: Who, me? Oh, I will. They said they were going to beat me up. What for? For truth?

P6: They wouldn't beat you up.

P4: And they will not kill me! Or...maybe...Let them kill me! I came out and said who they are! Nobody here told them. So I came out and did! And they tell me that they are going to beat me up? Never! (shows a gun and walks away). I am leaving. Your truth is just your truth. If you don't need me—Glory to Ukraine! But free! In Europe! Thank you, my daughter. (walks away)

Participant 7 (P7) (random passer-by): Glory to Ukraine!

Upon multiple reviews of the documentary, complexity of the citizens' narratives is what I found most puzzling and equally astonishing. As a bottom line, no narrative could be distinguished as the dominant one. To see 'Participant 4' drawing a line between himself and the rest of the crowd with exclamations such as "let them kill me" or "I came out and said who they are!", standing against the nationalist activists, and then suddenly proclaiming "Glory to Ukraine! But free! In Europe!", was odd enough to remain unnoticed. Despite most open condemnation of toppling of the Soviet statue, the man uses nationalist slogans[26] and shares broader political values of those destroying the monument—'free' and 'pro-European' path of Ukraine. Expression of the political, cultural or civic stances that could, at first, be classified as pro-Russian (or pro-Soviet) implies neither anti-Ukrainian nor anti-European preferences.

This episode is particularly reflective of the socio-political composition of (post)Euromaidan Ukraine, where political and cultural identities are highly intertwined and consist of elements that no longer follow the classical definition of the 'pro-Russian' (pro-Soviet) or 'pro-Ukrainian'. What I also found exceptionally pro-

---

26 "Glory to Ukraine! Glory to the heroes!" is a Ukrainian national salute that appeared at the beginning of the 20th century and became widely popular among ethnic Ukrainians during the Ukrainian war for independence (1917-1921). The motto acquired a new meaning during the Euromaidan revolution, where the participants themselves, not the nationalists from the past, were the heroes and proclaimed glory to themselves. Volodymyr Kadygrob, *#Euromaidan: History in the Making* (Osnovy Publishing, 2014), 196-197.

found is the prophetic nature of this dialogue—if necessary, the neglected activist (Participant 4) is ready to protect himself and his 'truth' with a gun. Six months later, in the summer of 2014, the world witnessed the military activities in the east unraveling along the somewhat similar scenario: with a hand from Russia, a number of locals in Donbas took arms to 'articulate' their stands against Kyiv, and object the 'pro-European' course that implied extirpation of the Soviet heritage.

But this is how it all started. Gornostai's documentary is the record of the origins of the grassroots multivocality on decommunization. As we are to see shortly, thousands of Ukrainians bear their own opinion on communist symbols, their own experience of the fall, and rather personal justification (or rejection) of de-Sovietization. The process of articulation of multiple 'meanings' of decommunization is taking place in ongoing juxtaposition of one element against another (Laclau 1985), as well as exclusion of certain elements in the name of the commonly supported political stands. Importantly, the fundamental split of the socio-political positions of the majority of the population is constructed around the *past*—communist statues, for instance, and not the present—the 'pro-European' course of Ukraine. In this context, the communist monuments, as well as empty plinths of the dismantled statues, become canvases for articulation of personal, grassroots messages to the government, fellow citizens, the Russian aggressor and, as was mentioned earlier, even Lenin himself.

Creative Remembering

With the exception of the monument of Lenin in Kyiv, which was the first to be toppled as part of the onset of the Euromaidan revolution, the overthrow of the communist statues in cities like Kryvyi Rih, Vinnytsia, Kharkiv or Zaporizhzhya followed its own pattern. The process of massive demolition, dismantling or damage of Lenin monuments took place in western and central regions already during the Euromaidan revolution. In central Ukraine, such as the cities of Lybny or Myrhorod, statues of Lenin were also dismantled in early- and mid-2014. Most of the communist monuments in the urban centers of the east, such as Kryvyi Rih or Zaporizhzhya, however, remained untouched until 2015 and spring/summer of 2016 (Fieldnotes. By Anna Kutkina. Dnipro, Zaporizhzhya, Kharkiv, 2015-2016).

Within the timespan of over four years, the demolition of Lenin monuments has turned into one of the central visual projects of major Ukrainian cities. Methodologically speaking, there was no impediment to observing the removal of communist statues. Since most of the Lenin statues were usually located at the central squares of cities (or villages), their transformation was immediately apparent. Compared to the early 1990s, the Leninfall developed within a complex mosaic of cultural appropriation techniques. The body of Lenin—Lenin-the-statue, was damaged, relocated and overwritten with different meanings. To facilitate the examination of major stages of engagement with Lenin statues (2014-2018), various techniques of appropriation of the monuments could be divided into the following phases:

1) Either violent or sanctioned toppling of statues of Lenin being followed by application of political messages via graffiti painted on the plinth;

2) Painting of the Lenin statues into vernacular yellow-blue colors or dressing them up in Vyshyvanka (Вишиванка)—embroidered shirt of Ukrainian national costume;

3) After the official implementation of the 2015 decommunization laws, an authorized removal of the communist symbols in all regions of Ukraine.

Broadly speaking, as a political and cultural phenomenon, Leninfall has raised questions on mechanisms of articulation and institutionalization of change. The "Leninopad," as it is often called by Ukrainians, revealed how toppling, preservation or re-location of the communist symbols become methods of political meaning-making that implies physical interaction with objects of the Soviet past as explicit means of articulation of one's political and cultural stands. The process of decommunization and removal (or preservation) of the Soviet symbols is not only an indicator of ideological or socio-political transitioning. It is also a marker of the formation of a discursive universe or the 'imagined communities,' where artistic preservation of Lenin statues is also the means for conducting a political dialogue—that of the ordinary citizens and the state.

After the toppling of the Lenin statue in Kyiv by a group of individuals claiming to be affiliated with the Svoboda Party[27], the spectrum of political creativity on the Lenin pedestal included replacement of the monument with extraordinary artistic creations as a means of presentation of diverse socio-political messages. They varied from the grassroots desire to fight corruption (e.g. a golden toilet, an emblem of former President Yanukovych's corruption was placed directly on the statue's pedestal) to redirection of the country's political course towards the EU (e.g. the EU and UPA flags placed on the statue's plinth), or presentation of a wider range of messages such as political and cultural partnership between the states (e.g. a giant blue hand named "Middle way[28]" installed beside the pedestal to symbolizing "friendship and cooperation").

---

27 The All-Ukrainian Union "Svoboda" (translated as "Freedom") is a Ukrainian nationalist political party that was founded in 1991 as the Social-National Party of Ukraine. It is positioned between the right-wing and the far-right of the political spectrum. It is widely considered a fascist and/or anti-semitic party, as well as simply a radical nationalist party. The party was reformed in 2004 and has been led by Oleh Tyahnybok (elected every two years). In the 2012 Ukrainian parliamentary elections, Svoboda won its first seats in the Ukrainian Parliament. It garnered 10.44% of the popular vote and the 4th most seats among national political parties. From 27 February 2014 till 12 November 2014 three members of the party held positions in Ukraine's government. The party won 6 seats in the late October 2014 Ukrainian parliamentary election. Accessed October 5, 2018. Source: https://svoboda.org.ua/.

28 Named "Middle Way," the giant blue hand was installed next to the pedestal of the toppled Lenin statue in Kyiv by the Romanian artist Bogdan Rață, best known for his distorted sculptures of the human body (2017-2018). The blue hand was placed at Taras Shevchenko Boulevard. Brought to the city by the Romanian Embassy and the Nasui Collection & Gallery as part of Kiev's "Moving Monuments" program, the sculpture divided locals, many of whom were celebrating that the installation was merely temporary. Davies, Katie Marie. "Kiev has replaced the city's Lenin statue with a giant blue hand." The Calvert Journal. September 28, 2018. https://www.calvertjournal.com/articles/show/10684/kiev-has-replaced-the-citys-lenin-statue-with-a-giant-blue-hand.

After the official termination of the Euromaidan revolution and following the removal of the tents, burned tires, wire and other relics of the revolution, examination of the pedestals became easier. In April 2014, when the protesters' camp was still installed, it was almost impossible to grasp the scale of the toppling: from an approximate distance of 10 meters, the plinth was still covered with soot. Darkened by the ash of the revolutionary fire, the postament of the 'great leader' has lost its centrality—no longer carrying Lenin, the pedestal has turned into a new symbol, in Bikov's terms—"the sign of change" (Bikov 2017: 38) (Figure 70). Still rooted deeply in the Ukrainian soil, communism in Ukraine was beheaded. Whether supported or objected, the impact of this toppling can be anything but underestimated—it commenced both physical and discursive pursuit of meanings—the process of creative replacement of the Soviet cult with diverse, personal, oftentimes artistic political narratives.

Symbolically, as one of the activists who was taking the statue down in December shared: "[toppling of Lenin figure] was the day the revolution started. Because Lenin on Bessarabska Square wasn't just a symbol of the past; it was also a symbol of everything that was going wrong in Ukraine…The whole of Maidan was so enthusiastic. This was the central act of the revolution, when people freed themselves from the past" (Halushka and Gobert 2017: 14). According to one of my interviewees, Evgen, "factually, when it came to making a decision of whether to remove the monument or not, the answer would traditionally be "yes" (Nazarchuk, Evgen. Interview. By Anna Kutkina. Kryvyi Rih. 2 March 2017). What comes as an important point of the toppling process is that the statue of Lenin also became a space for expression of the primarily anti-communist or anti-colonial positions. The 'torturer' or 'colonizer' ("Kat") (Figure 74) was observed as the primary graffiti message articulated on the pedestals of the Lenin statues across Ukraine.

The interviews confirm that toppling of the communist statues was one of the multiple forms of articulation of decommunization. Complete demolition of all remnants of the communist past became officially institutionalized by the state after termination of the Euromaidan revolution by means of passing of the official 2015 'decommunization laws'. This government-implemented legislative procedure implied (and installed) complete eradication of Lenin statues. It became a powerful legislative mechanism for articulation of what I argue to be the homogeneous hegemonic formation of the state--a complete demolition of the Soviet statues from the physical space of Ukraine.

As Ukraine transitioned into a large-scale clearance of its communist past, the ordinary citizens' stands towards the toppling of the Soviet insignia remained *diverse* (Fieldnotes. By Anna Kutkina. Ukraine. 2014-3018). Already in early 2015, prior to official implementation of the decommunization laws, I observed the empty plinths becoming canvases of predominantly anti-Soviet narratives, and yet carrying many *pro-Lenin* stands. Sébastien Gobert, Niels Ackermann, Yevgenia Belorusets and Alevtina Kakhidze are among the many who also acknowledge the multiplicity of sociopolitical positions of Ukrainains when it comes to decommunization. However, apart from revealing their views during interviews, the people who objected to decommunization or were taking rather neutral stands on the process were not recorded to make their views broadly known. Simply put, if one conducted analysis of the images of de-Sovietization in post-2013 Ukraine, such as photographs or debris of the toppled statues of Lenin or the plinths, both topographic and narrative findings would be representative of a rather one-sided, anti-communist position. The heterogeneous hegemonic formation that was being constructed at the grassroots level since the Euromaidan revolution, remained *silent* or visually undetectable. Had these views been made public or vocalized, the multivocal narratives of the ordinary Ukrainians would have carried potential for refinement of the 'black-and-white' picture of Ukraine being 'unified' by adversities of its communist past—the hegemonic formation supported and implemented by the state.

Overall, it could be argued that after the termination of the Euromaidan revolution, its winner—an ordinary Ukrainian, attained a right to demolish the figure of the oppressor, as well as to place him or herself at the wheel of the state—atop the pedestals of an overthrown Lenin. Massive public flashmobs of Ukrainians standing on the plinths have turned into a national phenomenon (Figure 74). Such events were recorded in Kyiv, Kharkiv, Poltava and other cities and villages across the country (Fieldnotes. By Anna Kutkina. Ukraine. June 2014-September 2018). The narratives vocalized within this process, however, were ambiguous. The interviewee from Kharkiv, Olexander, for instance, expressed the complexity of his civic convictions while sharing an image of himself standing on Lenin's plinth:

"It was the moment of absolute triumph. It was both a national and personal victory. My people have won the revolution! That was it! Lenin was gone and now, finally, an ordinary Ukrainian could take the dictator's place both politically and physically! Can you imagine? It was almost symbolic – you, being so tiny – a forgotten citizen of your state, standing on top of Lenin's giant shoes! What a euphoria! It was the moment of massive revenge as well. And the only thing that made me sad was watching older people standing aside and almost crying. One of those minutes when you understand that, as in any revolution, there will always be winners and losers" (Osintsev, Olexander. Interview. By Anna Kutkina. Kharkiv. 12 June 2016).

When asked about his opinion on the statue's demolition and his image and attitude toward the event a year later, Olexander expressed indifference, disappointment, and was rather critical of decommunization as a whole:

"Yes, all major media channels recorded the Leninfall in Ukraine. So what? It is way too easy to overthrow the stone. What about traditions, all the corruption, theft, all the crime that our country accumulated during decades of communism? Us, them…we come and destroy the signs. Same thing is happening to the streets. We rename them, but all the buildings, trees, houses – they are all static! You know what I mean? I do support popular graffiti – the communist regime was torturous. Of course! The question is – how do we get rid of its roots? Its culture? How do we record real change? That is a rather good, very good question" (Osintsev, Olexander. Interview. By Anna Kutkina. Kharkiv. 17 July 2017).

As the physical demolition of the communist past from the city landscape, therefore, the Leninfall involved articulation of contradictory political meanings that contributed towards a heterogeneous hegemonic formation at the grassroots level—that of support *and* objection to decommunization. Meanwhile, the means of articulation of such hegemonic formation—modes of interaction with symbols of the colonial past—were diverse. When both the visual and interview data were collected, there evolved a quest on how to measure decommunization as being 'complete.' In other words, there emerged a question of whether it could be argued that the fall of the Lenin statues was the sign of successful completion of decolonization. As one of my interviewees, Oles, has pointed, "there [existed] the danger of overthrowing the stone and having the remnants of the regime being left in multiple forms such as corruption or crime" (Krasko, Oles. Interview. By Anna Kutkina. Zaporizhzhya. 25 July 2017).

In his analysis of the 'Leninfall' in Ukraine, Sébastien Gobert defines the Leninfall as "a chaotic effort to break with the past and, accordingly, with Russia" (Gobert 2017: 4). He and his colleague, the photographer of the project *Looking for Lenin*[29] Niels Ackermann, further point to ideological and institutional justification of de-Sovietization: "official decommunization laws tried to provide a framework for the democratic movement" (Halushka and Gobert 2017: 22). However, according to the authors, "rather than offering answers, it raised only questions." The euphoria of the demolition was alternated with apathy and feelings of meaninglessness of decommunization as a mechanism of socio-political change. Particularly after 2016, when hundreds of Lenin statues have been taken down in major cities and villages, the questions of effectiveness and

---

29 *Looking for Lenin* (2017) is the artistic research project of the journalist Sebastien Gobert and the photographer Niels Ackermann. Originated as a quest to answer the question on 'where the toppled Lenin statue in Kyiv go?', authors of this project have hunted down and photographed the fallen statues of Lenin across Ukraine (2013-2016), revealing the monuments' inglorious fate. The statues were found in the most unexpected places such as scrap yards, store rooms, or bathrooms of ordinary Ukrainians, who were trying to save Lenin monuments from complete destruction. The visual content of the project was turned into an exhibition, which was installed both in Ukraine and internationally. Accessed February 8, 2018. Source: http://fuel-design.com/publishing/looking-lenin/.

modes of decommunization emerged as the primary areas of the ordinary citizens' concerns. Interestingly, the scepticism towards the state-run policies of decommunization was expressed by the representatives of diverse social and cultural strata. In his interview with Ackermann and Gobert, the deputy mayor of Chernihiv, Oleksandr Lomako, addresses the absence of real changes brought by the 'Leninfall':

"You are looking for Lenin? Good for you. I'll help you but let's move fast: I have a lot of work to do. I don't really care about decommunization. Neither do the city residents. In Chernihiv, there are few economic opportunities, we don't have many jobs to offer. Our city is neglected. We need to develop businesses and attract investments and provide future for our kids – that's our priority. They took Lenin away. Good. But this didn't change anything in our lives" (Halushka and Gobert, 2017: 94).

A farmer from Ivano-Frankivsk, Galyna Prokopenko, whose husband was an active participant of the Euromaidan revolution, expresses further concern of decommunization being nothing but a destructive manoeuvre of the state:

"I used to be a simple, non-politicized person until the day my husband went to Maidan. What a time that was – so much faith, passion, so much hope for a better future! Three years later…what do we have? Members of the parliament live their luxurious lives while ordinary people like us are forced to work like slaves to make our ends meet. And Lenin? He has always been a dead figure for us. Both during communist times and after the fall of the Soviet Union. This current government knows this…and is just trying to mask its crimes with those of Lenin. Nothing…nothing is changing. They should start punishing living criminals rather than the dead ones…" (Prokopenko, Galyna. Interview. By Anna Kutkina. Lviv. 5 February 2017).

As such, the post-Maidan de-Sovietization developed into a vicious cycle where dissatisfaction, yearning for change and even anger were motivators that triggered the toppling of communist symbols and, at the same time, were the terminal point of the 'Leninfall.' Ultimately, Gobert claims, "the process [became] illegible." Traditional stereotypes such as the Ukrainian-speaking intelligentsia from Lviv being devoted supporters of decommunization, or, on the contrary, Russian-speaking factory workers from Eastern

Ukraine being the opponents of the Leninfall, dissolved. The socio-economic conditions, fight against corruption, or regional improvement of the state apparatus evolved into a dominant narrative that accompanied the Leninfall at both the regional and national level. (Interviews. By Anna Kutkina. Lviv, Kyiv, Zaporizhzhya, Odessa, 2015-2018). The focal point of the Euromaidan revolution—subversion of criminal 'post-Soviet' elites and institutionalized demolition of corruption that, potentially, would lead to improvement of the living-standards of average Ukrainians, was identified by the interviewees as a sequel of decommunization.

Drawing of the analytical relationships between narratives, images and physical objects, such as the toppled statues of Lenin, revealed the figure of Lenin being a nodal point of multiple forms of meaning-making. As a symbol of the contested past, it is 'composed' of diverse personal meanings and is an ample emblem of change—it is both an object and method of exemption from the communist past. Additionally, the post-2013 decommunization is also a peculiar form of prolongation of the Euromaidan revolution, where the removal (or preservation) of communist symbols by the ordinary public serves as a tool for articulation of the grassroots political and cultural stands.

The Lenin Camouflage

The curator of the project the *Soviet Mosaics in Ukraine*, Yevhenia Moliar (2016), discusses three levels of decommunization: 'ideological decommunization,' where the officials inform of their ability to conduct reforms by using destruction of communist statues as a populist demeanor, 'gentle popular decommunization,' where local citizens take the initiative and adjust communist symbols via numerous artistic stands, and 'communist decommunization,' where the urban space undergoes alteration by private figures who view the remnants of the monuments as lithic ruins.

Although the 'gentle popular decommunization,' or what could be called 'artistic decommunization,' is mentioned in the literature on decommunization of post-Maidan Ukraine as a key element of de-Sovietization (Chervonenko 2016; Gilley 2015; Moliar

2016; Shevel 2015), the Leninfall in cities like Zaporizhzhya, Dnipro or Kryvyi Rih indicates peculiar tendencies of the preservation rather than demolition of the communist symbols. This could be seen as pursuing two primary objectives: use of humor and irony to illustrate ideological and practical flaws of decommunization, and preservation of the Soviet monuments by means of political art. In 2015, for instance, Ukrainian artist Oleksandr Milov transformed a rusting statue of Lenin in Odessa into a monument of *Star Wars* villain Darth Vader, where he covered old body of the 'leader' with stout material and added a helmet (Figure 71).

In his interview to BBC Culture, Milov calls himself "a child of a country that does not exist anymore" and explains his creation as the "desire to save the monuments of history" (McDonald 2015). He further defines his art as a metaphorical attempt "to clean up the operating system and to keep it on the hard drive of memory." Without physical eradication of the communist symbol—the body of Lenin, the signifier of the Soviet oppression, or the statue of Lenin, therefore, is 're-defined.' It escapes complete demolition with the help of an artistic collision of multiple meanings or sociopolitical narratives within the original space of the statue.

Complex *and* simple in its ideological essence, the statue of Milov addresses further generic questions on (im)possibility of immediate transformation of the state. Also, it presents important dilemma of "who represents the Dark Side better—Lenin or Darth Vader?"—the communist system or the ruling elites of post-2013 Ukraine. "Such poignant subversion fits well with the technology-savvy, progressive image the port city [of Odessa] strives to present to the world," argues Gobert (2017: 13). Similar to other examples of communist monuments that were reused as Cossacks, military commanders or superheroes (Figure 72), the statue of Darth Vader is one of the many instances where national reform of decommunization was carried out by private agents. Artistic ideas of the ordinary citizens are made public and political through creative imposition of communist symbols. And vice versa: political symbols of the communist regime are transformed into subjects of personal, closed domain, where painted or changed, they are reduced to objects of home décor (Figure 73).

The process of both public and private preservation of the communist statues by means of political art illustrates what I argue to be the construction of parallel 'imagined communities.' In classical terms of Benedict Anderson (1983), just as the members of any political community "will never know most of their fellow-members," the participants of the decommunization of post-2013 Ukraine are left virtually invisible to each other (with the exception of famous artists, researchers or journalists working on the matter: e.g. Milov or Gobert). At the same time, the ordinary citizens who are either toppling or preserving Lenin statues are unified into broader ideological (or cultural) formations that promote both demolition and preservation of the communist past. The process of such multivocal decommunization that has been taking place in Ukraine since the early days of the Euromaidan revolution became a national phenomenon and is an example of heterogeneous hegemonic formation of the grassroots level.

Within this context, political reading of the collected data illustrates further re-narration and re-construction of history that takes place so as to fit the political and cultural demands of the present. The figure of Lenin loses its original meaning and is turned into a Cossack, for instance (Figure 72) or even the object of personal interior (e.g. pieces of Lenin statue being used as a glass-holder). The narratives unraveled through 'Leninfall' are exceptionally diverse. As new meanings are articulated by multiple forms of creative interaction with the statues, the symbol of the political epoch is deconstructed to present multivocal readings of the communist past, as well as the country's 'democratic' present: the loyalty to the Soviet past, the democratic protest such as the Euromaidan revolution, or an overall, new creative approach of turning the monuments into objects of art. Such process epitomizes construction of what is a powerful hegemonic formation. It implies the phenomenon of meaning-making that challenges the simplicity of physical destruction of Lenin statues as the primary and only possible means of obliteration of the communist era. It also raises further questions on the possibility of individual ownership of the space and its political, historical objects, as well as the efficiency of political art as a means of articulation and implementation of the dialogical interaction.

In many places the preservation of Lenin statues has also assumed a form of 'Ukrainization.' In both the capital city of Kyiv and major industrial centers of the country (e.g. Zaporizhzhya and Kryvyi Rih) statues of Lenin were displayed in the traditionally Ukrainian attributes—painted in yellow and blue colors of the Ukrainian flag or dressed in Ukrainian embroidery shirt, Vyshyvanka. This visual 'nationalization' of communist monuments is an outcome of two conflicting views. In the case of painting of Lenin statues, the act was performed by nationalist groups who used colors of the Ukrainian flag (yellow and blue) as a means of *censorship* of the communist past (Kutkina 2018). In Zaporizhzhya, on the other hand, visual transformation of a vyshyvanka-dressed Lenin occurred upon the official approval of local administration that took the initiative to provide an "appeasing solution" to potentially conflicting groups (such instance, however, was an exception and did not reflect the general tendency of the state in dealing with communist symbols). Admired by older generations, the symbol of "prosperous communist past" was left intact and, at the same time, was dressed in the cogent emblem of "Ukrainianess"— Vyshyvanka. "If it was not for official decommunization laws, we would have kept our Lenin like that. It was such an important symbol of Zaporizhzhya—the city that remembers and honors its past, but yet is open to a solely Ukrainian future, most certainly," states one of the citizens of Zaporizhzhya who chose to remain incognito. The interviews that I conducted with members of NGOs, journalists, and ordinary citizens of the city record the widespread support for preservation of the communist statues in Zaporizhzhya and other regions of eastern and southern Ukraine (e.g. Kryviy Rih, Kharkiv, Odessa).

In broader terms, these instances of artistic preservation, or transformation of statues of Lenin reflect the socio-political and cultural change of the country's civic domain, where particularly after the Euromaidan revolution, traditional juxtaposition between 'east' and 'west' has *disappeared*. Either physical or ideological, the 'exterior' of an interviewee is illusive: a holder of the Ukrainian flag or a shirt can be Russian-speaking, remain respectful of the communist past, and, at the same time, be willing to sacrifice his or her life for territorial integrity and the independence of Ukraine. And vice versa. Importantly, when it comes to interaction with cultural heritage of the Soviet past, Ukrainian symbols became indicative of a diverse set of actions—*both* guarding and disruptive. At the grassroots level, the new hegemony of multivocality materialized through memorials, where articulation of one's cultural and political stands towards the Leninfall was left incomplete; it was an ambiguous marker of a citizen's political identity, and at the same time, an abrupt delineator of popular clichés (e.g. the correlation between one's geographic and political or cultural identity).

Compared to peaceful modes of preservation of the communist symbols—dressing up of the Lenin statues in the Ukrainian traditional t-shirts or painting of monuments in blue-and-yellow colors of the Ukrainian flag—the episodes of sporadic toppling of the Soviet statues attracted particular media attention (Shevel 2015). However, my research has shown that the vandalistic destruction of the communist monuments was still rare. Regardless of one's pro-Soviet or anti-communist opinions, Ukrainians of different regions expressed support for commemoration rather than complete destruction of their past. They showed initiative for the creation of a "Totalitarianism Museum" where the dismantled communist statues could be placed. At the same time, the inability of the state-apparatus to institutionalize change—to not only pass but to also track implementation of decommunization laws, and the toppling of Soviet symbols in particular, became distinctively apparent as of 2016-2017. According to former director of the Institute of National Remembrance and one of the most controversial drafters of the decommunization laws, Volodymyr Viatrovych "as of 2017 there was no official database on monuments in Ukraine. In particular, there [was] no single database when it came to smaller monuments that existed in villages or smaller cities of the country." According to Viatrovych, the local people themselves had to contact the government to report on monuments of Lenin still standing in their backyards. It is usually after the ordinary citizens' initiative that "the central government would address local authorities to enforce toppling of monuments down" (Nalivaiko, Maryna. Interview. By Anna Kutkina. Vinnytsia. 10 May 2018). As such, decommunization could be seen as a rather reactive phenomenon, where potential 'de-Sovietization' of the city's (or village's) public space relies on awareness and effort of its residents.

In all major cities of Ukraine, a high number of monuments were demolished during the first months of spontaneous decommunization — December 2013-March 2014 (Himka 2015; Motyl 2015; Zabyelina 2017). My research has shown that particularly at the local level, however, political loyalty of acting authorities to the symbols of the communist regime remained strong. In eastern parts of Ukraine, where the number of adherents to the Soviet past was still "notably high" (Motyl 2015), blocking decommunization was one of the primary means of winning political votes. Objecting to the national policy of decommunization, officials of the cities like Zaporizhzhya postponed toppling of Lenin statues as to both obtain loyalty of potential voters and appease the local population: the citizens who supported or objected removal of communist statues. In broader terms, besides unraveling the dilemma on what to do with the toppled statues, 'artistic' Leninfall exposed the possibilities for non-hierarchical negotiations — creative adaptation of the Soviet heritage from 'communal' to 'private.' Irrespective of the educational, economic or cultural background, everyone had their own experience and understanding of decommunization.

Years down the road from the Euromaidan revolution, "Lenin statues have gained certain ideological meanings that could not be reduced to specific evaluation of Lenin as a historical figure or that of the Soviet period in general," argue the authors of the study of the 'Leninfall' in the cities of Dnipro, Zaporizhzhya and Kharkiv (Gaidai/ Liubaretc 2016). A number of academic and media analysts of post-Euromaidan decommunization have taken their arguments as far as to state that "the fact that [Ukrainians] are taking down the monuments of the only successful revolutionary in the Eurasian history — anti-imperialist, Lenin, could be seen as one of the primary indicators of no real political revolution occurring in Ukraine" (Bikov 2017). The Curator of Art Projects of Izolyatsia

Foundation in Kyiv, Yevgenia Moliar (2017), on the other hand, points at the vexatious Ukrainian state ideology "that condemns any form of criticism." At the governmental level, decommunization could be seen as "turning into a risky civic procedure, as it demands at least partial re-definition of the citizens' cultural and political identity," Moliar argues further. One of the primary objectives of this chapter was to restrain from siding with any form of examination of decommunization as a completed phenomenon. The process of both the regional and national scale, the decommunization, and toppling of Lenin statues in particular, both maintains and challenges the political order: it implies implementation of the official decommunization laws at both the state and grassroots level, and at the same time, reveals multiple modes of preservation (or re-articulation) of the past by alternative, artistic means.

7. Filling the 'Pedestal'

> "Our life is war."
> —Ivan Franko

The increasing use of the past for political, commercial and cultural purposes is a national phenomenon of post-Euromaidan Ukraine (Motyl 2015; Kozyrska 2016; Shveda 2016). Derived from an extensive period of administrative chaos of the early years of Ukraine's independence—1991-onwards, the monopoly over interpretation of the past has been established through the institutionalization of national memory (Gerasimov and Mogilner 2015; Hofland 2015; Szeptycki 2011). Similar to the socio-political aftermath of the 2006 Orange Revolution, identity-making of post-2013 Ukraine involves condemnation of the Soviet past and re-articulation (or institutionalization) of the historical symbols that carry controversial meanings within the socio-political and cultural context of Ukraine. Upon the official termination of the Euromaidan revolution and toppling of most of the communist monuments, the 'resurrection' of Stepan Bandera, Semen Petliura or members of the Ukrainian Insurgent Army became particularly evident in both physical and discursive space of the country.

The process of substitution of Lenin 'with' Bandera occurred *prior* to official implementation of the decommunization laws that rendered historical figures of the OUN and UPA inviolable, and took place at both the grassroots and governmental level. The photo, video and interview data that I collected documents de-Sovietization commencing through absorption of visual spaces, such as the bookshelves or public squares, that became filled with images and narratives on Stepan Bandera as early as in spring 2014. Alongside the first waves of vandalistic toppling of the statues of Lenin across Ukraine, what I define as the final stage of post-Euromaidan de-Sovietization took multiple forms that ranged from state-promoted glorification of the military activities in Donbas to diverse means of artistic mourning of the grassroots level.

Photo and video data that I collected capture the appearance of images of Stepan Bandera as early as during the first weeks of the revolution. They were placed next to the visuals of the "Strike Poster" project (e.g. Figures 17 and 18), as well as alongside the hand-made graffiti and t-shirts of the protestors. Figure 89 is an example of such graffiti — the statements "Lviv has not calmed down yet," "Glory to Heroes," or "You are forever alive in a heated heart" formed a collage of the anonymously written messages that, as the revolution unraveled, achieved the status of the official slogans of the protest. Originated in Galicia in the 1930s as the slogan of the radical right Organization of Ukrainian Nationalists (OUN) (Himka 2015), "Glory to Ukraine! Glory to the heroes!" was one of the many discursive symbols of the Euromaidan revolution. It was popularized in the form of graffiti and posters and "became the voice for those who could not find their own words and thus joined the chorus of "Glory to Ukraine," argues one of the participants of the 2014 February protests in Kyiv (N.V. *Documenting Maidan*. 2014: 9).

Within the scope of war in Donbas and the official decommunization laws of 2015, meanings of the controversial figures such as Stepan Bandera or originally nationalist slogans were re-articulated. As I went to different cities to conduct fieldwork, I observed images of Bandera or Symon Petliura being placed next to the photographs of the participants of the Euromaidan revolution and soldiers who died in Donbas. Figure 90, for instance, illustrated this phenomenon. That photo was taken at the Sofiivska Square in Kyiv in June 2015. By that time, war in Donbas had been at its height for over a year, with multiple platforms for commemoration of soldiers killed in Donbas being installed by both the ordinary Ukrainians and the government. When this picture was taken, it was unclear whether the installation of the image of Petliura next to the commemoration-board of the Ukrainian soldiers killed in Donbas was the initiative of the ordinary citizens or the state. However, in this photograph, as a renowned nationalist leader who led Ukraine's struggle for independence in the early 20th century, Petliura is supplementing the chain of Ukrainians who died protecting freedom and independence of Ukraine. The text of the image of Petliura says: "On April 25th of 1926, in Paris, the Moscow-bolshevist agent murdered the head of the directory of the Ukrainian People's Republic, leading Ottoman Symon Petliura." Though indirectly, a discursive parallel is established between Petliura and modern Ukrainian soldiers who are defined as 'victims of Moscow.' In other words, against the background of the 2015 decommunization laws, the controversial historical figures are equated to modern heroes of Ukraine. Apart from challenging the democratic premise of the Euromaidan revolution, placement of images of Petliura next to pictures of the Ukrainian soldiers is raising further ethical questions on whether, if being alive, the soldiers of Donbas would be supportive of making the defenders of modern Ukraine synonymous with figures like Petliura.

From the poststructuralist perspective, identities do not pre-exist the moment of articulation: the way in which we tie the name to a field of references lends the identity to the name (Palonen 2018: 101). Looking at the collected data, there emerges a further question on the possibility of articulation of multiple identities within a single space that would be reflective of the heterogeneous nature of the elements and yet, remain unifying enough to create a sense of regional or national community. The photos, videos and interviews illustrate diverse means of dealing with such a complex task. While monuments of Lenin and other communist symbols were removed both as part of spontaneous nationalist raids and institutionalized state-sanctioned toppling, presentation of controversial figures of Bandera, Shukhevych or members of the UPA as founding fathers of 'pro-European' transition implies articulation of nationalist symbols into 'new' elements of modern democratic reforms. Here, I suggest examining particular instances of such practice by tracing what I argue to be the 'evolution of democratization' of nationalist discourse and its symbols within the context of post-2013 decommunization.

Bandera and the Nationalist Discourse

Decades after his assassination, Stepan Bandera still triggers debates in both academic and political circles of Ukraine and beyond. Before leaving office in early 2010, President Viktor Yushchenko awarded Bandera the rank of a Hero of Ukraine. On the one hand, this prompted a line of political speculation; on the other, it provoked academic debates where adherents of Bandera and OUN also took part. In his publication, *Strasti za Banderoui* ("Passions for Bandera"), Rossolinski-Liebe divides the participants of the academic debates into three groups: 1) Historians with critical approach to Bandera's legacy (John-Paul Himka, Franziska Bruder, David Marples, Per Anders Rudling or the author himself); 2) "liberal and 'progressive' Ukrainian scholars such as Yaroslav Hrytsak, Andrii Portnom, Vasyl' Rasevych or Mykola Riabchuk;" and 3) the defenders of Bandera (Volodymyr Viatrovych, Marco Levytsky or Askold Lozynskyj). In his analysis of the Rossolisnki-Liebe's classification, Yuri Radchenko evaluates the criteria used for the approach as "excessively vague" (Radchenko 2013: 14). According to Radchenko, Rossolisnki-Liebe "takes a sharply critical approach to the cult of the OUN, UPA and the SS "Galicia" division in Ukraine and among the Ukrainian diaspora...and [at the same time], discusses this subject very much from the perspective of an outsider; nor does he offer Ukrainian society any suggestion for a way out of this trap" (ibid: 15). Such criticism also could be applied to works on Bandera or cult (or denial) of the OUN and UPA as a whole. In post-Euromaidan Ukraine, where support or objection to the figure of Bandera, for instance, could be seen as an indicator of one's pro-European or pro-Russian stands, respectively, the existence of a dialogue is particularly important. Within such a stance, the academic circle remains one of the few spheres where explicit and manifold discussion is possible, and where discord is a distinctively positive phenomenon.

After the factual termination of the Euromaidan revolution, discretionary expression of one's political positions has declined. As I noted during field trips to different regions of the Ukraine in June 2014, February-April 2017, or October 2018, public discussion of decommunization was particularly apparent during political events such as Viche[30], the Presidential inauguration, or state-installed exhibitions. The special English-language issue of the magazine Prostory, "Documenting Maidan," that I collected at the Pinchuk Art Center in Kyiv in 2014, contains a series of opinion pieces of intellectuals, artists and ordinary citizens who raise fundamental questions on modes of articulation of history within the public space. In her essay "Translating the Euromaidan: A translator's view of reasoning strategies," Anastasia Afanasyeva outlines an integral problem of the Ukrainian political culture of post-2013 – the lack of transparent presentation of diverse regional narratives as part of a common, national discourse:

"We are dealing here with fundamentally different strategies of communication. While the Ukrainian side is convinced that the Maidan movement will be better legitimated when questionable elements are ignored, it is this very lack of a confrontation of these questionable issues that calls the entire movement's credibility into question for Western Europe. The failure to open up to criticism is considered blind ideologization. Returning to Doris Bachmann-Medick's question on finding strategies to solve a conflict of understanding, the answer once again lies in a demand for reflective negotiation. It is only possible for both sides of Ukraine to reach transcultural comprehension when both sides have recognized the other's strategies and each side's motivations have been discussed together" (Afanasyeva 2014: 36).

Prior to official recognition of the strategies of 'othering,' however, the very existence of multiple discourses or the socio-political and cultural stands should be acknowledged. What was observed in various types of my data is actually the opposite – monopolization of national discourse by the western Ukrainian symbols. This phenomena occurred as part of natural political evolution, where

---

30 As a reminder for the reader, *Viche* is the term that describes manifestation of popular rule, analogous to the popular meetings held in the cities of ancient Greece and in Western European cities during the Middle Ages. It obtained particular importance within the context of the Euromaidan Revolution when hundreds of ordinary citizens gathered at the Maidan Nezalezhnosti Square to express their socio-political demands and have an open dialogue with the state officials. Accessed December 12, 2019. Source: http://www.encyclopediaofukraine.com/ display.asp?linkpath=pages%5CV%5CI%5CVicheIT.htm.

the empty space of post-revolutionary domain has been filled with narratives of the most politically-active. In his diary dated November 21 2013, one of the participants of the Euromaidan revolution, Zhenya, wrote that "when [he] saw that people in Kyiv were coming out to protest, [he] thought about how in Donetsk no one would come out. People might be up for going to some festival or other but to come out and declare your political position—no one was interested in that." According to Zhenya, "[he] wrote to a few people [he] knew but they all wrote back saying things like "well, wait and see what happens in Kyiv, maybe it's no big deal." Well, fine then, [he] said. I'll go on my own" (*Documenting Maidan*, 2015). Large-scale demonstrations that followed in Donetsk and other areas of eastern Ukraine composed the integral part of an overall narrative of the Euromaidan protests. However, when it comes to utilization of the physical and discursive space of the cities as a platform for multiple modes of decommunization, it commenced with the capital and was then followed by other regions. The streets, buildings and monuments of Kyiv were the first to experience official, massive rearticulation with the shift of political epochs—to function as both the object and scheme of political identification. The transitioning from 'communism' to 'Europe' took place as an evolution of meanings: the multivocal posters or graffiti of Maidan, as well as communist symbols such as statues of Lenin, were replaced by Bandera, Petliura or members of the UPA, who 'resurrected' as heroes of the new time.

In geographic terms, scholars argue that the legitimization of symbols of early-mid twentieth century Ukrainian struggle for independence or nationalist movement evolved not only into regional, but also national occurrence (Katchanovsky 2010; Marples 2006; Motyl 2010; Narvselius 2015). As was cited earlier, first, openly displayed posters of Bandera and the insignia the Right Sector ('Pravyi Sektor[31]') appeared at Maidan Nezalezhnosti square in

---

31 The organization the "Right Sector" ("Правий сектор") is a far-right Ukrainian nationalist movement and party. It was established in late November 2013 as a confederation of street fighting soccer fans and right-wing nationalist groups: the Social-National Assembly, Trident (Dmytro Yarosh), UNA/Yuriy Shukhevych, Patriot of Ukraine (Andriy Belitsky), White Hammer, and Carpathian

December 2013. The photographs of the black-and-red flags of the Right Sector (Figures 96 and 97) were taken at Khreschatyk Street and Maidan Nezalezhnosti Square in Kyiv in May 2014. Back then, the flags of the Right Sector were placed on the walls and balconies of the buildings, tents, bridges and monuments when the tents and other emblems of the participants of Maidan, such as the images of the "Strike Poster" project, were still displayed.

It is important to note that during the Euromaidan, the insignia of the Right Sector was one of the *many* elements of the visual narrative of the protest. Since 2013, however, the nationalist groups obtained the role of civic elements that were transforming the perception of nationalist formations in Ukraine. Being one of the most active participants of the revolution, and later one of the core battalions of the Ukrainian army in Donbas, the right wing's apprehension was transformed from radical or nationalist entity to that of the primary units *representing* political demands of Ukrainians. Leaving aside an overall estimation of the far right participation in the Maidan protests, since spring 2014, the troops of the Right Sector have been one of the most active participants of war in Donbas, protecting independence and territorial integrity of Ukraine.

In this sense, it is of no surprise that two years into military operation in Donbas, members of the Right Sector were defined as "patriots" and "fearless protectors of Ukraine," both by the state and the majority of ordinary Ukrainians. The photograph that was taken as part of my field trip to Kharkiv in June 2016 (Figure 98) captures the Right Sector insignia as the primary element of the military agitation campaign. It is composed of chromatic colors of the Right Sector flag (originally, the red and black colors of the UPA flag) and the Ukrainian flag (blue and yellow), and presents the following message: "Right Wing: Who, if not me? When, if not right now?" ("Правый сектор: Як не я—то хто? Як не тепер—то коли?"). It also contains images of heroes of the "Holy Hundred" —

Sich. It was named after the effort of the groups to protect the right side of the Euromaidan protesters. The Right Sector became one of the primary actors of the Euromaidan revolution, and later one of the core units of the Ukrainian army in Donbas. Accessed July 7, 2015. Source: https://pravyysektor.info.

protestors of Euromaidan who gave their lives for Ukraine, as well as the image that symbolizes traditional Ukrainian woman—"The Ukrainian woman: Protector of the family and the land" ("Українка—берегиня роду та краю"). This poster was part of the exhibition located directly across the former central monument of Lenin, which was dismantled by the officials of Kharkiv in June 2016. Similarly, the images of Bandera and flags of the Right Sector were observed at the central squares of central, northern and eastern oblasts of Ukraine and, in particular, the empty pedestals of the communist statues (Fieldnotes. By Anna Kutkina. Kyiv 2016/2018, Chernihiv 2016, Lybny 2016, Kharkiv 2016, Nosivka 2018). Presented as posters, graffiti or public artistic installations, the symbols constructed a new hegemonic formation, where the term or figure of a 'nationalist' obtained a coherently new meaning—that of a hero, protector or patriot.

However, particularly in the eastern regions, idealization of nationalist figures and their insignia were contested. Along the slogans that articulated an openly pro-European or pro-Ukrainian position, the Nazi insignia were a common element of the graffiti. In June 2014, for instance, I took a picture of graffiti in Zaporizhzhya that encouraged usage of Ukrainian instead of Russian (Figure 99). The message of the graffiti—"Language [in Ukrainian] and not Language [in Russian]" ("Мова а не язык"), was an openly pro-Ukrainian narrative conveyed by the swastika. Another photograph taken in Lybny in June 2016 captures two controversial statements: "Stop to junta[32]: NO to War" ("Хунту STOP Нет Войне") (written in Russian in red) and "Junta will be! Yes to Nazism" ("Хунта буде. Да нацизму" (written Ukrainian in blue) (Figure 100). Both of these graffiti articulate the phenomenon where bearers of the pro-Russian and pro-Ukrainian stands are involved in an artistic form of public dialogue. An opponent of war (text in red) calls

---

[32] A junta is a military government that has taken power by force, and not through elections. Within the socio-political context of (post)Euromaidan Ukraine, the term "junta" has been used by the opponents of the Euromaidan revolution who used this term to refer to the participants of the protests in Kyiv and other cities. Accessed July 17, 2015. Source: https://www.collinsdictionary.com/dictionary/english/junta.

for termination of military activities by addressing the pro-Ukrainian side as 'Junta' — the term that was also commonly used by the Russian propaganda media campaign during and shortly after the Euromaidan revolution. The 'answer' that follows (text in blue written on top of original graffiti) confirms persistence of 'junta' by implying continuation of presence of the Ukrainian forces in Donbas. At the same time, the latter graffiti (Figure 100) contains affirmation of Nazism—"Yes to Fascism." Similar to political posters of the early days of the Euromaidan revolution (e.g. images of the "Strike Poster" project), these graffiti are examples of heteroglossic hegemonic formation of the grassroots level: the citizens of Ukraine are involved in articulation of their diverse political stands through multiple forms of artistic 'dialogism' (Bakhtin 1981). Taken as a whole, the grassroots political discussion is meant to spark social change and is articulated within the physical framework of objects in both urban and rural environments.

During the fieldwork trips, multiple forms of dialogism or the juxtaposition of the homogeneous and heterogeneous hegemonic formations were observed as the primary mode of meaning-making. Numerous graffiti that combined *both* the appeasing discourses of national unity and symbols of nationalist content such as swastika or UPA/OUN were recorded across Ukraine. In Figure 101 — the image taken in Lviv in February of 2017, for instance, we see a quote from a famous Ukrainian singer Kuzma written on the wall of one of the buildings. Despite all the political turmoil, it is a statement of hope for a better future for Ukraine: "If wherever you look is darkness and color-black that means you fell asleep and tomorrow will be better." In this picture, the word 'Lviv' is written to hint a swastika which is placed next to an uplifting message of Kuzma. Similar instances of depiction of nationalist symbols next to politically neutral, more socially-oriented messages for democratization of Ukraine were also recorded in eastern and central oblasts. Figure 102 is another visual that captures exaltation of nationalist elements: the graffiti painted in Kryviy Rih, it defines the Organization of Ukrainian Nationalists as that of "power and honor." The graffiti "Glory to Ukraine," accompanied by swastika (Figure 103), was also observed in Poltava, where another graffiti that promotes national unity was painted next to this image (Figure 105) — "West and East are together forever. P.R.O. - D. Shukhevych." Examining the style of these images, it could be assumed that both of these messages were painted by the same author(s). As such, though contestational in nature, messages of diverse political content constructed a powerful hegemonic formation, which was expressed at the grassroots level in the form of graffiti, political posters and other forms of political art.

Broadly put, the city-contexts of post-Euromaidan Ukraine, therefore, provided the space for new interpretation of the controversial symbols of the past. The objects of urban topoi (such as walls of the buildings or pedestals of the monuments) were used as canvases for articulation of political meanings which further created a framework of the 'imagined communities' — without meeting or interacting with each other face-to-face, the authors of graffiti (or the participants of toppling or preservation of the communist statues) associated themselves with each other, constructing the space where articulation of political stands became an act of regional and national identity-making. Within such a context, construction of heterogeneous hegemonic formation took place by overlapping one meaning with another — articulation of multilayered discursive formations. As both nationalist and anti-Bandera (or anti-UPA narratives) co-existed within the same graffiti or poster, for instance, the borders between political elements or stands became blurred.

The Bookshelves: Mirroring Decommunization

To render the examination, post-2013 decommunization can be classified into two primary articulations: the substitution of empty space of the Lenin statues by historic nationalist figures of 20th century Ukrainian, and active articulation of the communist (or Russian) history and present as the colonial 'other.' Besides appearing as posters, graffiti or sporadic images such as that of Shukhevych placed next to photographs of soldiers of Donbas (Figure 90), the controversial figures of the Ukrainian past were introduced by the government in diverse forms. The first explicit visual evidence of what I refer to as 'nationalization' of decommunization was observed in May and June 2014 in Kyiv, Vinnytsia, Kharkiv, Zaporizhzhya, Kryvyi Rih and Lviv. In particular, I noticed a tendency of the glorification of Bandera, Shukhevych and members of the UPA on book-covers exhibited in the windows of major bookstores. At first, I noticed this phenomenon in Kyiv in early May once the facades of the stores that were damaged by the revolutionary activities were restored. While the tents, as well as posters were still part of the Maidan Nezalezhnosti square, central bookstores, such as *Knygarnya E* (*Книгарня Є*) in Kyiv, were particularly explicit in re-articulation of nationalist figures into new heroes or role models of post-Euromaidan Ukraine. The books with images of Bandera, Klyachkisvsky or Kuk (leaders of the Ukrainian Insurgent Army) on their cover were placed at the forefront of all major bookstores of Kyiv, as well as cities and towns across Ukraine. Since high number of bookstores in Kyiv, Zaporizhzhya or Lviv, for instance, are located at the busiest streets and occupy prominent parts of the buildings — usually capacious halls with wide exhibitory windows, the books composed an explicit visual frontier: by virtue of bright, artistic presentations of Bandera or members of the UPA as heroes of Ukraine, they articulated a clear narrative of admiration and praise.

The exterior of *Knygarnya E* (*Книгарня Є*), for instance, is an example of such kind. Founded in 2007 by the Austrian company ECEM Media GmbH, which is also the founder of the popular magazine "Ukrainian Week," shortly after the Euromaidan revolution, *Knygarnya E* expanded to 25 bookstores in 12 most populated cities. In Kyiv alone, as of 2017, it held 10 bookstores, three in Lviv, one in Dnipro, two in Kharkiv, as well as stores in Ivano-Frankivsk, Volodymyr-Volynsk, Vinnistia, Ternopil, Rivne, Lutsk, Khmelnytskyi, and Sumy. At that point, it was one of the largest book-chains of Ukraine, famous for specializing in Ukrainian literature, as well as being a meeting-point of numerous cultural gatherings — book-presentations, round tables, literary and academic assemblies. In 2014-2015, as war in Donbas reached its peak, referring to both the

20th century and early Kievan Rus'[33] history became another distinctive feature of decommunization of the public and intellectual space.

The political significance of such literature was clear: the majority of the books had Stepan Bandera in their titles and were related to his figure (or members of the OUN/UPA) either directly or collaterally. For example, the half-open book with white cover and image of Stepan Bandera (Figure 91) is entitled "Stepan Bandera…when one says: 'Glory to Ukraine!'" (Posivnych 2015). To its left is another book of the Ukrainian writer Halyna Gordasevych, called "Stepan Bandera: The Human and Myth." Other books which are captured within this photograph are entitled "Baptism of Rus'", "The Epoch of Kozacksdorm in the Ukrainian Literature," "The Hetmanate[34]," or "National Ukraine." The lower shelf contains books of the following titles: "Legends of Lviv" (Vynnychuk 2014), "Ukrainian Traditions and Habits," "History of the Ukraine-Rus'" (Arkas 2012), "Project-Ukraine" (Yanevski 2015), "Project. "Ukraine" (Lytvin 2015), "Country-Moksel or Moskovia" (Bilinski 2006), and, once again, "Ukraine-Rus'" (Bilinski 2013).

The images of the bookshelves of another store of *Knygarnya E* in Kyiv (June 2015) (e.g. Figures 92 and 93) also display narratives dedicated primarily to the OUN and UPA, as well Symen Petlura — the founding statesman of the Ukrainian People's Republic. They are entitled "Forest Guys: Prose of UPA" (Tonyk 2014), and "The

---

33   Kievan Rus' was a federation of East Slavic and Finnic peoples in Europe (9th-13th century) under the reign of the Varangian Rurik dynasty. The modern nations of Ukraine, Russia and Belarus claim Kievan Rus' as their cultural and socio-political birth-place. Accessed July 28, 2015. Source: http://resource.history.org.ua/cgi-bin/eiu/history.exe?&I21DBN=EIU&P21DBN=EIU&S21STN=1&S21REF=10&S21FMT=eiu_all&C21COM=S&S21CNR=20&S21P01=0&S21P02=0&S21P03=TRN=&S21COLORTERMS=0&S21STR=Kyivska_Rus.

34   The Ukrainian State, sometimes also called the Hetmanate, was an anti-socialist government that existed on most of the modern territory of Ukraine from April 29 to December 14, 1918. As Ukraine turned into a provisional dictatorship of Hetman of Ukraine Pavlo Skoropadskyi, the Hetmanate outlawed all socialist-oriented political parties, creating an anti-Bolshevik front. The Hetmanate is one of the primary symbols of political independence and nationhood of Ukraine. Accessed November 5, 2018. Source: incognita.day.kyiv.ua › get-manat-ta-jogo-rol-v-istoriyi.

Emperor of the United States: Big Escape from Galychyna (Pollak 2014). Linguistic choice of words such as "khlopci" ("хлопці"), or 'guys,' gives an effect of proximity or familiarity of main characters—members of the UPA, as if to bring them 'closer' to ordinary Ukrainians and make them part of modern national discourse. Stepan Bandera (Figure 91) is also deprived of his military uniform and is dressed in a jacket, shirt and a tie. The portrayal of the political leaders as approachable or 'close to people,' Aulich and Sylvestrova argue (1999), is a popular method of the communist propaganda. In this sense, methodologically speaking, the discursive facade of post-Euromaidan Ukraine has not experienced radical transformations.

As a space for intellectual representation, as well as the element of the architectural frontier of the cities, bookstores were also used for articulation of 'us' and 'them'—arguably, that of the 'west' and 'east,' Ukraine and Russia (or former Soviet Union). On June 18 2016 I interviewed a colleague of the artistic director of *Knygarnya E* in Kyiv, Oksana Levkova. One of the primary objectives of the interview was to discover the criteria used for selection of books by the stores such as *Bukva* or *Knygarnya E*. When asked about the possibility of ideological censorship for selection of books, Levkova replied that "the only criteria [they] followed [was] to not let separatist ideas in." In other words, all the narratives presented at the bookstores at that time were to correspond to the official 'pro-Ukrainian' ideology of the state. Upon completion of the interview, the question on what constitutes separatist narratives has emerged. In particular, I was curious about the space (if any) that was given to Ukrainians who did not share the explicitly anti-Soviet stands or were not adherents of the OUN or UPA. At that point, one thing certain was that, as an attempt to re-politicize the transforming post-revolutionary space, 'nationalization' of the bookshelves was one of the *many* forms used by the state, as well the authors, to re-articulate history, and as such, the nation itself.

The second dominant narrative that materialized within the bookshelves was that of war in Donbas: an extensive number of books on "war in the east" were exhibited simultaneously with those on Bandera and the UPA. The image of the bookshelf of *Knygarnya E* in Kyiv taken in June 2015 (Figure 94) captures the following titles: "The Awakening" (Ruslan San-Marino 2015), "Three Hours Without War" (Butchenko 2015) and "Nadia: Strong Name" (Savchenko 2015), autobiographical diary of Nadiya Savchenko[35]. Most texts on war in Donbas were collections of personal stories of the soldiers. Oftentimes, the style of narratives of these texts was personal and reminded of a diary that was made public through reference to a broader socio-political context. The primary 'messages' of these books were related to heroism, as well as inevitability of mental and physical trauma that developed hand-in-hand with the increase of the spirit of patriotism. Finally, extensive literature on war in Donbas was used by the government and civic activists to include *all* discourses "from the east"—"we are by no means excluding eastern narratives…all the war stories are published and ready to be heard by the Ukrainian public," Levkova asserted in our interview in June 2016.

Therefore, articulated in the same physical and discursive space of the bookstores, the narratives of glorification of controversial figures of the country's history were unified with modern, personal stories of the Ukrainian soldiers: the struggle for independence and territorial integrity was articulated into a broader, heroic horizon of the state. It should be noted, however, that as the items of both intellectual and artistic domain, books were one of the *many* elements of the meaning-making process. Sold across the country, they accustomed Ukrainians to the idea of nationalist figures being the role models of the country's struggle for independence, and at the same time, served as an ideological blanket of a state unified by war, both distant and eminently personal.

---

35 Nadiya Savchenko is a Ukrainian politician and a first lieutenant in the Ukrainian Ground Forces. During the war in Donbass, Savchenko served as an instructor of the Aidar Battalion—a voluntary infantry unit. She was captured by the pro-Russian forces in eastern Ukraine in June 2014 and was then imprisoned in Russia under the accusation of directing artillery fire that caused the death of two Russian journalists. Savchenko remained in the Russian jail until May 2016. She was released from jail as part of an exchange in a prisoner swap and was awarded a Hero of Ukraine/Order for Courage (2017). Accessed October 27, 2018. Source: https://www.ukrinform.ua/tag-savcenko.

In broader terms, the books on Donbas formed a collection of personal stories of soldiers, volunteers, journalists and ordinary citizens who experienced raw, vivid exposure to the military actions. One of the primary characteristics of these texts was that their authors—the ordinary Ukrainians, were willing to share intimate stories on the traumatizing effects of war. Stylistically, the stories varied from diary entries of everyday activities such as training, preparing ammunition, eating, cleaning or resting to broader, novel-like narratives on specific military tasks—famous battles such as the Ilovaisk Massacre[36] or the storming of the Donetsk airport (September 2014). Similar to posters and artistic exhibitions presented at the Maidan Nezalezhnosti Square or the Pinchuk Art Center in Kyiv (2014-2017), books on Donbas articulated the heterogeneous hegemonic formation of the grassroots level. By exposing diverse, multivocal perceptions of war, they promoted patriotism by making a localized military confrontation a national, personal story of all Ukrainians. At the same time, brutalities of war were also externalized and romanticized, as posters and books on Donbas constructed glorifying narratives of heroes who "went to the east to bring the victory home." In this sense, the 'east' (even if that of the homeland—Donbas) was presented as the 'other,' and at the same time, as an integral site of national value.

The books on Stepan Bandera and the UPA, on the other hand, raised a number of questions on socio-political and cultural objectives of glorification of the heroic figures. In particular, as the author of *Stepan Bandera*, Mykola Posivnycha asserted, the primary

---

36 The Battle of Ilovaisk started on August 7 2014, when the Armed Forces of Ukraine began a series of attempts to capture the city of Ilovaisk against the pro-Russian insurgents affiliated with the self-proclaimed Donetsk People's Republic (DPR/DNR). On August 18 2014, the Ukrainian forces entered the city, when they became encircled between 24-26 August by overwhelming Russian military forces that crossed the border to join the battle. As of August 14 2015, 366 Ukrainian soldiers have died, 429 were injured, 128 were captured by the pro-Russian groups, and 158 people went missing. The Ilovaisk massacre is considered one of the bloodiest moments of war in Donbas. Accessed November 23, 2016. Source: https://www.radiosvoboda.org/a/ilovajsk-spohady/30136220.html.

goal of his work was to "enrich the existing debates on who Bandera truly was, and to address the dilemma of whether he was a hero, a traitor, or a true symbol of the Ukraine's fight for independence" (Fieldnotes. By Anna Kutkina. *Knygarnya E*. Public seminar. Kyiv. 12 July 2015). Another author, Bilinskii argues that one of the objectives of books on Bandera, as well as works on the origins of Ukraine and Kievan Rus', for example, is "to demolish myths of the Soviet and Russian historians and political scientists who fuel cynical propaganda on common origins of Russia and Ukraine" (Bilinski 2013: 25). Therefore, the further from the revolution we proceed time-wise, the more diversity we observe in the articulation of the 'other' within the intellectual and political context of Ukraine. Often explicit and bold in its form, the othering of Russia and its Soviet heritage varied from political statements of the official state representatives (e.g. the Independence Day speech of President Petro Poroshenko[37] on August 24, 2018) to multiple forms of political acts and cultural expressions, be it the demolition of the communist statues or renaming of the streets. The primary concepts that emerged as key thematic lines in the post-2013 Ukrainian literature could also be found within the international literary scope: nationalism, regional polarity or identity formation (Chikhi 2014; Owczarzak 2010; Wilson 2014). Putting the details aside, I recall walking the streets of Kyiv and being astonished with the scale of the ideological filtration-campaign: as the hegemony of a free and independent Ukraine was vigorously established, the old, ironically Soviet methods of softer, yet explicit homogenization of heroes, as well as the 'other,' were apparent.

"One Hundred Years of Fighting for Independence"

Since the Euromaidan revolution, re-articulation of memory and national identity became the dominant visual and discursive narra-

---

37 Radio Svoboda. "Independence Day of Ukraine. Military Parade." #radiosvoboda #РадіоСвобода #Ukraine. August 23, 2017. YouTube video, 1:37:50. https://www.youtube.com/watch?v=6XbxxN-_G-Y.

tive. It evolved through articulation, juxtapositioning and contestation of different elements of the country's history and association of the socio-political course of Ukraine with its past. In his article "Russia as Ukraine's 'Other': Identity and Geopolitics," Mikhail Molchanov defines "vilification of Russia in Ukraine [as] reaching unusual proportions" (Molchanov 2015: 4). He addresses the socio-political developments of post-2013 Ukraine as "nationalist othering of Russia" and claims that the origins of this process "go long way back to the mid-nineteenth century." He further argues that "the othering of the opponent serves as a potent instrument of war mongering on the part of the Ukrainian government today" (ibid: 5). Similar stands on the Ukrainian-Russian relations are found within both international and, to a lesser degree, Ukrainian scholarly community (Ernst 2014; Prostakov 2014; Tsygankov 2009).

To some degree, I align with the claim of modern Ukrainian-Russian relations being rooted in the countries' common and combative past. To assert that othering of Russia has not been one of the dominant mechanisms of political meaning-making in Ukraine would be an underestimation. However, the process of articulating Russia as the 'other' is a far more *complex* phenomenon. It has been practiced by the nationalist elements such as radical minority groups toppling the Lenin statues, the post-Euromaidan government and the ordinary citizens of *diverse* political and cultural tenets. According to Laclau and Mouffe (1985), the othering takes place through construction of discourses as an attempt to fix meanings within a particular political domain. Multiple meanings that emerge through contestation are articulated into a dominant horizon of social orientation, or hegemony. Within such a process, every element (or world-view) conditions one another and, as Bakhtin argues, "must be taken into consideration by means of dialogical interaction" (Bakhtin 1981: 13).

It is important to note that the othering of Russia within the socio-political context of post-2013 Ukraine is not exclusively an act of nationalism. Instead, as I unravel further, glorification of Bandera or UPA, or what could be seen as a negative portrayal of Russia, is an attempt to find *new* national meaning(s). By means of both juxtaposition and collision of particular elements of history (and/or the present), decommunization takes place to construct new cultural, political and social symbols that, in theory, are meant to address the ideological demands of the present. Nationalist figures are used by the government to emphasise historical continuity of Ukraine's strive for independence. Whether the amalgamation of visuals (or figures) of the past with those of the present is an effective mechanism of democratic transitioning of a culturally and politically heterogeneous state, however, is a different question.

And so, as was stated earlier, the analysis of the collected data shows that replacement of old communist symbols with controversial figures of the Soviet-Ukrainian history is the prevailing characteristic of post-Euromaidan decommunization. Particularly after the official implementation of the 2015 decommunization laws, Stepan Bandera (as well as members of the OUN or UPA) emerged as primary symbols of anti-colonial transitioning. They became part of both visual and discursive narrative of the state that seeks to define the nation by *mixing* diverse elements of both present and past to construct a potentially "unified future." At the governmental level, one of the most peculiar characteristics of the first three years of the official decommunization policies (2015-2018) was the articulation of the Ukrainian nation-building process as a *centuries-long struggle* against the Russian aggressor. As more Lenin statues were toppled and streets, metro stations, and parks shed their Soviet titles away, the talks on reasoning behind the popularity of Bandera or members of the UPA, as well as modes of commemoration of heroes of Maidan and war in Donbas, have turned into a national public debate.

In his analysis of the academic biography of Stepan Bandera, written by Rossolinki-Liebe, the Director of the Center for Interethnic Relations in Eastern Europe, Yuri Radchenko, condemns rehabilitation of communist figures like Stalin in contemporary Russia and eastern Ukraine. He points at the rise of right-wing radicalism in countries like Poland as one of the forms of the juxtaposition of two opposing tendencies of the post-Soviet space: glorification of the tyrannical Soviet leaders in Russia and praise of relentless nationalists of the former territories threatened (or controlled) by the Russian or Soviet empire. As Radchenko points, radicalization is a pervasive phenomenon that goes extensively beyond the Ukrainian borders. In his description of the cult surrounding the Polish right-wing politician Roman Dmowski[38], Rossolinki-Liebe asserts that the manner in which Dmowski was commemorated by the Polish diaspora during the Cold War is very similar to the Ukrainian diaspora's veneration of Bandera.

Like the Bandera worshipers, Dmowski admirers have denied or diminished the anti-Semitic and extremist views expressed by him and the Endecja movement and have prized his patriotism and his devotion to the process of establishment a nation state. They have also propagated distorted nationalist versions of Polish history. They have denied the Polish involvement in the Holocaust and have presented the Poles as tragic but brave heroes and martyrs, and the victims of their neighbors, in particular Germans and Russians (Rossolinki-Liebe 2014: 527).

To some degree, the cult of Ustaša of Ante Pavelić in independent Croatia could also be compared to that of Bandera and OUN. Within the context of war for independence and the rule of the first President of Croatia Franjo Tuđman, the cult became particularly popular, while the Serbs came to be addressed as "Četnici" and Croats as "Ustaše" by the opposing parties' propaganda. Considerably, similar phenomenon could be observed in the context of war in Donbas, where the volunteers and soldiers of the Ukrainian army are often called "banderites" or followers of Bandera. However, comparison of glorification of the OUN and UPA to that of Croatian or Serbian formations is rather ambiguous. The Ustaše received their statehood directly from Hitler and were actively collaborating with the Nazis until the end of the war (Radchenko 2015: 12). By contrast, members of the UPA and OUN were both collaborators *and* victims of the Nazi regime. Arguably, it is for that reason that, aware of their atrocities towards the Poles, Jews and Ukrainians themselves, the population of Ukraine remains divided in its

---

38 Roman Dmowski (1864-1939) was a vocally anti-semitic Polish politician and the co-founder of the right-wing National Democracy political movement. He stood against control of the Polish territories by the German and Russian empires, and promoted articulation of Polish national identity along the ethnic and religious (Roman Catholic) lines. Accessed December 12 2018. Source:. https://www.britannica.com/biography/Roman-Dmowski.

evaluation of the OUN and UPA's role in the formation of the Ukrainian nation. In particular, the interviews that I conducted both with the ordinary citizens and state officials in Lviv, Kyiv, Vinnytsia, Kharkiv and Zaporizhzhya reveal equalization of the OUN and UPA with the figure of Stepan Bandera.

Already during the official inauguration of President Petro Poroshenko (June 7, 2014), the following dialogue was captured on camera as part of my fieldwork trip to Kyiv. The video shows a spontaneous conversation of two men awaiting for the arrival of the President at the Sofiivska Square in Kyiv. The ordinary Ukrainians are involved in an intensive debate on the role Bandera played in the formation of the Ukrainian state, and the relevance of his person to the socio-political context of post-Euromaidan Ukraine. The video records several positions on Bandera, as well as a vivid vocalization of the long-lived stereotypes — offensive ways of calling someone Ukrainian or Russian, a 'Banderovite' and 'Katsap' (or 'Moskal'), respectively. To some extent, idealization of nationalist figures is a resurrected rather than an innovative discursive condition that can become explicit and intensify during the regime-change. In the video, we can also grasp a popular cliche of the supporters of Bandera being native Ukrainian-speakers of the anti-Russian political stands (as in this video, also dressed in a traditional Ukrainian shirt, vyshyvanka), and the adherents of the pro-Soviet (or pro-Russian) views being the Russian-speakers. Below is the dialogue quoted in full:

Man 1: We need a unitary Ukraine. Look, Katsapy are saying that we are Banderovites. And they are the Vlasovites[39]! And that is much worse!

---

39 Andrey Vlasov was a Russian Red Army general and collaborationist. He fought in the battle for Moscow and was captured to lift the siege of Leningrad, after which he defected to Nazi Germany and headed the so-called Vlasov Army or ROA. At the end of WWII he changed sides again, but was convicted of treason and hanged. As such, 'Vlasovec' became an appalative used in Ukraine to call someone a 'Russian Nazi collaborator'. Accessed July 2, 2019.

Man 2: *Well, they are saying we do not have our own propaganda. We do! Bandera has cheated Hitler! For the sake of an idea! And what was the idea? To create a nation-state. Because he knew that politicians are always cheating. And he used that! That is why he is the wisest politician in the world! To obtain the trust of others and to create a nation-state! That was happening during times when other nations were collapsing. He has created one! And the problem is that we do not have the right propaganda. We do not have the means to promote that!"*

Man 1: *Yes, so that we could win the informational war!*

Man 2: *And Hitler has cheated Stalin with his pact. And Bandera cheated Hitler himself!*

Man 1: *Yes, and Vlasovites [Russians] sold themselves down to the Gestapo.*

Man 2: *Well, Vlasovites were pawns. One should not even compare Vlasovites to Bandera. Bandera cheated the owner of the world – Hitler!*

Man 1: *No, no I am not comparing. I am just saying that they call us Banderovites, and they are the Vlasovites, and now they are also Putinovites!*

Man 2: *So, yes, the problem is that we do not have the right propaganda. Bandera is the wisest politician!*

Woman 1: *"Thank you! Keep telling this to everyone! Especially the youth!*

Besides referring to Bandera as the promoter of an idea of creation of the nation-state and a gifted political leader who "cheated

---

Source: https://www.britannica.com/biography/Andrey-Andreyevich-Vlasov.

Hitler himself," the dialogue exposes the Ukrainians' need to react to Russia's appeal to Ukrainians as nationalists. An ordinary Ukrainian—'Man 2' in the conversation cited, acknowledges the idealized role of Bandera as a tool of modern political propaganda, and meanwhile, suggests the impossibility of standing up for Ukraine without using nationalist symbols. At the same time, we can tell that not all the observers of the dialogue share loyalty to and admiration of Bandera. The video captures the evolution of the debate where some citizens express little to no interest in the discussion, while others vocalize their multiple positions in most active terms:

> ***Man 3:*** *"Comrades ("Tovarishi"), would you please stop your propaganda! Your propaganda of Bandera! Today is the inauguration of our President Poroshenko! What does Bandera have to do with that? Today is a great holiday! You should not touch that history. And today is also the national commemoration day. And you are propagating your Bandera. Go to the graveyard and commemorate him there. No, better do that at the Church.'*
>
> ***Woman 2****: Are you Stepan Bandera by any chance? [addressing 'Man 3']*
>
> ***Man 3:*** *No.*
>
> ***Woman 2****: Oh, too bad. We would have kneeled in front of you, if you were Bandera.*
>
> ***Woman 4****: I am also for Bandera. Not sure about the rest. The difference is that I am not talking about him publicly.*
>
> ***Man 4:*** *'Yes, we all will turn into Banderovites soon. Because we love our land. And Bandera loved our land as well. Now let Katsapchyky [Russians] be afraid of us! Yes, moskalyky! [synonym to 'Katsjapchyky']. Because they will shiver once they hear this word — 'Bandera!'*
>
> ***Man 3:*** *What I suggest to you, gentlemen [uses the 'Russian' word 'gospoda' (господа)] Oh, sorry, gentlemen! [uses*

> the Ukrainian word for gentlemen – 'pany' ('пани')] – go to the grocery store, get a bottle and have a drink for the health of President Poroshenko. That is the best thing that you can do today...We are all sick of this history by now. It is already about 55 years since Bandera was murdered and they keep remembering...calling and calling his name."

The contestation of remembrance of Bandera as a hero of Ukraine illustrates what I came to discover as the primary characteristic of post-Euromaidan de-Sovietization—*multivocality* of the citizens' political stands when it comes to 'reintegration' of the past into the present. The following statement of one of the participants is crucial for understanding the binary nature of Bandera—a personal (and, for some, national) symbol of independence, it carries *multiple* meanings depending on one's political or cultural disposition. For Ukrainians recorded on the video, glorification of Bandera is a natural state of political positioning where a citizen who "loves" his or her state is implicitly turning into 'Banderovite'—because "Bandera loved [his] land as well." Devotion to the concept of nationhood or sovereignty of Ukraine is articulated into a national idea of de-Sovietization or de-Russification. Here, the controversial figures of the Ukrainian past obtain an explicitly positive connotation: they are redefined as heroes who paved political ground for present and future generations of patriotic Ukrainians.

A particularly important question is asked by 'Man 3': "Today is the inauguration of our President Poroshenko...What does Bandera have to do with that?" Indeed, this query is one of the primary puzzles of post-Euromaidan decommunization. What does Bandera or any other controversial figure or symbol of the past have to do with establishment of the post-Soviet, democratic nation? And more specifically, why did Bandera's persona become so important especially during and after the Euromaidan revolution? If voicing multiple opinions is the phenomenon of post-Yanukovych's post-revolutionary thaw, what makes an aftermath of the Euromaidan different from that of the Orange Revolution? Both the 2004 and

2014 revolts were followed by increased freedom of speech. However, an openly nationalist rhetoric has penetrated both visual and discursive space of Ukraine primarily after the Euromaidan. As of 2018, besides Ukrainian and international academic and media circles, no official, institutionalized opposition to glorification of the OUN and other nationalist figures existed in Ukraine. At the grassroots level, however, the contestation of re-articulation of controversial figures of the past into modern heroes has burst with visual and discursive diversity.

The 'Other,' the Ukrainian, and the State

In an attempt to fixate on the revolutionary meanings of 'democratic development,' 'freedom' and 'independence,' the post-Euromaidan officials passed the decommunization laws that were deployed to unify Ukraine against the external aggressor—the Russian Federation. As war in Donbas endured, along with eradicating the communist insignia from both urban and cultural topoi, the government of Ukraine started using political art to illustrate the intensity *and* continuity of Ukraine's fight for independence. Particularly after the occupation of Crimea and the escalation of the military activities in the east, visual and discursive articulation of the Russian Federation as both the historic and modern aggressor has intensified.

Already in September 2014, Ukrainian artist and political activist, Yevgenia Belorusets, held an exhibition at the *Pinchuk Art Center* in Kyiv. In her work, she defined decommunization along the following lines: "Lenin has been romanticized during the historical period and [is being] completely demonized today" (Figures 78 and 79). In February 2016, I took a picture of a poster at Maidan Nezalezhnosti square that manifested Ukraine as an absolute good and Russia as blazing evil (Figures 108 and 109). The visual was placed on the columns of the Independence Statue between the hand-made posters that commemorated Ukrainian soldiers killed in Donbas. It portrayed Jesus dressed in the Ukrainian flag arm-wrestling Satan covered with the Russian banner. The image was made part of a larger poster that disclosed the following message:

"The Republic of Maidan: Dignity Against Permissiveness" ("Республіка Майдан: Гідність Проти Свавілля"). At the left corner of the poster, a dove is carrying a Ukrainian flag as an olive branch or a symbol of peace. The portrait of a famous Ukrainian writer and the proponent of Ukrainian independence, Lesya Ukrainka, is the central image of the poster. It is surrounded by pictures of the protestors killed during the Euromaidan Revolution— "Nebesna sotnya" or "The Heavenly Hundred." A collage of different images, the poster contains both historic and modern figures and is the self-explanatory portrayal of Ukraine fighting an absolute evil—the Russian Federation. Though it is unclear whether this poster was a state-promoted or the ordinary citizens' creation, placed at the central square of the country, it carried a powerful message of positioning of Ukraine (or 'us') against Russia (or the 'other').

In October 2017, I conducted a fieldwork trip to Kyiv to interview authors of the book *Looking for Lenin*, Sébastien Gobert and Niels Ackermann, and to participate in the public discussion of their study of the 'Leninfall.' The discussion involved the primary drafter of the 2015 decommunization laws, Volodymyr Viatrovych, as well as prominent political figures and artists of Ukraine— Yevgenia Belorusets, Lada Nakonechna and Vlada Ralko. As a brief observational note, Volodymyr Viatrovych was the only figure that evening who expressed vigorous, openly anti-Soviet and anti-Russian stands. The artists, journalists and the audience of the talk conveyed less uniform and more politically neutral positions: explicit othering of Russia and the Soviet Union was either judged or taken cautiously. One of the primary points raised addressed the "impossibility of erasing the Soviet cultural and political legacy from the Ukrainian present and past" (Ralko 2017). Another acute question, "whom to replace Lenin with?" was brought up by Sébastien Gobert. As I recorded that day, the audience, as well as the artists, have also stated the necessity of "finding a symbol that would replace Lenin at the national scale—the one that would unify the 'pro-European' and 'pro-Russian' citizens of Ukraine" (Fieldnotes. By Anna Kutkina. Public Discussion. Kyiv. October 11, 2017).

All that being said, I observed questioning of decommunization as being primarily a grassroots phenomenon, however. At the state-level, eradication of the Soviet political and cultural legacy was an attainable occurrence. Two years after passing the decommunization laws, the phenomenon became even more pronounced both in visual and discursive terms. Of all exhibitions that I documented during more than 20 fieldwork trips to Ukraine, a state-installed poster exhibition of October 2017, "100 Years of Fighting for Independence" or freedom (Figures 111-122), was probably one of the most monumental public installations. The exhibition was composed of meters-tall images of the Ukrainian soldiers of the Anti-Terrorist Operation in Donbas that were placed hand-in-hand with poster-stands on history and images of the UPA, Bandera and other political activists of the 20th century Ukraine. Containing detailed texts and archival images of the OUN, UPA and their comrades, the exhibition carried both educational and ideological objectives. It introduced the viewer to the persistence of the Ukrainian fight for cultural and political sovereignty. Not only its title, "100 Years of Fighting for Independence," but also its images articulated this point clearly. Figure 113, for example, captured the stand-poster that uses color as means for illustrating continuity of the fight: the soldiers of early-mid 20th century Ukraine form one line with fighters of modern Ukrainian army – the black-and-white image is turning into a colored one, implying interconnectedness of the past and the present. Another narrative on the origins of the "new army" of Donbas (Figures 114-119) comes across through the posters: in this instance, the time-span of the Ukrainians' struggle for freedom is expanded further back to the times of the Kievan Rus (882 AD). As such, placement of posters of Kievan Rus next to those of the UPA or OUN, that are then followed by photographs of soldiers of Donbas, is an example of both visual and discursive chain where the struggle for the country's independence is presented as not only decades, but centuries old, and is a politically and culturally *inherited* phenomenon.

What could be seen as a general 'message' of the exhibition, formation of "The New Army" (Figures 118 and 119), is a national objective of post-Euromaidan Ukraine – the primary goal that was set by President Poroshenko during his Independence Day speech on August 24 2018. The images of the "New Army" present a visual narrative of *unity* of ancient and recent past of Ukraine as both a discursive and practical instance: the symbols of Kievan Rus', such as the iron hand with the sword, for example, become the symbol of the tank division of the Ukrainian army in Donbas (Figure 116). Acknowledging modern elements of the socio-political transformations within the states, such as increased inclusion of women in military activities (Figure 121), the exhibition also embraced a broader message of "Freedom [being Ukraine's] Religion" (Figure 122). If one took a picture of Maidan Nezalezhnosti square in October 2017, the viewer would capture *all* visual elements of the state-promoted campaign: the past (nationalist figures of the OUN or UPA) and the present (images of the Ukrainian soldiers in Donbas) being articulated into a national hegemonic formation of the country's decades-long fight for independence – the process of cultural and political liberation of Ukraine from the imperial 'other.'

Finally, the data collected during my fieldwork trip in September-October 2018 illustrate further re-articulation of the Ukrainians' fight for independence, and in particular, the struggle against the Soviet (or Russian) aggressor as not only national, but also *international* phenomenon. Figures 123-127 are images of the poster-exhibition titled "For your and our freedom 1968-2018" ("За вашу і нашу свободу 1968-2018") (Kyiv. 19 September 2018). This exhibition is another political move of the state that draws a connection between present and past and, this time, also promotes the relevance of the Ukrainian resistance to Russian (or Soviet) dominance on the international scale. The poster-stands include a visual row of archival images of the European states that underwent the Soviet or Russian domination (Figure 124). Each of these posters is a narrative on specific individuals who opposed the USSR or the Russian Federation, and suffered physical and political repressions. The countries included in the exhibition range from Ukraine (Figure 125) to Yugoslavia (Figure 127), and even Russia itself – Figure 126, "Political prisoners of the Soviet Russia, 1968."

Simultaneously with the "For your and our freedom 1968-2018" exposition, I viewed another installation, "Maidan: Landscape of Memory" at the Maidan Nezalezhnosti square on October 17, 2018 (Figures 128-130). The latter contained photographs of different moments of the Euromaidan revolution posted on the metal frameworks that were shaped as the silhouettes of the protestors. Both personal and anonymous—persons presented by the pictures or the silhouettes of the protestors, respectively, the exhibition offered space for commemoration of the past *and* re-articulation of the present. The past was turned into a continuous process of the political and cultural struggle. It was preserved and glorified to show acknowledgement of those who sacrificed their lives for the country and, potentially, to justify the ongoing war in Donbas as an act of continuing the tradition—that of a centuries-old patriotism and national bravery perfected via resistance to the Russian dominance.

A careful examination of the posters, however, revealed the grassroots demand for political dialogue between the ordinary citizens and the state. Many of the posters of the "Maidan: Landscape of Memory" exhibition, for instance, contained the grassroots 'corrections' of the state-promoted narrative: the title of one of the posters, "Artifacts of the Revolution of Dignity Museum," included the word "dignity" ("гідності") which was supplemented with paint by placing three letters in front of the word so as to turn it into "profit" ("вигідності") (Figure 132). Despite the graffiti being anonymous, which means that no interview with the author was possible to affirm the original intention of the text, I would argue in favor of this statement being critical of the aftermath of the Euromaidan revolution. The creative re-articulation of the word "dignity" into "profit" shows awareness of Ukrainians of the continuation of corruption and the potential failure of the government to deliver political and cultural promises made during Maidan.

Another example of challenging the state-articulated narratives with grassroots political art was the exhibition project in Kyiv called "The reality of modern war". The collection of posters, photographs and personal objects of the Ukrainian soldiers in Donbas was opened in July 2016, and installed at the entrance hall of the National Museum of the History of Ukraine in the Second World

War. The exposition was held simultaneously with a permanent museum collection of "World War II." During my visit to the museum, I took over 100 pictures of both the "The reality of modern war" and the "World War II" exhibitions. The analysis of the pictures reveals striking similarities of the images of these two displays. Juxtaposed to the visuals of the decades-old "World War II" exhibition, the pictures of "The reality of modern war" capture the soldiers and objects of war in virtually identical positions and backgrounds. Whether intentionally or not, the state of post-Euromaidan Ukraine constructed a powerful hegemony of reading the country's present through the prism of its past. What could be seen as a response of the ordinary citizens are the creative, yet equally political installations. The images of the third exhibition were exposed in June 2016 at the National Museum of the History of Ukraine in the Second World War, hand-in-hand with the previously discussed installations. The exhibition illustrates an alternative, artistic reading of war in Donbas, where both artists and ordinary citizens use daily objects of war to create peace-promoting articles of public or home decor. The bullets, guns and other pieces of ammunition are transformed into chairs, plate-holders and picture frames. According to the overseer of the exhibition (who chose to remain anonymous), the primary objective of such creative installations "[was] to bring the military conflict of Donbas closer to the rest of Ukraine and, at the same time, to offer extensive space for political discussion and re-articulation of war as a new rather than traditional, old phenomenon" (Interview. By Anna Kutkina. Kyiv. 19 June 2016).

Artistic utilization of objects of war, as well as those of the Euromaidan revolution, into the ordinary, daily space of Ukrainians was observed in diverse public settings and different regions of the country. Figures 86 and 87, for instance, capture the installation of shields, bullets, helmets and flags of Maidan into "Porter Pub" in Kyiv (July 2016). A helmet pierced by a bullet (possibly taken from a body of a protestor shot by a sniper in February 2014) was placed on the wall of the pub right next to the flag of the Right Sector. Diverse and arguably controversial in their original meanings, these and similar objects were spotted in different cities across Ukraine.

As artistic political installations of the grassroots level, they constructed the heterogeneous hegemonic formation, where the Euromaidan revolution and its aftermath, including war in Donbas, were given manifold, both grievous and optimistic connotations. Irrespective of the geographic location of the city (or village), the state-promoted replacement of the Soviet statues with monuments on war in Donbas (e.g., Figure 82), or controversial characters like Bandera took place simultaneously with contextually and stylistically diverse grassroots articulation of war, the Euromaidan revolution, history, present or future. On both its regional and national scale, decolonization of Ukraine has turned from vandalized (or sanctioned) toppling of the communist statues and passing of the official decommunization laws to a visually (and contextually) manifold search for new political and cultural meanings. Either spontaneously or intentionally articulated, it implied both physical and discursive resurrection of controversial figures of the past and creative *merging* of these symbols with objects and symbols of the contemporary, daily domain.

Both visual and discursive state-run installations that were grounded on the idea of othering, or the fight against the Soviet and Russian patronage, therefore, is what I define as the 'final' visual stage of post-Euromaidan decommunization. It includes the state promoting patriotism thriving on extracting figures from the Ukrainian past that are known for their explicitly negative stands against any form of foreign patronage and, in particular, that of the Russian Empire and the Soviet Union. Clearly, I acknowledge that this research cannot claim to present volumes of grassroots criticism of the state-sponsored exhibitions that glorified figures of Bandera or UPA, or national public protests against the toppling of the communist statues. At the same time, as I hope to have shown, open criticism of the romanticization of war, as well as verbal objection to re-articulation of Bandera into a hero of modern Ukraine, was no doubt present. At the grassroots level, patriotism-raising, for instance, involved commemoration of the participants of the Euromaidan revolution and carried no signs of resurrection of the controversial past. The poster-stands of Lviv (Figure 133), Vinnytsia

(Figures 134 and 135), or Kharkiv (Figures 136 and 137) were identical in their visual and discursive style: they implied the formation of a *common*, national narrative that articulated figures of the Ukrainian *present* as the key elements of new, democratic transitioning.

At the same time, narrated through slogans rooted in the nationalist past—"Heroes do not die" (Figure 138), the heroes of the grassroots Ukraine were diverse. They did *not* follow the state-suggested model of replacement of one cult figure such as Lenin (or Shchors, Figure 81) by another—Bandera. In other words, the ordinary citizens' positions on modes of socio-political and cultural transformation of post-Euromaidan Ukraine were *manifold*. They varied from radical toppling (or preservation) of the communist statues (Figure 69) to the unifying graffiti "West and East are together" or "Return Your Crimea" that were followed by the swastika sign (Figures 105 and 106, respectively). They also included commemorative posters of heroes of war in Donbas or the Euromaidan revolution (Figures 59 and 134, respectively). Multivocal in its meanings, the grassroots hegemonic formation called for unification of Ukraine around the idea of *diversity*. The hegemonic formation of the state, on the other hand, offered the model of national unity that still contained elements of the one-sided reading of the country's past—figures like Stepan Bandera or members of the UPA, who, according to the many, fall short in being national symbols of a democratic state (Plokhy 2011; Rossolinski 2014; Struve 2016).

As a final remark of this chapter, it should be noted that irrespective of ambiguousness of his figure, the reappearance of Bandera marked the beginning of explicit transformation of the Ukrainian political domain where, arguably, for the first time since 1991, there occurred open mastering of the country's discursive and physical space by western Ukrainian symbols. It remains important to add, however, that particularly in the context of an ongoing hybrid war in Donbas, as well as occupation of Crimea, decommunization still assembles a broader meaning of liberation of Ukraine from the double-headed imperial yoke. At the same time, while neither the Ukrainian nor international community holds doubts on

Russia's presence and its stirring of an armed conflict in Donbas, detection of the 'other' renders difficult the further into history one goes. While the physical demolition of the Soviet heritage assumed the creation of a community where citizens were expected to be unified around destruction of the 'other,' photo, video and interview data discussed delineates decommunization as a *complex* process of continuous meaning-making. It implies struggle or contestation of diverse political positions, and at the same time, does *not* necessarily mean dominance of one position over the other. As a bottom line, if there were to be one reflection only that I suggested the reader extracts from this book, it would be the conclusion that political or cultural multivocality does *not* necessarily imply conflict. Alternatively, it can be indicative of a *dialogue* rather than the discursive or physical domination of one political unit over the other — the "polyphony" Bakhtin does not apply to literature only.

Conclusion

"He who frees himself, will be free"
— Lesya Ukrainka

In his discussion of the Euromaidan revolution and its aftermath, the founder of the Ukrainian-German Civil Society Forum "Kyiv Dialogue," Tobias Munchmeyer raises the fundamental question of "how does democracy look like?" At first glance, both as the public space of the protest and the political action that brought corrupt government of President Viktor Yanukovych to an end, Maidan is a classic example of a democratic practice. It was both a physical and discursive expression of self-organization and alliance of the people. It was the domain of diversity of socio-political and cultural positions and, at the same time, a symbol of unity around the universal values of peace, equality and freedom.

It is important to keep in mind that within the historic spectrum, the Euromaidan revolution was the fourth national attempt to articulate the decades-long objective of sovereignty and detachment from the legacy of the Soviet Union. In 1990, the central square of Kyiv, (as locals call it often— "Maidan") became the space of a national student strike. At first, primarily students from Western Ukraine, and later all regions of the country, the participants arrived at that-time October Square to object the political influence of the Soviet Union on Ukraine and, in particular, the military draft of Ukrainian students into the Soviet army. The hunger strike of the students lasted until the resignation of the prime minister and signing of the Ukrainian Parliament agreement to meet the protesters' demands. Ten years later, renamed after the disintegration of the USSR, Maidan Nezalezhnosti was once again the centerpiece of a massive protest—this time against the corrupt government of President Leonid Kuchma. What became known as the "The Ukraine without Kuchma[40]" campaign, the revolt resulted in the presidential election of Viktor Yanukovych as means of avoiding criminal responsibility of Kuchma administration's murdering of the journalist Georgiy Gongadze[41] (2000) and numerous arrests of the protestors. In 2004, the Orange Revolution was the first successful overthrow of President Viktor Yanukovych: in a series of protests that took place at the Maidan Nezalezhnosti square in Kyiv and across the country, people objected to the lead of Viktor Yanukovych at the 2004 presidential elections, rising up against the universal corruption of the state. Little did the Ukrainians know back then that the world was yet to witness Maidan Nezalezhnosti justifying its name once again, also almost ten years later, but this time—in full.

Clearly, the Maidan of 2004 and the Euromaidan of 2014 have many features in common. The most obvious one, of course, is that both in 2004 and 2014 the political target of the protests was the same person, Viktor Yanukovych. As Hrytsak notes in *#Euromaidan: History in the Making,* "some already ascribe Yanukovych an exceptionally important role in Ukrainian history. In 2004, Yanukovych made Ukrainians understand what they did not want—his presidency. In 2014, he helped Ukrainians to understand what they wanted—not just a new President, but an overhaul of the entire system that he embodied" (Hrytsak 2014: 27). And that is certainly so.

---

40 "Ukraine without Kuchma" was a mass protest that took place in Ukraine in 2000-2001. The primary demand of the protestors was the resignation of that time President, Leonid Kuchma. The protests were triggered by the release of an audio that proved involvement of Kuchma's government into murdering of the journalist Georgiy Gongadze. Unlike the Orange Revolution, Ukraine without Kuchma was implemented by the government enforcement units, and followed by wide-scale arrests of the opposition. Chemerys, Volodymyr. "Ukraine without Kuchma." NGO Institute Respublica. December 30, 2006. https://inrespublica.org.ua/en/novyny/ukrayina-bez-kuchmi.html.

41 Georgiy Gongadze was a Ukrainian opposition journalist and founder of the internet newspaper *Ukrayinska Pravda,* who was murdered in September of 2000 after expressing open criticism of President Leonid Kuchma and producing online reports on high-level corruption. The decapitated body of Gongadze was found in the forest November 3 2000. Accessed July 7, 2015. Source: https://inlviv.in.ua/ukraine/georgi j-gongadze-voyin -i-zhurnalist -shho-zagynuv-za-svobodu-slova-v-ukrayini.

No doubt, the Euromaidan revolution is the most ambitious embodiment of Ukraine's post-Soviet transition. Unlike all previous protests of post-1990 and, in particular, the Orange Revolution, however, "at which the name of the president elect "Yush-shen-ko" was chanted ... [and yet where] values [were] defined with a geographic adjective" (Belorusets 2014: 25), the Euromaidan is a symbol of both democratic and, to some extent, even an anarchist utopia. Hands down, the Maidan of 2014 was a statement of national consolidation—a political move of millions who came together leaving linguistic, religious and political differences aside, and stepping up in unison for the universal values, be it human rights, independence or freedom from corruption. Hrytsak owes this shift in collective consciousness to the emergence of a new generation: the "Independence Generation," born between 1985 and 1995, they are "free from Soviet mentality" and, for this reason, "reject vertical hierarchy and are the generation of "horizontal connections" — similar to those in Facebook or Twitter" (ibid: 28). Indeed, it is hard to disagree that, as a movement that started with the student protest, Euromaidan of 2014 was this generation's revolution.

What I still have issues tackling, however, is the ease with which novelty overshadows the clearly existing, still living and actively present past—here, I am coming back to the primary puzzle which is the oversimplification of complexity of the 2014 revolution and to an equal, if not greater extent, its political and cultural aftermath. If we are to transfer from communism to democracy, how do we do so without excluding or muting those who might still be *both* 'Soviet' and 'European?' According to the 2020 Ukraine Demographics[42], we are still talking about at least 16.7 percent of Ukrainians aged 65 and older and 67.36 percent between 15 and 64 residing in Ukraine. The citing of these figures is not at all meant to make communism more alive or significant than it is. Nowadays there are very few people both in Ukraine and outside its borders who would go as far as to claim communisms' tangibility for the post-Soviet space. If we tend to explain the Euromaidan through

---

42 "Ukraine Demographics." Worldometer. June 12, 2021. https://www.worldometers.info/demographics/ukraine-demographics/.

the prism of the "Independence generation" only and ignore political echoes of the past, however, we risk falling into a trap of undermining the role of the 'Soviet' together with the 'anti-Soviet,' *not* the one of the present, but that of the USSR.

Whether one acknowledges it or not, to some extent, the face of post-Euromaidan decommunization still wears a mask of the 20th century. Renaming the Moscow Avenue to Stepana Bandery Avenue or Kartvelishvili Street to Volodymyr Pokotylo Street[43], for example, is an act of appealing to the past, still. Shortly after the Euromaidan revolution, one of the most commonly cited arguments within the scholarly and political community of Ukraine was that it was unknown how long the protests could actually continue should there be no "Right Sector" which switched the struggle into a phase of active fighting. According to Hrytsak, the Maidan of 2014 brought us to an important conclusion: "nationalists and extremist nationalism have no chance to win a democratic revolution — but the Ukrainian revolution hardly stood a chance without its nationalism and nationalists" (ibid: 30). He further states that, in other words, citing Ann Applebaum, "nationalism is exactly what Ukraine needs. Democracy fails when citizens don't believe their country is worth fighting for." In this regard, I would argue in favor of drawing a clear distinction between nationalism as a 'one-time' political tool of overthrowing the corrupt regime, and the discursive or symbolic ground for construction of a new post-revolutionary identity. For the latter, to flourish in a direction of democracy rather than the ideologically homogeneous regime (of any kind), the political texture of the state is to be sensitive to *diversity*. Down the road, this is what the Euromaidan was about.

I do hope that with the finishing of this book, the reader is left with a sensation that the broader objective of this work was not to define particular political groups that exist within a society, or to undermine cultural formations that support or object decommunization. The goal was to look at multiple mechanisms of a selection

---

43 Bigg, Claire. "Kyiv Renames 'Moscow' Avenue After a Contentious Nationalist Figure." Radio Free Europe. June 15, 2021. https://www.rferl.org/a/ukraine-kyiv-avenue-renamed-moscow-to-bandera/27844918.html.

of the discursive and physical elements that were included (or erased) from the physical space of (post)Euromaidan Ukraine. In this regard, identification of the primary political and cultural means of the citizens' and ruling elites' consolidation of a politically and culturally diverse state was particularly engaging. By using Ukraine as a case-study, I hope to have illustrated how the process of disengagement with the 'other' could be defined by two primary categories: the physical and the discursive. The former includes both the vandalism and sanctioned eradication of remnants of the oppressive communist regime—the monuments of the Soviet leaders, for example, as a form of expression of the protest against both former and present political regimes, as well as drawing of an ideological distinction between past and present. Within processes of such kind, diverse forms of political art, such as posters, graffiti or videos are often used for articulation of the political operation that contributes to establishment of multiple hegemonic formations. The latter—the discursive (or ideological) mechanism of decommunization—has been shown to take place through articulation of both opposing and supporting positions on the country's political, cultural and economic course.

Six years down the road, I still argue that the evolution of post-Euromaidan de-Sovietization should be examined beyond the framework of passing and implementation of the 2015 decommunization laws. In their study of the reforms and decommunization in post-Euromaidan Ukraine, Anna Oliinyk and Taras Kuzio argue that "for the first time, decommunization removed and changed the Soviet narrative and in the process distanced Ukraine from Russia (with which it was now at war) as part of an agenda of building what [the Ukrainian] political forces understood to be a 'normal' European country (Oliinyk and Kuzio 2021: 26). Absolutely, the socio-political and cultural transformations of (post) 2013 Ukraine have carried an objective of 'Europeanization' of Ukraine at both the state and ordinary citizens' level. Meanwhile, we might also want to hold off somewhat more on defining decommunization as an act that "removed" the Soviet narrative—at least at the mentality level, the phenomenon of full-fledged transformation, especially as deeply ingrained as that of the 'Soviet genome,' reckons time.

As I intended to illustrate, the process of all-national decommunization is a multilayered phenomenon with several stages. It commenced as an artistic expression of the grassroots, ordinary citizens' positions on Europeanization of Ukraine and found its way in a vivid, provocative, and powerful political art. The grassroots narratives drew out and into imaginative and thought-stirring posters, graffiti, and performances. Printed, painted or installed across the cities, towns and villages, the 'change' proliferated in numerous formats—from clothing prints, to postcards, cell phone cases and other memorabilia. It was inspired and carried by the ordinary citizens' desire to detach from the President Yanukovych's regime, and, as such, the Russian political and cultural patronage. At the same time, the grassroots vision of democratization was grounded on a broad array of political meanings that ranged from personal demands of "being heard"—such as the hand-made posters of the "Strike Poster" project—to national requests for termination of Russian military aggression or promotion of human rights. Both during and after the Euromaidan revolution, political and cultural diversity of the grassroots stands was being articulated into a powerful hegemonic formation of a heterogeneous nature. After the official termination of the revolution, however, we saw the process of decommunization taking an official or governmental form, and with that—the homogenization of meanings.

Starting in the summer 2014, decommunization evolved towards a simple and more complex form: in one respect, it narrowed post-Euromaidan democratization to passing of the decommunization laws that legitimized national demolition of physical and ideological elements of the Soviet heritage. After the annexation of Crimea and Russian military involvement in war in Donbas, we observed othering of Russia as means for unification of Ukraine against the external aggressor being justified by the state as a necessary political move (Allison 2014; Kulyk 2016; Ryabchuk 2014; Shevel 2015; Shveda 2016; Wilson 2015). Once again, in practical terms, the state-institutionalized de-Sovietization acquired the form of canonization of the controversial figures of the past such as Stepan Bandera, Semen Petliura or members of the UPA. Replacing the discursive and physical symbols of the communist regime, such as statues of Lenin, these controversial figures of Ukrainian history have undergone the discursive or narrative re-articulation: defined as 'national heroes,' they obtained new meanings of contributors to the modern fight for the country's independence. Simultaneously, staging of regional and national poster exhibitions, as well as publishing books that promote visual and discursive collision, or equalization of controversial historical figures with soldiers of war in Donbas, were the primary mechanisms of the state-promoted decommunization. The central puzzle of the phenomenon was that, aiming at 'unifying,' such process constructed a powerful hegemonic formation that implied political and cultural symbols of the primarily western regions of Ukraine and, therefore, tended to be exclusive of both pro-Russian *and* pro-European (anti-nationalist) parts of the country's population.

While the analysis of the grassroots level decommunization illustrates contentious articulation of the manifold, multivocal positions on dealing with the Soviet heritage, it is important to remember that artistic means of preservation of the communist relics, such as dressing monuments of Lenin in nationally embroidered shirts or hiding statues in the backyards, is but a tip of the Ukraine's 'diversity' iceberg. At both the regional and national level, the decommunization unraveled the possibility of combining controversial (e.g., nationalist) elements of the past with nationally honored figures of the present (e.g., heroes of Maidan or war in Donbas) into a dominant horizon of social orientation or action. Within such a process, the nationalist symbols were contested and, at the same time, new meanings of both regional and national scale were articulated. Like during other world-scale political transformations, such as the Russian Revolution of 1917, WWII, or the collapse of the Soviet Union, artistic intervention into political space of the state in transition has been an effective mode of citizens-state interaction; it involved diverse forms of the citizens-state encounter that vary from the top-down articulation of the homogeneous state-promoted narratives to the openly contested meanings of the grassroots level. Ultimately, the process of state-grassroots interaction could be defined as that of achieving social consensus, where 'dialogism' (Bakhtin

1981), I argue, is the primary component of hegemonic meaning-making.

The bridging of the theory of hegemony (Cox 2019; Gills 1994; Laclau 1985), the theory of heteroglossia (and monologism) (Bakhtin 1981) and that of the 'imagined communities' (Anderson 1983), in this sense, has shown to be an effective theoretical method of analysis of a state in transition. As every worldview conditions another and the existence of hegemonic formation presupposes the existence of that of a counter-hegemonic nature, the only means of construction of a peaceful, democratic development are those of conducting a dialogue. The possibility of a successful completion of such a task, however, can be increased by deepening our knowledge of the socio-political and cultural stands of the ordinary citizens. That being said, I come back to emphasizing the importance of taking a step further and narrowing the point of reference of the imagined communities from the "nation" (Anderson 1983) to that of a 'region': examination of the ordinary citizens' or communities' stands on what is presumed to be a relatively simple or black-and-while socio-political phenomenon, such as decommunization, carries potential of unraveling (or creating) new formula of construction of national identity—the one that acknowledges having no common voice as *being* the common voice.

Certainly, as scholars and analysts argue, the victory of Euromaidan confirms the old rule: "revolutions with a nationali dimension have a greater chance of winning" (Hrytsak 2014: 29). Articulated as part of the narrative of the heroic combat of Ukraine against the historic and modern patronage of Russia, on the other hand, the controversial figures of Bandera or members of the UPA are no longer 'fighting' the communist regime. Extracted from the past, they are made part of the country's visual and discursive present. Both during the Maidan and official decommunization that followed, as symbols of 'nationalism,' they acquired new democratic meanings by being either voluntary or enforced elements of modern discursive articulations. Importantly, when it comes to proceeding with analysis of such processes, further expansion of the existing theoretical frameworks may be required to address the local nature of the imagined communities—to study political diversity as a mosaic of particular, *personal* voices.

For the reader who may still have questions on either motives or objectives of this book, claiming it to be an encyclopedic study of (post)Euromaidan Ukraine is by all means outside my intentions. Rather, this work is an outcome of a specific fieldwork conducted by a researcher who arrived in the field—the physical space of the Euromaidan in Kyiv—as to test the 'black-and-white' media-promoted hypothesis: the "Euromaidan being a gathering of fascists and nationalists" (1st Channel, Russia, 2013-onwards) or it being the socio-political space that is "representative of all regions and citizens of Ukraine" (5th Channel, Ukraine, December 2013-early 2014). Neither during the first days of my stay in the field, nor over seven years later would I argue for either of these polarized claims to be true. What I feature as one of the primary conclusions is the importance of examining decommunization as both micro *and* macro politics. Be it the demolition or preservation of the communist symbols, the Ukrainian decommunization is foremost an act of personal statement. Yet, articulated by the many in what was observed to be a creative way, it becomes a statement of the many. The toppling of the Lenin statue in Kyiv in December 2013, or massive years-long demolition of communist symbols at the regional level is but a selective representation of public opinion. To be complete, the analysis of post-2013 decommunization requires examination of both the sporadic (e.g. 'nationalist') and systemized (e.g. state-implemented) modes of eradication of the past.

Indeed, while the effectiveness of decommunization of the post-Soviet space such as that of Ukraine is being examined by scholars, analysts, politicians, artists, media or thousands of ordinary people who choose to care, full comprehension of decommunization at both the external (physical) and internal (mentality) level remains a quest. What do the 'post-Soviet' citizens want to do with vestiges of their past? What does uncertainty of physical destiny of the monuments, as well as controversial attitudes towards concepts like 'communism' or 'democracy' tell us about the efficiency of decommunization as such? Finally, does decommunization necessarily lead to democratization and if so, what is the economic, political or cultural scale for the estimation of its completion? The acquisition of an explicit answer to all of these questions within the socio-political context of Ukraine is possible only *over time*. As a political phenomenon of a national scale, decommunization requires cultural and political adaptation to particularities of the country's population. With the demolition of communist statues, renaming of the streets, or popularization of controversial figures of the past in books or political poster exhibitions, we can grasp how particular names (or places) hold distinctive value for both politicians and the public. At the same time, we can also witness the empty plinths of the Soviet monuments enabling articulation of new sets of meanings—potentially, the ideas of a henotic value.

Following Laclau, Palonen argues, "we might say that, in the moment of naming, the inherent multiplicity of the "people" becomes one—if only temporarily." Calling the political transformations of (post)Euromaidan Ukraine 'decommunization' worked the opposite way: framing of the assumed political course as 'anti-Soviet' (or 'anti-communist') exposed the narratives of the *many*. And there we stand today—remembering, forgetting, dwelling...

Meanwhile, the over 90-year-old 'hypothesis' of the Soviet poet Vladimir Mayakovsky, "Lenin lived, Lenin lives and Lenin will live forever" ("Komsomolskaya," 1924) is yet to be tested.

References

Adas, Michael. "Imperialism and Colonialism in Comparative Perspective." *International History Review* 20, no. 2 (2010): 371-388. https://doi.org/10.1080/07075332.1998.9640829.

Afanasyeva, Anastasia. "To See Things With Clarity." *Atlanta Review* 21, no. 2 (2015): 35-36.

Ahvenjarvi, K. Hiltunen, and J. Turunen. "Using our Pasts, Defining our Futures: Debating Heritage and Culture in Europe." *International Journal of Heritage Studies* (2019): 975-978. https://doi.org/10.1080/13527258.2019.1700391.

Aitamurto, Kaarina. "Russian Paganism and the Issue of Nationalism: A Case Study of the Circle of Pagan Tradition." *Pomegranate* 8, no. 2 (2007): 184-210. https://doi.org/10.1558/pome.v8i2.184.

Akinsha, Konstantin. *Permanent Revolution. Ukrainian Art Today*. Hungary: Ludwig Muzeum, 2018.

Allison, Roy. "Russian 'Deniable' Intervention in Ukraine: How and Why Russia Broke the Rules." *International Affairs* 90 (2014): 1255-1297. https://doi.org/ 10.1111/1468-2346.12170.

Anderson, Benedict. *Imagined Communities*. London: Verso, 1983.

Anderson, Benedict. *Imagined Communities: Reflections on the Origin and Spread of Nationalism*. London: Verso, 1991.

Andrukhovych, Jurii. "From Twelve Circles." *Boundary 2. An International Journal of Literature and Culture* (July 2014): 1-24.

Anlar, Aslihan. "Ukraine's Euromaidan. Analysis of a Civil Revolution." *Europe-Asia Studies* 68, no. 8 (2016): 1450-1451.

Arendt, Hannah. *On Revolution*. New York: Penguin, 1984.

Arrighi, Giovanni. *The Long Twentieth Century: Money, Power, and the Origins of Our Times*. New York: Verso, 2010.

Arkas, Mykola. *Istorija Ykrajiny-Rusi (The History of Ukraine-Rus')*. Kyiv: Nash Format, 2012.

Ash, Timothy Garton. *Trials, Purges and History Lessons. From the book History of the Present: Essays, Sketches, and Dispatches from Europe in the 1990s*. London: Penguin, 2000.

Atwood, M. "Resisting the Veil: Reports from a Revolution." *The Walrus* 1 (2003): 86-89.

Aulich, James and Marta Sylvestrova. *Political Posters in Central and Eastern Europe*. UK: Manchester University Press, 1999.

Baker, Catherine. *Nation in Formation: Inclusion and Exclusion in Central and Eastern Europe*. London: School of Slavonic and East European Studies, 2007.

Bakhtin, Mikhail. *The Dialogic Imagination: Four Essays*. Texas: University of Texas Press, 1981.

Bakhtin, Mikhail. *Problems of Dostoevsky's Poetics*. University of Minnesota Press, 1984.

Bakhtin, Mikhail. *Art and Answerability: Early Philosophical Essays*. University of Texas Press, 1990.

Bames, Trevor. *The Logics of Dislocation: Models, Metaphors and Meanings of Economic Space*. New York: Guildford, 1996.

Bames, Trevor, and James Duncan. *Writing Worlds: Texts, Discourses and Metaphors in the Interpretation of Landscape*. London: Routledge, 1992.

Barnes, Trevor J. *On Theory, History, and Anoraks*. Antipode, 2001.

Bateson, Ian. "A People without a History Won't Fight": The Battle to Control Ukraine's Past." *World Policy Journal* 34, no. 1 (2017): 42-46. https://doi.org/10.1215/07402775-3903712.

Baysha, Olga. "Ukrainian Euromaidan: The Exclusion of Otherness in the Name of Progress." *European Journal of Cultural Studies* 18, no. 1 (2014): 3-18. https://doi: 10.1177/1367549414557806.

Bazylevych, In. "Public Images, Political Art, and Gendered Spaces." *Journal of Contemporary Anthropology* 1 (2010): 1-16.

Beauchemin, Cris and Amparo González-Ferrer. "Sampling International Migrants with Origin-based Snowballing Method: New Evidence on Biases and Limitations." *Demographic Research* 25, no. 3 (2011): 103-134. http://doi: 10.4054/DemRes.2011.25.3.

Beichelt, Timm. *Transnational Ukraine? Networks and Ties That Influence(d) Contemporary Ukraine*. New York: Columbia University Press, 2016.

Belorusets, Yevgenia. *Documenting Maidan*. Kyiv: ProStory, 2014.

Belorusets, Yevgenia. *Let's Put Lenin's Head Back Together Again*. Kyiv: Pinchuk Art Center, 2015.

Berdyaev, Nikolai. *Syd'ba Rosii (The Destiny of Russia)*. Moscow: Astrel Publishers, 2010.

Bhabba, Homi K. "Signs Taken for Wonders: Questions of Ambivalence and Authority Under a Tree Outside Delhi, May 1817." *Critical Inquiry* (1985): 144-165.

Bhabba, Homi K. "Culture's in Between. *Art Forum.*" 32 (1990): 167-211.

Bikov, Dmitri. *Dva Lenina*. Profile Press, 2017.

Bieler Andreas and Adam David Morton. "A Critical Theory Rout to Hegemony, World Order and Historical Change: Neo-Gramscian Perspectives in International Relations." *SAGE Journals* 28, no. 1 (2004): 85-113. https://doi.org/10.1177/030981680408200106.

Bilinsky, Volodymyr. *Krajina-Moksel or Moskovia* (*Country-Moksel or Moskovia*). Kyiv: Olena Teliga Publisher, 2006.

Bilinsky, Volodymyr. *Ykrajina-Rus'* (*Ukraine-Rus'*). Ternopil: Bohdan, 2013.

Blaut, J. M. "Colonialism and the Rise of Capitalism." *Science and Society* 53, no. 3 (1989): 260-296.

Blommaert, Jan. "Critical Discourse Analysis." *Anthropol* 29 (2000): 447-466. https://doi.org/10.1146/annurev.anthro.29.1.447.

Bohdanova, Tetyana 2014. "Unexpected Revolution: The Role of Social Media in Ukraine's Euromaidan Uprising." *European View* 13, no. 1 (2014): 133-142. http://doi: 10.1007/s12290-014-0296-4.

Bondarchuk, Roman and Kateryna Gornostai. *Euromaidan. Rough Cut.* IDFA, 2014.

Bonnel, Victoria. *Iconography of Power. Soviet Political Posters Under Lenin and Stalin.* Berkeley: University of California Press, 1999.

Bottici, Chiara and Benoit Challand: *Imagining Europe: Myth, Memory, and Identity.* New York: Cambridge University Press, 2013.

Bowen, H.V. *Revenue and Reform: The Indian Problem in British Politics, 1757–1773.* Cambridge: Cambridge University Press, 1991.

Branham, R.Bracht. *Rethinking Theory: Bakhtin and the Classics.* Illinois: Northwest University Press, 2002.

Bremmer, Jan N. "From Heroes to Saints and from Martyrological to Hagiographical Discourse." *Nomos* 1, no. 6 (2017): 35-66.

Briggs, Daniel, Ivan Gololobov, and Aimar Ventsel. "Ethnographic Research Among Drinking Youth Cultures: Reflections From Observing Participants." *Folklore* 61 (2015): 157-176. https://doi.org/10.7592/FEJF2015.61.youth_culture.

Brockmeier, Jens. "Remembering and Forgetting: Narrative as Cultural Memory." *Culture and Psychology* 8, no. 1 (2002): 15-43. https://doi.org/10.1177/1254067X02008001617.

Brubaker, Rogers. "Nationhood and the National Question in the Soviet Union and Post-Soviet Eurasia: An Institutionalist Account. Citizenship and National Identity: from Colonialism to Globalism." *SAGE* (1997): 85-119.

Bruner, Edward. *The Anthropology of Experience*. The University of Chicago Press, 1984.

Budryte, Dovile. "Memory, War, and Mnemonical In/Security: A Comparison of Lithuania and Ukraine." *Palgrave Macmillan* (2018): 155-177.

Burakovskiy, Aleksandr. "Holocaust Remembrance in Ukraine: Memorialization of the Jewish Tragedy in Babi Yar." *Nationalities Papers* 39, no. 3 (2011): 371-389. https://doi.org/10.1080/00905992.2011.565316.

Burchill, Scott, and Andrew Devetak. *Theories of International Relations*. New York: Palgrave Macmillan, 2005.

Bussmann, Margot and John R. Oneal. "Do hegemonies distribute private goods? A test of power-transition theory." *Journal of Conflict Resolution* 51 (2007): 89-110.

Butchenko, Maksym. *Tri Chasa Bez Voyni (Three Hours Without War)*. Kyiv: Folio, 2015.

Butler, Judith. *Precarious Life. The Powers of Mourning and Violence*. New York: Verso, 2004.

Buttino, Marco E. *In a Collapsing Empire: Underdevelopment, Ethnic Conflicts, and Nationalisms in the Soviet Union*. Milan: Feltrinelli, 1993.

Buyskykh, Iuliia. "Carnival in Urban Protest Culture: The Case of Kyiv Early Euromaidan." *Lietuvos Etnologija* 16 (2016): 69-89.

Carroll, William. "China in the Shanghai Cooperation Organization: Hegemony, Multi-Polar Balance, or Cooperation in Central Asia." *International Journal of Humanities and Social Science* 1, no. 18 (2011): 1-8.

Candlin, C. and Maley Y. *The Construction of Professional Discourse*. London: Routledge, 1997.

Cassirer, E. *The Myth of the State*. New Haven: Yale University Press, 1986.

Cederstrom, Carl and Andre Spicer. "Discourse of the Real Kind: A Post-Foundational Approach to Organizational Discourse Analysis." *Organization* 2 (2013): 178-205.

Chad, Elias. *Posthumous Images: Contemporary Art and Memory Politics in Post-Civil War Lebanon*. Durham: Duke University Press, 2018.

Chadaga, Julia. "Light in Captivity: Spectacular Glass and Soviet Power in the 1920s and 1930s." *Slavic Review* 66, no. 1 (2007): 82-105.

Chase-Dunn, Christopher. "Commentary on "Globalisation and Development: The Relevance of Classical 'Dependency' Theory for the World Today." *International Social Science Journal* (2018): 1-4.

Chatterjee, Partha. *The Nation and Its Fragments: Colonial and Postcolonial Histories*. NJ: Princeton University Press, 1993.

Chervonenko, Vitalij. "Bez Lenina: Yspehi i provali dekommunizacii (Without Lenin: Successes and Failures of Decommunization)." *BBC Ykraina* (2016): 1-3. http://bbc.in/2gCVCX1.

Chikhi, Sabrina. "Ukraine Conflict: Resolution Through Negotiation. *USA: University for Peace and Conflict Monitor*." (2014): 1-7.

Christmann,, Gabriela B. "The Power of Photographs of Buildings in the Dresden Urban Discourse. Towards a Visual Discourse Analysis." *Forum: Qualitative Social Research* 9, no. 3 (2008): 1-14.

Cohen, Josh. "The Historian Whitewashing Ukraine's Past." *Foreign Policy Association* (2016): 1-9.

Collier, Malcolm. "Approaches to Analysis in Visual Anthropology." *SAGE* (2001): 36-62.

Connerton, Paul. *How Societies Remember*. Cambridge University Press, 1989.

Covert, Hannah H. and Mirka Koro-Ljungberg. "Layers of Narratives, Images, and Analysis." *Qualitative Research Journal* 15 (2014): 306-318. https://doi: 10.1108/QRJ-08-2014-0042.

Cox, G.W. *The Politics of Divided Government*. Routledge, 2019.

Coynash, Halya. "Decommunization" Laws: Deeply Divisive and Destined for Strasbourg." *Krytyka* (2015): 1-7.

Crane, Susan. *Participatory Action Research*. Central Queensland University Press, 1997.

Crang, M. *Cultural Geography*. London: Routledge, 1998.

Curry Dion, and Matthew Vincent Flinders. "Deliberative Democracy, Elite Politics and Electoral Reform." *Policy Studies* 29, no. 4 (2008): 371-392. https//doi:10.1080/01442870802482075.

Custer, Dwayne. "Autoethnography as a Transformative Research Method." *USA: Sofia University* 19 (2014): 1-13. https://doi:10.46743/2160-3715/2014.1011.

Danen, Bram. "Russia and Ukraine: A Post-Colonial Perspective on the Ukraine-Russia Conflict." *Leiden University Press* (2016): 1-36.

Danylenko, Viktor. *Ukraine 1989-1991: The Last Chapter of the Soviet History.* Institute of History: NAN, 2016.

Darwin, John. *After Tamerlane. The Rise and Fall of Global Empires 1400-2000.* London: Allen Lane, 2007.

D'Anieri,, Paul. "Structural Constraints in Ukrainian Politics. *East European Politics and Societies* 25, no. 1 (2011): 28-46. https://doi.org/ 10.1177/ 0888325410388559.

Delanty, Greg. *The European Heritage. A Critical Re-Interpretation.* New York: Routledge, 2017.

Deluca, Kevin. "Articulation Theory: A Discursive Grounding for Rhetorical Practice" *Philosophy and Rhetoric* 32, no. 4 (1999): 334-348.

Derian, James Der. "Anti-diplomacy, Intelligence Theory and Surveillance Practice." *Intelligence and National Security* 8, no. 3 (1993): 29-51.

Destradi, Sandra. "Regional Powers and Their Strategies: Empire, Hegemony and Leadership." *Review of International Studies* 36, no. 4 (2010): 903-930. https://doi.org/10.1017/S0260210510001361.

Dewan, Mayukh. "Understanding Ethnography: An 'Exotic' Ethnographer's Perspective." *Springer* (2015): 185-203.

Dietsch, Johan. *Making Sense of Suffering: Holocaust and Holodomor in Ukrainian Historical Culture.* Lund: Media Tryck, 2006.

Dikovitskaya, Margarita. *Visual Culture: The Study of the Visual after the Cultural Turn.* Cambridge: The MIT Press, 2005.

Diuk, Nadia. "Euromaidan: Ukraine's Self-Organizing Revolution." *World Affairs* 176 (2014): 9-16.

Dobko, Taras. "Learning to Be Free: Freedom and its Counterfeits in Post-Soviet Ukraine." *Lviv: Ukrainian Catholic University Publishers* (2014): 1-14.

Duara, Prasenjit. *Rescuing History from the Nation: Questioning Narratives of Modern China.* The University of Chicago Press, 1996.

Dudek, Andriana. "Poland and Russia at the Turn of XXI Century. Between a Liberal Illusion and Imperial realism." *UNISCI Journal* 96 (2016): 1-24.

Dudovskiy, John. "Snowballing Sampling." *Research Methodology* (2012): 1-8.

Dugin, Alexander. *The Fourth Political Theory.* London: Arktos, 2012.

Dugin, Alexander. *The Last of the World-Island: The Geopolitics of Contemporary Russia*. London: Arktos, 2014.

Dunne, Tim, Milja Kurki and Steve Smith. *International Relations Theories*. Oxford: OUP, 2007.

During, Simon. *The Cultural Studies*. London: Routledge, 1993:

Edelman, Murray. *The Symbolic Uses of Politics*. Urbana. University of Illinois Press, 1985.

Eliade Mircea. *Images and Symbols*. Princeton: Princeton University Press, 1991.

Enwezor, Okwui. "The Postcolonial Constellation: Contemporary Art in a State of Permanent Transition." *Indiana University Press* 34, no. 4 (2003): 57-82. http://www.jstor.org/stable/4618328.

Eriksen, Thomas H. *Ethnicity and Nationalism. Anthropological Perspectives*. London: Pluto Press, 1993.

Ernst, Douglas. "Merkel on Putin: He acts the way he does to 'prove he's a man.'" *The Washington Times* (2014): 1-7. https://www.washingtontimes.com/news/2014/dec/9/angela-merkel-vladimirputin-he-acts-way-he-does-p/.

Esherick, Joseph and Jeffrey Wasserstrom. "Acting Out Democracy: Political Theater in Modern China." *Journal of Asian Studies* 49 (1990): 836-866.

Etkind, Alexander. *Internal Colonization: Russia's Imperial Experience*. UK: Polity Press, 2011.

Etkind, Alexander. *Warped Mourning: Stories of the Undead in the Land of the Unburied*. California: Stanford University Press, 2013.

Evans, Alfred. "Putin's Legacy and Russia's Identity." *Europe-Asia Studies* 60, no. 6 (2008): 889-912. https://www.jstor.org/stable/20451565.

Fairclough, Norman. *Discourse and Social Change*. London: Longman, 1992.

Fanon, Frantz. *Concerning Violence*. Paris: Seuli, 1985.

Farinas, Rebecca. "The Icon Moves: Diversity Through Pragmatic/Religious Aesthetics of the Euromaidan." *UK: Pragmatism Today* 6 (2015) 23-33.

Fèdinec, Csilla and István Csernicskó. "(Re)conceptualization of Memory in Ukraine after the Revolution of Dignity." *Central European Papers* 5, no. 1 (2017): 46-71. https://doi.org/10.25142/cep.2017.003.

Fedirko, Olexander. "Methodological Background of Post-Soviet Regionalism: The Case of Ukraine." *Baltic Journal of European Studies* 4 (2014): 20-33.

Fedor, Julie, Markku Kangaspuro, Jussi Lassila, and Tatiana Zhurzhenko. *War and Memory in Russia, Ukraine and Belarus*. Palgrave Macmillan Memory Studies, 2017.

Fejto, Francois. *History of People's Democracies*. Pall Mall Press, 1971.

Femia, Joseph. "Hegemony and Consciousness in the Thought of Antonio Gramsci." *Political Studies* 23, no. 1 (1975): 29-48. https://doi.org/10.1111/j.1467-9248.1975.tb00044.x.

Finlayson, A. and Valentine J. "Politics and poststructuralism: An introduction. Edinburgh." *Edinburgh University Press* 224 (2002): 142-169.

Finlayson, Graham. *Removing Shadows from Images*. New York: Springer, 2002.

Fitzpatrick, Sheila. *Everyday Stalinism: Ordinary Life in Extraordinary Times. Soviet Russia in 1930s*. New York: Oxford University Press, 1999.

Foucault, Michel. *The Order of Things: An Archaeology of Human Sciences*. London: Tavistock Publications, 1970.

Fraser, Nancy. *Justice Interruptus: Critical Reflections on the 'Post-Socialist' Condition*. London: Routledge, 1997.

Freedman, Lawrence. "Ukraine and the Art of Limited War. Survival." *Global Politics and Strategy* 56 (2014): 7-38. https://doi.org/10.1080/0039638.2014.985432.

Gaidai, A. and A. V. Liubarets. "Leninfall: Elimination of the Past as a Way of Constructing the Future (on the Materials of Dnepropetrovsk, Zaporozhye and Kharkov)." *Perm University Herald* 2 (2016): 28-41.

Galeotti, Mark and Andrew S. Bowen. "Putin's Empire of the Mind." *Foreign Policy* (2014): 16-19.

Galz, Ference. "Backwardness, Nationalism and Historiography." *East European Quarterly* (1983): 31-42.

Gandhi, L. *Postcolonial Theory: A Critical Introduction*. New York: Columbia University Press, 1998.

Geertz, Clifford. *The Interpretation of Cultures*. New York: Basic Books, 1973.

Georgakopoulou, Alexandra. *Small Stories, Interaction and Identities*. Amsterdam: John Benjamins, 2007.

Gerard, Genette. *Narrative Discourse*. Oxford: Blackwell, 1990.

Gerasimov, Ilya and Marina Mogilner. "Deconstructing Integration: Ukraine's Postcolonial Subjectivity." *Slavic Review*. Cambridge University Press 74, no. 4 (2015): 715-722. https://doi.org/10.5612/slavicreview.74.4.715.

Gessen, Maria. "Powerlessness and Pretense." *New York: New York Times* (2013): 1-12.

Gilley, Christopher. "Laws 2558 and 2538: On Critical Inquiry, the Holocaust, and Academic Freedom in Ukraine." *Politychna Krytyka* (2015): 1-8.

Gilley, Christopher. "Painting Imperialism and Nationalism Red: The Ukrainian Marxist Critique of Russian Communist Rule in Ukraine 1918-1925." *Revolutionary Russia* 29, no. 1 (2016): 101-107.

Gills, Barry K. "Hegemonic Transitions in the World System: Accumulation and the Making of World Order." *Review* 15 (1994): 620-687.

Glatz, Ferenc. "Backwardness, Nationalism, Historiography." *East European Quarterly* (1993): 17-28.

Gobert, Sébastien. "Lenin's Tumble: The Iconoclasm of Ukraine's Decommunization." *The Odessa Review* (2017): 1-6. http://odessareview.com/lenins-tumble-iconoclasm-ukraines-decommunization/.

Gomza, Ivan and Nadiia Koval. "The Winter of Our Discontent: Emotions and Contentious Politics in Ukraine During Euromaidan." *Kyiv-Mohyla Law and Politics Journal* (2014): 39-62. https://doi: 0.18523/kmlpj52673.2015-1.39-62.

Gordesevych, Galyna. *Stepan Bandera: Ljudyna i Mif (Stepan Bandera: A Human and a Myth)*. Kyiv: Apriori, 2008.

Gramsci, Antonio. *Selections from the Prison Notebooks of Antonio Gramsci*. New York: International Publishers, 1971.

Gratza, Agnieszka. "Approaching the Brink: Manifesta 10 and the Standoff over Crimea." *PAJ: A Journal of Performance and Art* 38, no. 1 (2016): 71-78. https://doi. 10.1162/PAJJ_a_00297.

Grytsak, Yaroslav. *Strasti za Natsionalizmom. Istorychni Esseyi (The Passion for Nationalism. Historical Essays)*. Kyiv: Krytyka, 2004.

Gubrium, Jaber, and James A. Holstein. *Analyzing Narrative Reality*. London: SAGE, 2009.

Gudkov, Lev. "Russian Public Opinion in the Aftermath of the Ukrainian Crisis." *Russian Politics and Law* 53 (2015): 32-44.

Gunning, Dave. *Postcolonial Literature*. Edinburgh University Press, 2013.

Halbwachs, Maurice. *On Collective Memory.* The University of Chicago Press, 1992.

Hall, Stuart. "Race, Articulation and Societies Structured in Dominance." *Paris: Sociological Theories: Race and Colonialism* (1980): 305-345.

Hall, Stuart. *The West and the Rest: Discourse and power. Modernity: An Introduction to Modern Societies.* MA: Blackwell, 1996.

Halushka, Myroslava and Sébastien Gobert. *Looking for Lenin.* FUEL Design & Publishing, 2017.

Hammersley, Martyn and Paul Atkinson. "Ethnography and Participant Observation." *Strategies of Qualitative Inquiry* (1998): 1-14.

Hardt, Michael and Paolo Virno. *Multitude.* MA: The International Encyclopedia of Revolution, 2000.

Hartmond, Myroslava. "Godhead Dethroned: Leninfall as Collective Esoteric Practice." MU Editorial 2 (2016): 1-24. http://bit.ly/2yhwD5i.

Harvey, Don. *Spaces of Hope.* Berkley: University of California Press, 2000.

Hatherley, Owen. "Rewriting the Past: must Rhodes Fall?" *Apollo. The International Art Magazine* (2016): 1-7. https://www.apollo-magazine.com/rewriting-the-past-must-rhodes-fall/.

Herman, David. *Narratologies: New Perspectives on Narrative Analysis.* Ohio State University Press, 1999.

Hodkin, Katharine and Susannah Radstone. *Contested Pasts: The Politics of Memory.* London: Routledge, 2003.

Hofland, Christi Anne. *Institutions of Activism: Museums and Ukraine's Revolution of Dignity.* Seattle: University of Washington, 2015.

Holloway, John. *Change the World Without Taking Power.* London: Pluto, 2005.

Holms, Stephen. "The End of Decommunization." *Heinonline* (2004): 33-38.

Holquist, Michael and Vadim Liapunov. *Art and Answerability: Early Philosophical Essays by M.M.Bakhtin.* University of Texas Press: Austin, 1990.

Howe, Stephen. *Empire. A Very Short Introduction.* Oxford: OUP, 2002.

Himka, John Paul. "Legislating Historical Truth: Ukraine's Laws of 9 April of 2015."*Politics of Memory* (2015): 1-10.

Himka, John Paul. "The History behind the Regional Conflict in Ukraine." *Kritika: Explorations in Russian and Eurasian History.* Slavica Publishers 16, no. 1 (2015): 129-136. 10.1353/kri.2015.0008.

Himka, John Paul. "The Lviv Pogrom of 1941: The Germans, Ukrainian Nationalists, and the Carnival Crowd." *Canadian Slavonic Papers* 53 (2015): 209-243. https://doi.org.10.1080/00085006.2011.11092673.

Hitrova, Tetyana. "Discourse 'Decommunization' in a Public Plane of Contemporary Ukrainian Information Space." *International Letters of Social and Humanistic Sciences* (2016): 1-6.

Hirsch, Francine. *Empire of Nations: Ethnographic Knowledge and the Making of the Soviet Union.* London: Cornell University Press, 2005.

hooks. Bell. *Yearning: Race, Gender, and Cultural Politics*. Boston: South End Press, 1990.

Hrytsak, Yaroslav. "The Post-Colonial Is Not Enough." *Slavic Review* 4 (2015): 732-737.

Hurrell, Andrew. "Hegemony, liberalism and global order: What space for would-be great powers?" *International Affairs* 82, no. 1 (2006): 1–19.

Huntington, Samuel P. "Democracy's Third Wave." *Journal of Democracy* 2 (1991): 12-34.

Hutcheon, Linda. "Circling the Downspout of Empire: Post-Colonialism and Postmodernism." *Ariel: A Review of International Literature* 4 (1999): 149-175.

Hymes, Dell. *Ethnography, Linguistics, Narrative Inequality*. London: Taylor and Francis, 1996.

Inayatullah, Naeem and David L. Blaney. "Realizing Sovereignty." *Review of International Studies* 21, no. 1 (1995): 3-20. https://www.jstor.org/stable/20097393.

Ivanova, Olena. "Collective Memory of the Holocaust and National Identity of the Student Youth in Ukraine." *Danyliw International Seminar* (2007): 1-6.

Ishchenko, Volodymyr. "Far Right Participation in the Ukrainian Maidan Protests: An Attempt of Systematic Estimation." *Routledge* (2016): 1-21.

Ishchenko, Volodymyr. "Fighting Fences vs Fighting Monuments: Politics of Memory and Protest Mobilization in Ukraine." *Debatte: Journal of Contemporary Central and Eastern Europe* 19 (2011): 369-395. https://doi.org/10.1080/0965156X.2011.611680.

Isajiw, Wsevolod. *Society in Transition: Social Change in Ukraine in Western Perspectives*. Toronto: Canadian Scholars' Press, 2006.

Jakubanecs, Alexander, Magne Shupphelln and Helge Thorbjorsen. "Slavic Brothers or Rivals? Effects of Consumer Ethnocentrism on the Trade Between Ukraine and Russia." *Journal of East-West Business* (2005): 55-78.

Jeffrey, Bob and Geoff Troman. "Time for Ethnography. *BERJ: British Educational Research Journal* 30 (2013): 535-548. https://doi.org/10.1080/0141192042000237220.

Jorgensen, Marianne and Louise Phillips. *Discourse Analysis as Theory and Method*. NY: SAGE, 2002.

Jung, C. *Man and His Symbols*. London: Arkana, 1990.

Kadri, Liik and Andrew Wilson. "What Will Happen With Eastern Ukraine?" London: ECFR (2014): 1-18. http://bit.ly/2kNQofB.

Kadygrob, Volodymyr. *Euromaidan: History in the Making*. Kyiv: Osnovy Publishing, 2014.

Kakhidze, Alevtina. *Thinking Visually*. Kyiv: Installation. 2015.

Kalb, Don and Herman Tak. "Polish Floods: Clues for Civil Society and the State in Post-Communism." *Etnologia Europaea* 31 (2001): 63-74.

Kalb, Don. "Conversations with a Polish Populist: Tracing Hidden Histories of Globalization, Class, and Dispossession in Postsocialism (and Beyond)." *American Ethnologist* 36 (2009): 207-23.

Kalb, Don. "Theory from the East? Double Polarizations Versus Democratic Transitions." *Baltic Worlds* 3 (2015): 17-29.

Kalb, Don. "Trotsky Over Maus: Anthropological Theory and the October 1917 Commemoration." *Dialectical Anthropology* 42 (2018): 327-343.

Kangas, Anni. "From Interfaces to Interpretants: A Pragmatist Exploration Into Popular Culture as International Relations." *Sage Publications* (2012): 317-343.

Kangaspuro Markku and Jeremy Smith. *The Bolshevik Modernization Project: Modernization in Russia Since 1990*. Tampere: Studia Fennica Historica, 2006.

Kasraeims and Pouzesh Shirazi. "LACLAU and Mouffe's Discourse Theory as an Effective Tool for Understanding and Explaining Political Phenomenon." *Journal of Politics* (2009): 339-360.

Katchanovksy, Ivan. "Terrorists or National Heroes? Politics of the OUN and the UPA in Ukraine." *The Annual Conference of the Canadian Political Science Association* (2010): 1-14.

Kattago, Siobhan. "War Memorials and the Politics of Memory: The Soviet War Memorial in Tallinn." *Constellations* 16, no. 1 (2009): 150-166. https://doi.org/10.1111/j.1467-8675.2009.00525.x.

Kebede, AlemSeghed. "Grassroots Environmental Organizations in the United States: A Gramscian Analysis." *Sociological Inquiry* (2005): 12-32.

Kharkhordin, O. *The Collective and the Individual in Russia*. Berkeley: The University of California Press, 1999.

Knierbein, Sabine and Tihomir Viderman. *Public Space Urban Emancipation and the Post-Political Condition*. New York: Routledge, 2018.

Knoblauch, Hubert, Alejandro Baer, Eric Laurier, Sabine Petschke, and Bernt Schnettler. "Visual Analysis. New Developments in the Interpretative Analysis of Video and Photography." *Forum: Qualitative Social Research 9* (2008): 28-57.

Knorr, Klaus. *The Power of Nations: The Political Economy of International Relations*. NY: Basic Books, 1985.

Kolakowski, Leszek. "What Is Left of Socialism." *First Things: A Monthly Journal of Religion and Public Life* (2002): 42-54.

Kolsto, Pål. *Political Construction Sites. Nation-Building in Russia and the Post-Soviet States*. Boulder: Westview Press, 2000.

Kolsto, Pål and Helge Blakkisrud. *The New Russian Nationalism: Imperialism, Ethnicity and Authoritarianism 2000-2015*. Edinburgh: Edinburgh University Press, 2016.

Kopenkina, Olga. *Circling the Square: Maidan and Cultural Insurgency in Ukraine*. New York: Cicada Press, 2014.

Koronenko, Valerii. "Decommunization as a Legal or Political Assessment of the Consequences of the Communist Regime: Ukrainian Experience in General European Context." *The Journal of Eastern European Law* (2019): 1-19.

Korostelina, Karina. "War of Textbooks: History Education in Russia and Ukraine." *Communist and Post-Communist Studies* 43, no. 2 (2010): 129-137. https://doi.org/10.1016/j.postcomstud.2010.03.004.

Korostelina, Karina. "Mapping National Identity Narratives in Ukraine." *The Journal of Nationalism and* Ethnicity 41, no. 2 (2013): 293-315. https://doi.org.10.1080/00905992.2012.747498.

Korostelina, Karina. "Ukraine Twenty Years After Independence: Concept Models of the Society." *Communist and Post-Communist Studies* 46, no. 1 (2013): 53-64. https://www.jstor.org/stable/48610373.

Kotlyar, Yuriy. "Decommunization of Ukraine in the Context of Generation Change." *Central and Eastern European Online Library* (2017): 99-108.

Kozak, Nazar. "Art Embedded into Protest: Staging the Ukrainian Maidan." *Art Journal* 76, no. 1 (2017): 8-27.

Kozyrska, Antonina. "Decommunization of the Public Space in Post-Euromaidan Ukraine." *Central and East European Online Library* (2016): 130-144.

Krasko, Arianna. *Responsibility and Responsiveness in the State Governance: Case of Ukraine*. Univerzita Karlova, 2017.

Krasner, Stephen. *Problematic Sovereignty*. Columbia University Press, 2001.

Kravchuk, Leonid. *Ukrajina: Nova Epoha: 1991-2011 (Ukraine: The New Epoch: 1991-2011)*. Kyiv: KM Publishers, 2011.

Kuhn, M. and D. Weidemann. *Internationalization of the Social Sciences: Asia-Latin America-Middle East-Africa-Eurasia*. Bielfield, 2010.

Kulyk, Volodymyr. "National Identity in Ukraine: Impact of Euromaidan and the War." *Europe-Asia Studies* 68, no. 4 (2016): 588-608. https://doi.org/10.1080/09668136.1174980.

Kuromiya, Hiroaki. *Freedom and Terror in the Donbas: A Ukrainian-Russian Borderland, 1870s-1990s*. Cambridge: Cambridge University, 2003.

Kutkina, Anna. "To Europe 'via' Lenin?: The Fall of the Communist Statues in Ukraine." Politiikasta (2018): 1-8.

Kuzio, Taras. *Ukraine: State and Nation Building*. NY: Routledge, 2002.

Kuzio, Taras. "History, Memory and Nation-Building in the Post-Soviet Colonial Space." *Nationalities Papers* 30 (2002): 241-264. https://doi.org/ 10.1080/00905990220140649.

Kuzio, Taras. "Nation Building, History Writing and Competition Over the Legacy of Kyiv Rus in Ukraine." *Nationalities Papers* 33, no. 1 (2005): 29-58. https://doi.org/10.1080/00905990500053960.

Kuzio, Taras, and Marc Nordberg. "Nation and State Building, Historical Legacies and National Identities in Belarus and Ukraine: A Comparative Analysis." *Canadian Review of Studies in Nationalism* 26 (1999): 69-90.

Kuzio, Taras. *Ukraine: Perestroika to Independence*. New York: St. Martin's Press, 2000.

Kuznetsov, Anatoly. *Babi Yar: A Documentary Novel*. New York: Dell Publishing, 1987.

Kvit, Serhiy. "The Ideology of Euromaidan." *Social, Health, and Communication Studies Journal* 1 (2014): 27-40.

Kymlicka, Will. *Multicultural Citizenship: A Liberal Theory of Minority Rights.* Oxford: Oxford University Press, 1995.

Laclau, Ernesto. *Emancipation(s).* London: Verso, 1996.

Laclau, Ernesto. *On Populist Reason.* New York: Verso, 2005.

Laclau, Ernesto and Chantal Mouffe. *Hegemony and Socialist Strategy: Towards a Radical Democratic Politics.* London: Verso, 1985.

Lassiter, Luke Eric. "Collaborative Ethnography and Public Anthropology." *Current Anthropology* 46, no. 1 (2005): 83-106.

Lasswell, Harold D. *Politics: Who Gets What, When, How.* New York: McGraw Hill, 1936.

Lasswell, Harold D. and Nathan Leites. *Language of Politics: Studies in Quantitative Semantics.* Cambridge: The MIT Press, 1968.

Lefebvre, Henri. *The Production of Space.* Oxford: Blackwell Press, 1991.

Lenin, W. I. *What is to be Done?* London: Penguin, 1989.

Lewicki, Saunders, and D. M. Milton. *Essentials of Negotiation.* New York: McGraw-Hill/Irwin, 2007.

Lipset, Seymour Martin. "The State of American Sociology." *Sociological Forum* 9 (1994): 199-220.

Lisle, Debbie. *The Global Politics of Contemporary Travel Writing.* Cambridge University Press, 2006.

Liubarets, Andriy. "The Politics of Memory in Ukraine in 2014: Removal of the Soviet Cultural Legacy and Euromaidan Commemorations." *Kyiv-Mohyla Humanities Journal* 3 (2016): 197-214.

Loomba, Ania. "Early Modern or Early Colonial?" *Project Muse* 14 (2015): 143-148.

Loyko, Sergij. *Ad: Istorija Myzhnosti, Braterstva i Samopozhertvy (Hell: History of Courage, Brotherhood and Self-Sacrifice).* Kharkiv: Ukraine Crisis Media Center, 2016.

Lusebrink, H. and R. Reichardt. *The Bastille: A history of a Symbol of Despotism and Freedom.* Durham and London: Duke University Press, 1997.

Lytvyn, Mykola. *Proekt "Ykrajina": Galychyna v Ykrajinskij Revoljucii 1917-1921 (Project "Ukraine": Galychyna in the Ukrainian Revolution 1917-1921).* Kyiv: Folio, 2015.

Macdonald, Fiona. "The Man Who Turned Lenin into Darth Vader." *BBC Culture* (2015): 1-6.

Mack, Natasha, Cynthia Woodsong, Kathleen M. MacQueen, Greg Guest, and Emily Namey. *Qualitative Research Methods: A Data Collector's Field Guide*. Research Triangle Park: Family Health International, 2005.

Mackinnon, Catherine. *Only Words*. Cambridge: Harvard University Press, 1993.

Matsuzato, Kimitaka. *Russia and Its Northeast Asian Neighbours: China, Japan and Korea 1985-1945*. Washington: Lexington Books, 2017.

Malyarenko, Tetyana and Stefan Wolff. *The Dynamics of Emerging De-Facto States: Eastern Ukraine in the Post-Soviet Space*. Routledge, 2015.

Mankoff, Jeffrey. "Russia's Latest Land Grab. How Putin Won Crimea and Lost Ukraine." *Foreign Affairs* 93 (2014): 60-68.

Manning, P. "Metaphors of the Field: Varieties of Organizational Discourse." *Administrative Science Quarterly* 4 (1979): 660-671.

Marchart, Oliver. *Post-Foundational Political Thought*. Edinburgh: Edinburgh University Press, 2007.

Marples, David. "Stepan Bandera: The Resurrection of a Ukrainian National Hero." *Europe-Asia Studies* 58, no. 4 (2006): 555-566. https://doi.org/ 10.1080/09668130600652118.

Marples, David. "Volodymyr Viatrovych i Ykrajinski Dekomunizacijni Zakony (Volodymyr Viatrovych and the Ukrainian Decommunization Laws)." *Krytyka* (2015): 1-8.

Marples, David. "Russia's Perceptions of Ukraine: Euromaidan and Historical Conflicts." *European Politics and Society* 17 (2016): 424-437. https://doi.org/ 10.1080/23745118.2016.1154129.

Martin-Barbero, James. *Communication, Culture and Hegemony*. Newbury Park CA: Sage, 1993.

Marx, Karl. *Capital: A Critique of Political Economy*. Translated by B. Fowkes. New York: Anchor Books, 1977.

Massey, Doreen. *For Space*. London: SAGE Publications Ltd., 2005.

Massey, Doreen and Jess. "Places and Their Pasts." *History Workshop Journal* 39 (1995): 182-192. https://doi.org/10.2307/4289361.

Mayerchyk, Mariya. "Ukrainian Feminism at the Crossroad of National, Postcolonial, and (Post)Soviet: Theorizing the Maidan Events 2013-2014." *Roadbound University Press* (2015): 1-4.

Mcbride, Jared. "How Ukraine's New Memory Commissar Is Controlling the Nation's Past." *The Nation* (2015): 1-8.

Mcclintock, Anne. *Imperial Leather: Race, Gender, and Sexuality in the Colonial Context*. Routledge, 1995.

Mcdowell,, Daragh. "Ukraine after the Euromaidan: Challenges and Hopes." *International Affairs* 3 (2015): 653-665.

McGowan, T. *The End of Dissatisfaction: Jacques Lacan and the Emerging Society of Enjoyment*. NY: Suny, 2004.

McGlynn, Jade. "Historical framing of the Ukraine Crisis through the Great Patriotic War: Performativity, Cultural Consciousness and Shared Remembering." *SAGE Journals* (2018): 1-17. https://doi.org/10.1177/1750698018800740.

McKee, Yates. *Strike Art: Contemporary Art and the Post-Occupy Condition*. New York: Verso, 2011.

Michalski, Sergiusz. *Public Monuments: Art in Political Bondage 1870-1997*. London Reaktion Books, 1998.

Michnik, Adam. *The Church and the Left*. University of Chicago Press, 1993.

Minakov, Mikhail. "Utopian Images of the West and Russia among Supporters and Opponents of the Euromaidan." *Russian Politics and Law* 53, no. 3 (2015): 68-85. https://doi.org/ 10.1080/10611940.2015.1053785.

Mink, Louis. *Historical Understanding*. Ithaca and London: Cornell University Press, 1997.

Mirzoeff, Nicholas. *An Introduction to Visual Culture*. London: Routledge, 1999.

Mitchell, Katharyne. "Monuments, Memorials, and the Politics of Memory." *Urban Geography* 24, no. 5 (2013): 442-459. https://doi.org/10.2747/0272-3638.24.5.442.

Mitchell, Timothy. "The Stage of Modernity." *Questions of Modernity* (2000): 1-34.

Mitchell, William J. *The Reconfigured Eye: Visual Truth in Post-Photographic Era*. The MIT Press: Cambridge, 1994.

Mitrokhin, N. "Infiltration, Instruction, Invasion: Russia's War in the Donbas." *Journal of Soviet and Post-Soviet Politics and Society* 1 (2015): 219-250.

Modelski, George and David Wilkinson. "Hegemony and Social Change." *International Studies Association* (2005): 1-17.

Mogilner, Marina and Ilya Gerasimov. "Deconstructing Integration: Ukraine's Postcolonial Subjectivity." *Slavic Review* 74, no. 4 (2015): 715-722. https://doi.org/10.5612/slavicreview.74.4715.

Moliar, Evgenia. Transformacii Publichnogo Mystectva: Radyanske Ta Suchasne (Transformation of Public Art: The Soviet and Modern). Kyiv: *Reporter*, 2016.

Morozov, Viatcheslav. *Russia's Postcolonial Identity. A Subaltern Empire in an Eurocentric World*. New York: Palgrave Macmillan, 2015.

Motyl, Alexander. *Thinking Theoretically about Soviet Nationalities: History and Comparison in the Study of the USSR*. New York: Columbia University Press, 1992.

Motyl, Alexander. "Facing the Past: In Defense of Ukraine's New Laws." *World Affairs* 178, no. 3 (2015): 58-66. https://jstor.org/stable/24888116.

Motyl, Alexander. "Ukraine, Europe, and Bandera." *Cicero Foundation Great Debate Paper* 10, no. 5 (2010): 11-14.

Moore, David. "Is the Post-in Postcolonial the post- in Post-Soviet? Toward a Global Postcolonial Critique." *Special Topic: Globalizing Literary Studies* 116, no. 1 (2001): 111-128. https://www.jstore.org.stable/463645.

Mrozik, Agnieszka and Stanislav Holubec. "Historical Memory of Central and East European Communism." *Routledge* (2015): 1-12.

Mutch, Alistair. "Critical Realism, Agency and Discourse: Moving the Debate Forward." *Organization* 12, no. 5 (2005): 781-786. https://doi.org/10.1177/130508405055948.

Munchmeyer, Tobias. "Kiev Dialogue." *Prostory* (2015): 25-26.

Munslow, Alun. *Narrative and History*. Basingstoke and New York: Palgrave, 2007.

Mullaney, Julie. *Postcolonial Literatures in Context*. New York: Continuum International Publishing Group, 2010.

Musliu, Vjosa and Olga Burlyuk. "Imagining Ukraine: From History and Myths to Maidan Protests." *East European Politics and Societies: and Cultures* 33, no. 3 (2019): 631-655. https://doi.org/10.1177/0888325418821410.

Nakonechna, Lada. "Blind Spots." *Prostory* (2014): 1-7.

Narvselius, Eleonora. "The "Bandera Debate": The Contentious Legacy of World War II and Liberalization of Collective Memory in Western Ukraine." *Canadian Slavonic Papers* 54, no. 3-4 (2015): 469-490. https://doi.org/10.1080/00085006.2012.1192718.

Neyland, Daniel. *Organizational Ethnography*. London: SAGE Publications Ltd., 2008.

Nikolayev, Alexander. *International Negotiations, Theory, Practice, and the Communication With Domestic Politics*. UK: Roman and Littlefield Publishers, 2018.

Nora, Pierre and David Jordan. *Rethinking France: Les Lieux de Mémoire*. Chicago: Chicago University Press, 2004.

Nuzov, Ilya. "The Dynamics of Collective Memory in the Ukraine Crisis: A Transitional Justice Perspective." *International Journal of Transitional Justice* 11, no. 1 (2016): 132-153. https://doi.org/10.1093/ijtj/ijw025.

Ochman, Ewa. "Soviet War Memorials and the Re-construction of National and Local Identities in Post-communist Poland." *The Journal of Nationalism and Ethnicity* 38, no. 4 (2010): 509-530. https://doi.org/10.1080/00905992.2010.482130.

Ochs, Elinor and Lisa Capps. *Living Narrative. Creating Lives in Everyday Storytelling*. Cambridge: Harvard University Press, 2001.

Onuch, Olga. "EuroMaidan Protests in Ukraine: Social Media versus Social Networks." *Problems of Post-Communism* 62, no. 4 (2015): 217-235. https://doi.org/ 10.1080/10758216.2015.1037676.

Oliinyk, Anna and Taras Kuzio. "The Euromaidan Revolution, Reforms and Decommunization in Ukraine." *Europe-Asia Studies* 73, no. 5 (2021): 807-836. https://doi.org/10.1080/09668136.2020.1862060.

Olsavsky, Bohdan. *Pereselentsi: Ljudy Jaki Ne Zagubyly Sebe (The Displaced Persons: People Who Have Not Lost Themselves)*. Kyiv: Discourse Publishers, 2016.

Overbeek, Henk. "Hegemony and Social Change." *The Forum* (2019): 368-270.

Palonen, Emilia. "The city-text in post-communist Budapest: Street Names, Memorials and the Politics of Commemoration." *GeoJournal* 73, no. 3 (2008): 219-230. https://doi.org/10.1007/s10708-008-9204-2.

Palonen, Emilia. "Political Polarisation and Populism in Contemporary Hungary." *Parliamentary Affairs* 62, no. 2 (2009): 318-334. https://doi.org/10.1093/pa/gsn048.

Palonen, Emilia. "Millennial Politics of architecture: myths and Nationhood in Budapest." *The Journal of Nationalism and Ethnicity* 41, no. 4 (2013): 536-551. https://doi.org/10.1080/00905992.2012.743509.

Paic, Zarko and Kresimir Purgar. *Theorizing Images*. UK: Cambridge Scholars Publishing, 2016.

Panizza, Francisco, and Romina Miorelli. "Taking Discourse Seriously: Discursive Institutionalism and Post-Structuralist Discourse Theory." *Sage Journals: Political Studies Association* 61, no. 2 (2012): 301-318. https://doi.org/10.1111/j.1467-9248.2021.00967.x.

Parry, Benita. *Problems and Current Theories of Colonial Discourse. Postcolonial Studies: A Materialist Critique.* London: Routledge, 2004.

Pearson, Raymond. *The Rise and Fall of the Soviet Empire.* London: Palgrave, 1997.

Peters, Michael A. *Postructuralism, Marxism, and Neoliberalism: Between Theory and Politics.* Boston: Rowman and Littlefield Publishers, 2001.

Petro, Nicolai. "The Real War in Ukraine: The Battle Over Ukrainian Identity." *The National Interest* (2014): 1-8. https://nationalinterest.org/feature/the-real-war-ukraine-the-battle-over-ukrainian-identity-11782.

Phillips, Nelson and Cynthia Hardy. *Discourse Analysis: Investigating Processes of Social Construction.* Sage University Paper, 2002.

Pirie, Paul S. "National Identity and Politics in Southern and Eastern Ukraine." *Europe-Asia Studies* 48, no. 7 (1996): 1079-1104. https://slavistik-portal.de/datenpool/ebsees-db.html?data=48889.

Plakhotnik, Oleh. "Issues of Preventive and Alternative Measures Application in the Criminal Procedure of Ukraine." *The Journal of Eastern European Law* (2016): 104-118.

Pollak, Martin. *Tsezar Ameryky: Velyka Vtecha z Galychyny* (*The Cesar of the United States: Big Escape from Galychyna*). Meridian Czernowitz, 2014.

Popova, Maria. "Why the Orange Revolution Was Short and Peaceful and Euromaidan Long and Violent." *Taylor and Francis Online* 61, no. 6 (2015): 64-70.

Portnov, Andriy. "On Decommunization, Identity, and Legislating History, From a Slightly Different Angle." *Krytyka* (2015): 1-4.

Portnov, Andriy. "How to Bid Goodbye to Lenin in Ukraine." *Krytyka* (2016): 1-7.

Portnov, Andriy. "On Decommunization, Identity, and Legislating History, from a Slightly Different Angle." *Krytyka* (2017): 1-5.

Posivnych, Mykola. *Stepan Bandera...Koly Odyn Skazhe: Slava Ykrajini* (*Stepan Bandera...When One Says: Glory to Ukraine*). Kyiv: Discursus, 2015.

Prozorov, Sergej. *The Ethics of Post-Communism.* Basingstoke: Palgrave, 2009.

Purgar, Krešimir. *W. J. T. Mitchell's Image Theory.* London: Routledge, 2017.

Pushnova, Tetiana. *Evromaidan Ochyma TSN (Euromaidan by the Eyes of TSN)*. Kyiv: Osnovy Publishers, 2014.

Pytlas, Bartek. *Radical Right Parties in Central and Eastern Europe: Mainstream Party Competition and Electoral Fortune*. Abingdon: Routledge, 2015.

Rao, Nagesh. *"Neocolonialism" or "Globalization"?: Postcolonial Theory and the Demands of Political Economy*. USA: Penn State University Press, 2014.

Radchenko, Yuri, "Demythologizing Bandera: Towards a Scholarly History of the Ukrainian Nationalist Movement." *Journal of Soviet and Post-Soviet Politics and Society* 1 (2015): 411-420.

Radchenko, Yuri. "Accomplices to Extermination: Municipal Government and the Holocaust in Kharkiv, 1941-1942." *Holocaust and Genocide Studies* 27, no. 3 (2013): 443-463. https://doi.org/10.1093/hgs/dct054.

Radcliffe, Sarah and Sallie Westwood. *Remaking the Nation*. Routledge, 1996.

Rapkin, David P. "Empire and its discontents." *New Political Economy* 10 (2005): 393-261.

Rear, David and Johns. "Laclau and Mouffe's Discourse Theory and Fairclough's Critical Discourse Analysis: An Introduction and Comparison." *Critical Political Studies*. 4 (2013): 1-28.

Rermnick, Daniel. *Lenin's Tomb. The Last Days of the Soviet Empire*. New York: Vintage, 1994.

Remy, Johannes. "The Valuev Circular and Censorship of Ukrainian Publications in the Russian Empire (1863-1876): Intention and Practice." *Canadian Slavonic Papers* 46, no. 1/2 (2007): 87-110. https://www.jstor.org/stable/40871165.

Ricoeur, Paul. *Time and Narrative*. Chicago: The University of Chicago Press, 1994.

Robinson, Andrew. "Bakhtin: Diology, Polyphony and Heteroglossia." *Ceasefire* (2011): 1-10. https://ceasefiremagazine.co.uk/in-theory-bakhtin-1/.

Robinson, Fiona. *The Ethics of Care: The Feminist Approach to Human Security*. Temple University Press, 2011.

Robinson, Paul. "Russia's Role in the War in Donbass, and the Threat to European Security." *European Politics and Society* 17, no. 4 (2016): 506-521. https://doi.org/ 10.1080/23745118.2016.1154229.

Rose-Redwood, Reuben, Derek Alderman, and Maoz Azaryahu. *The Political Life of Urban Streetscapes: Naming, Politics, and Place*. New York: Routledge, 2018.

Rossolinski-Liebe, Grzegorz. *Stepan Bandera: The Life and Afterlife of a Ukrainian Nationalist: Fascism, Genocide, and Cult*. Stuttgart: Ibidem Press, 2014.

Rotberg, Robert. *When States Fail: Causes and Consequences*. New Jersey: Princeton University Press, 2003.

Rozycki, Bartlomiej. "Renaming Urban Toponymy as a Mean of Redefining Local Identity: The Case of Street Decommunization in Poland." *Open Political Science* 1 (2018): 20-31. https://doi.org/10.1515/openps-2017-0004.

Rubchak, M. *Women in Russia and Ukraine*. Cambridge University Press, 1996.

Rudling, Anders and Christopher Gilley. "Laws 2538-1: On Critical Inquiry, the Holocaust and Academic Freedom in Ukraine." *Politychna Krytyka:* (2015): 1-10.

Ryabchuk, Anastasia, "Right Revolution? Hopes and Perils of the Euromaidan Protests." *Debate: Journal of Contemporary Central and Eastern Europe* 22, no. 1 (2014): 127-134. https://doi.org/10.1080/0965156X.2013.877268.

Ryabchuk, Mykola. "The Ukrainian Friday and Russian Robinson. The Uneasy Advent of Post-Coloniality." *Canadian-American Slavic Studies* 44 (2010): 7-42.

Said, Edward. *Culture and Imperialism*. New York: Vintage Books, 1993.

Said, Edward. *Orientalism*. New York: Vintage Books, 1979.

Sakwa, Richard. *Frontline Ukraine: Crisis in the Borderlands*. London: I.B. Tauris, 2016.

Sanford, Levinson. *Written in Stone: Public Monuments in Changing Societies*. Durham: Duke University Press, 1998.

San-Marino, Ruslan. *Probudzhennya: Pro Revoljuciyu z Pershyh Vyst* (*The Awakening: About the Revolution Firsthand*). KM-Buks, 2015.

Saryusz-Wolski, Jacek. "Euromaidan: Time to Draw Conclusions." *European View*. 13, no. 1 (2014): 11-20. https:// doi.org/10.1007/s12290-014-0290-x.

Sassoon, Anne. *Gramsci's Politics*. New York: St Martin's, 1980.

Savchenko, Nadia. *Sylne Im'ja Nadia* (*Strong Name Nadia*). Kyiv: Ustinian, 2015.

Schopflin, Gyorgy. *Politics in Eastern Europe*. Cambridge: Blackwell Publishers, 1993.

Searle, John. *The Construction of Social Reality*. New York: Free Press, 1955.

Semchenko, Maria. *Perfunctory Decommunization*. Kyiv: Day Kyiv, 2015.

Senel, Nese. "A Postcolonial Reading of Wide Sargasso Sea by Jean Rhys." *Journal of Language and Literature Education* 11 (2014): 38-45.

Sereda, Viktoriya. "Ukraine after Euromaidan: What Difference Does a Revolution Make?" *Atlantic Council* (2015): 1-12.

Shapoval, Yuri. "On Ukrainian Separatism: A GPU Circular of 1926." *Harvard Ukrainian Studies* (2001): 14-38.

Shekhovtsov, Anton and Andreas Umland. "The Maidan and Beyond: Ukraine's Radical Right." *Journal of Democracy. John Hopkins University Press* 25, no. 3 (2014): 58-63.

Shevel, Oksana. *Decommunization in Post-Euromaidan Ukraine: Law and Practice*. UK: Ponars Eurasia, 2015.

Shevel, Oksana. "The Battle for Historical Memory in Post-Revolutionary Ukraine." *University of California Press: Current History* 115, no. 783 (2016): 258-263. https://doi.org/10.1525/curh.2016.115.783.258.

Shipenkov, Maxim and Natasha Pelevina. "The Fight to Survive. *FP Argument*. 1-6.

Shkandrij, Myroslav. *Russia and Ukraine: Literature and the Discourse of Empire from Napoleonic to Postcolonial Times*. McGill Queen's University Press, 2001.

Short, John R. *Imagined Country: Environment, Culture and Society*. Syracuse University Press, 1991.

Shveda, Yuriy. "Ukraine's Revolution of Dignity: The Dynamics of Euromaidan." *Journal of Eurasian Studies* 7, no. 1 (2016): 85-91. https://doi.org/10.1016/j.euras.2015.10.007.

Signh, Amrijit, and Peter Schmidt. *Postcolonial Theory and the United States: Race, Ethnicity, and Literature*. Jackson. University of Mississippi Press, 2000.

Simon, R. *Gramsci's Political Thought*. London: Lawrence and Wishart, 1982.

Slack, Frances and Jennifer Rowley. "Conducting a Literature Review." *Management Research News* 27, no. 6 (2004): 31-39.

Smith, Anthony D. *Nations and Nationalism in a Global Era*. Cambridge: Polity Press, 1996.

Smith, Anthony D. "Towards Global Culture?" *Theory, Culture and Society* 7, no. 2-3 (1990): 171-191. https://doi.org/10.1177/026327690000 7002011.

Smith, Laurajana. *Uses of Heritage*. New York: Routledge, 2006.

Snyder, Timothy. "Holocaust: the Ignored Reality." *The New York Review* (2009): 1-8.

Snyder, Timothy. "The Form: Bloodlands as European History." *The New York Review* (2008): 149-168.

Snyder, Timothy. *Integration and Disintegration: Europe, Ukraine, and the World*. Cambridge University Press, 2015.

Snyder, Timothy. "Integration and Disintegration: Ukraine, Europe, and the World." *Slavic Review* 74, no. 4 (2015): 695-707. https://doi.org/10.5612/slavicreview.74.4.695.

Solchanyk, Roman. "The Politics of State-building: Centre-periphery Relations in Post-Soviet Ukraine." *Europe-Asia Studies* 46, no. 1 (1994): 47-68. https://doi.org/ 10.1080/09668139408412149.

Solzhenitsyn, Aleksandr. Rebuilding Russia. *Reflections and Tentative Proposals*. New York: Harpers Collin, 1991.

Soroka, George. *Ukraine After Maidan: Revisiting Domestic and Regional Security*. Ibidem-Verlag, 2018.

Spengler, Oswald. *The Decline of the West: Perspectives of World History*. New York: Knopf, 1922.

Spicer, David and H. Eddy. "Soft Power" and the Negotiation of Legitimacy: Collective Meaning Making in a Teacher Team." *Mind, Culture, and Activity* 2 (2001): 150-169.

Spivak, Gayatri Chakravorty. *A Critique of Postcolonial Reason: Toward the History of the Vanishing Present*. Harvard University Press, 1999.

Spry, Tami. "Performative Autoethnography: An Embodied Methodological Praxis." *Qualitative Inquiry* 7, no. 6 (2001): 706-732. https://doi.org/10.1177/107780040100700605.

Stan, Lavinia. *Transitional Justice in Eastern Europe and the Former Soviet Union: Reckoning with the Communist Past*. London: Routledge, 2009.

Statiev, Alexander. "The Soviet Counterinsurgency in the Western Borderlands." *Cambridge: CUP* (2010): 124-130.

Stavrakakis, Yannis. *Lacan and the Political*. London: Routledge, 1999.

Stepanenko, Viktor and Yaroslav Pylynskyi. *Ukraine after the Euromaidan: Challenges and Hopes*. Switzerland: Peter Lang, 2015.

Stoddart, Mark. "Ideology, Hegemony, Discourse: A Critical Review of Theories of Knowledge and Power." *Social Thought and Research* 28 (2007): 191-225.

Subtelny, Orest. *Ukraine: A History.* London: University of Toronto Press. 2009.

Sviatnenko, Sviatoslav and Alexander Vinogradov. "Euromaidan Values from a Comparative Perspective." *Social, Health, and Communication Studies Journal* 1, no. 1 (2014): 41-61.

Swanstrom, Niklas, and Mikael Weissmann. *Conflict, Conflict Preservation, Conflict Management and Beyond: A Conceptual Exploration.* Washington, DC: Central Asia-Caucasus Institute, 2015.

Szeptycki, Andrzej. "Ukraine as a Postcolonial State?" *The Polish Quarterly of International Affairs* (2011): 5-29.

Szmagalska-Follis, Karolina. "Repossession: Notes on Restoration and Redemption in Ukraine's Western Borderland." *Cultural Anthropology* 23, no. 2 (2008): 329-360. https://doi.org/10.1111/j.1548-1360.2008.0011.x.

Tarifa, Fatos and Jay Weinstein. "Overcoming the Past: De-communization and Reconstruction of Post-communist Societies." *Studies in Comparative International Development* 30 (1995): 63-77.

Taylor, Charles. "Multi-Paradigmatic Research Design Spaces for Cultural Studies Researchers Embodying Postcolonial Theorising. *Cultural Studies of Science Education* 3, no. 4 (2008): 881-891. https://doi.org/10.1007/s11422-008-9140-y.

Tolochko, P. *Davna Istoriya Ukrayiny (Old History of Ukraine).* Kyiv: Lybid, 1994.

Tonyk, Antos. *Lisovi Khloptsi: Proza pro UPA (Forest Guys: Prose of UPA).* Discursus, 2014.

Tooze, Roger. *The Progress of International Functionalism.* UK: Cambridge University Press, 2014.

Torfing, Jacob. *New Theories of Discourse: Laclau, Mouffe and Zizek.* USA: Blackwell Publishers, 1999.

Tornquist-Plewa, Barbara and Yuliya Yurchuk. "Memory politics in contemporary Ukraine: Reflections from the postcolonial perspective." *SAGE Journals* 12, no. 6 (2017): 669-720. https://doi.org/10.1177/1750698017727806.

Trotsky, Leon. *Permanent Revolution and Results and Prospects.* New York: Pathfinder, 1969.

Trubina, Elena. "Street Art in Non-Capital Urban Centres: Between Exploiting Commercial Appeal and Expressing Social Concerns." *Cultural Studies* 32, no. 5 (2018): 676-703. https://doi.org/10.1080/09502386.2018.1429002.

Trubina, Elena. "Past Wars in the Russian Blogosphere: On the Emergence of Cosmopolitan Memory." *Digital Icons: Studies in Russian, Eurasian and Central European New Media* (2010): 63-85.

Tsyganov, Andrei. *Russophobia. Anti-Russian Lobby and American Foreign Policy*. New York: Palgrave McMillan, 2009.

Tumarkin, Nina. *Lenin Lives! The Lenin Cult in Soviet Russia*. Cambridge: Harvard University Press, 1997.

Tuminez, Astrid. *Russian Nationalism Since 1856: Ideology and the Making of Foreign Policy*. Oxford: Rowman and Littlefield Publishers, 2000.

Turnbull, Nick. "Political Rhetoric and Its Relationship to Context: a New Theory of the Rhetorical Situation, the Rhetorical and the Political." *Critical Discourse Studies* 14, no. 2 (2017): 115-131. https://doi.org/10.1080/17405904.2016.1268186.

Tyshchenko, Igor. "A Return to Public Space." *Urban Studies* 3 (2017): 1-12.

Ulam, Adam B. *Lenin and the Bolsheviks: The Intellectual and Political History of the Triumph of Communism in Russia*. London: Fontana/Collins, 1969.

Usenko, Natalia. "Political Issues in Contemporary Art of Ukraine." *The Journal of Education Culture and Society* 5, no. 2 (2020): 180-192. https://doi.org/10.15503/jecs20142.180.192.

Venediktova, I. "Consolidation of Regulatory Provisions of the Civil Code of Ukraine on Protected by Law Interests." *Heinonline* (2014): 80-91.

Verdery, Katherine. *What Was Socialism and What Comes Next?* Princeton: Princeton University Press, 1996.

Verdery, Katherine. *The Political Lives of Dead Bodies: Reburial and Postsocialist Change*. New York: Columbia University Press, 1999.

Viatrovych, Volodymyr. "Volodymyr Viatrovych: Real and Fictional History in Ukraine's Archives." Kyiv Post (2016): 1-5. https://www.kyivpost.com/article/opinion/op-ed/volodymyr-viatrovych-real-and-fictional-history-in-ukraines-archives-413382.html.

Vogel, David. "The Globalization of Business Ethics: Why America Remains Distinctive." *SAGE Journals* 35, no. 1 (1992): 30-49. https://doi.org/10.2307/41166711.

Voloshinov, V. N. *Marxism and the Philosophy of Language*. Harvard University Press, 1986.

Vorona, V. and Mykola Shulga. *Ukrains'ke Suspilstvo 1992-2010 (The Ukrainian Society 1992: 2010)*. Ukraine: Social Monitoring Society, 2010.

Vynnychuk, Yuri. *Legendy Lvova*. Kyiv: Folio, 2014.

Warner, Marina. *Monuments and Maidens: The Allegory of the Female Form*. University of California Press, 2001.

Weeks, Harry. "Re-cognizing the Post-Soviet Condition: the Documentary Turn in Contemporary Art in the Baltic States." *Studies in Eastern European Cinema* 1, no. 1 (2014): 57-70. https://doi.org/10.1386/seec.1.1.57/1.

Weiner, Amir. "In the Long Shadow of War: The Second World War and the Soviet and Post-Soviet World." *Diplomatic History* 25, no. 3 (2001): 443-456. https://www.jstor.org/stable/24914127.

Welsh, Helga A. "Dealing with the Communist Past: Central and East European Experiences after 1996." *Europe-Asia Studies* 48 (2007): 413-428.

Westdal, Christopher and Jeremy Kinsman. "On the Edge of Peace or Catastrophe in Ukraine." *IPolitics* (2015): 1-3. https://ipolitics.ca/2015/03/02/on-the-edge-of-peace-or-catastrophe-in-ukraine/.

Whittle, Andrea. "Preaching and Practicing 'Flexibility': Implications for Theories of Subjectivity at Work." *Human Relations* 58, no. 10 (2005): 1301-1322. https://10.1177/0018726705059859.

Williams, James. *Understanding Poststructuralism*. London: Routledge, 2014.

Williams, Patrick, and Laura Chrisman. *Colonial Discourse and Post-Colonial Theory: A Reader*. New York: Columbia UP, 1994.

Williams, Raymond. *Marxism and Literature*. New York: Oxford University Press, 1977.

Wilson, Andrew. *Ukraine Crisis: What It Means for the West*. New Heaven: Yale University Press, 2014.

Wilson, Andrew. *Ukrainian Politics Since Independence*. UCL Press, 2015.

Winter, Tim. "Clarifying the Critical in Critical Heritage Studies." *International Journal of Heritage Studies* 19, no. 6 (2013): 532-545. https://doi.org/10.1080/13527258.2012.720997.

Wise, Andrew Kier. "Postcolonial Anxiety in Polish Nationalist Rhetoric." *University of Illinois Press* 55, no. 3 (2010): 285-304. https://www.jstor.org/stable/25779884.

Woll, Alexander and Harald Wydra. *Democracy and Myth in Russia and Eastern Europe*. London: Routledge, 2008.

Wydra, Harald. *Communism and the Emergence of Democracy*. Cambridge: Cambridge University Press, 2007.

Wydra, Harald. "The Power of Symbols—Communism and Beyond." *International Journal of Politics, Culture and Society* 25, no. 1-3 (2011): 1-18. https://doi.org/10.1007/s10767-001-9116-x.

Yakovenko, Natalia. *Ukrainian Nobility from the End of 14th to the Mid of 17th Century*. Kyiv: Krytyka, 2008.

Yanevskij, Danylo. *Proekt-Ykrajina* (*Project-Ukraine*). Kyiv: Folio, 2015.

Yekelchyk, Serhy. *The Conflict in Ukraine: What Everyone Needs to Know*. NY: Oxford University Press, 2015.

Yurchak, Alexei. "Suspending the Political: Late Soviet Artistic Experiments on the Margins of the State." *Duke University Press: Poetics Today* 29, no. 4 (2008): 713-733. https://doi.org/10.1215/03335372-082.

Yurchuk, Yulia. "Reclaiming the Past, Confronting the Past: OUN-UPA Memory Politics and Nation Building in Ukraine (1991-2016)." In *War and Memory in Russia, Ukraine and Belarus*, edited by Julie Fedor, Markku Kangaspuro, Jussi Lassila and Tatiana Zhurzhenko, 107-137. Palgrave Macmillan Memory Studies, 2017.

Zelinska, Olga. "Ukrainian Euromaidan Protest: Dynamics, Causes, and Aftermath." *Sociology Compass* 11, no. 3 (2017): 1-12. https:doi.org/10.1111/soc4.12502.

Zhurzhenko, Tatiana. "The Myth of Two Ukraines: A Commentary on Mykola Riabchuk's "Ukraine: One State, Two Countires?" *Eurozone* (2002): 1-7.

Zhurzhenko, Tatiana. *Borderlands into Bordered Lands: Geopolitics of Identity in Post-Soviet Ukraine*. Stuttgart: Ibidem-Verlag, 2010.

Zhurzhenko, Tatiana. "A Divided Nation? Reconsidering the Role of Identity Politics in the Ukraine Crisis." *Berliner Wissenschafts-Verlag* 89, no. 1/2 (2014): 249-267. https://www.jstor.org/stable/24868495.

Zhurzhenko, Tatiana. "From Borderlands to Bloodlands." *Eurozine* (2014): 1-12.

Žižek, Slavoj. *The Sublime Object of Ideology*. London. Verso, 1989.

Žižek, Slavoj. *Ethics of the Real: Kand, Lacan*. London: Veros, 2000.

APPENDIX

List of Illustrations

Figure 1: "Stalin's Monument" 231
Figure 2: "Unified Country"/"Єдина країна/Единая страна" 231
Figure 3: "I love Ukraine"/"Я люблю Україну" 232
Figure 4: "Ukraine is not Russia!"/"Україна не Россія" 232
Figure 5: "We are the brotherhood with Russians blood-wise, butare never as brotherly-slavery, Sevastopolian"/"Мы с русскими по крови--братство, но никогда — по братству рабства-Севастополец" 233
Figure 6: "Go home!" 233
Figure 7: "No to War!"/"Нет войне!" 234
Figure 8: "No to War!"/"Нет войне!" 234
Figure 9: "Brothers?" 235
Figure 10: "Human Rights"/"Права людини" 235
Figure 11: "Love Russians despise Putin"/"Любим русских презираем Путина" 236
Figure 12: "People, think"/"Люди, задумайтесь" 236
Figure 13: "We need a Ukrainian President. PS: A Banderovite"/"Нам потрібний президент українець. ПС: Бандерівець" 237
Figure 14: "To Europe without Yalynkovych!"/"В Європу без Ялинковича!" 237
Figure 15: "The Communist party"/"Компартия" 238
Figure 16: The "Strike Poster" exhibition 238
Figure 17: "Я крапля в океані"/"I am a drop in the ocean"/The "Strike Poster" 239
Figure 18: "Euromaidan is the best thing that could have happened to Ukraine"/"Евромайдан- лучшее, что могло случиться с Украиной"/The "Strike Poster" 239

Figure 19: "The Yanukovych Nose"/"Ніс Януковича"/The "Strike Poster" 240
Figure 20: "We are being beaten at our own expense"/"Нас бьют за наши деньги"/ The "Strike Poster" 240
Figure 21: "We do not need such hockey"/"Такой хоккей нам не нужен"/The "Strike Poster" 241
Figure 22: "Imagine – there is no Putin"/The "Strike Poster"/The "Strike Poster" 241
Figure 23: "Constitution of Ukraine (Article 5): The only source of power in Ukraine are the people"/"Коституція України стаття 5: Єдиним джерелом влади в Україні є народ"/The "Strike Poster" 242
Figure 24: "Shame for the entire world"/"Сором на весь світ"/The "Strike Poster" 242
Figure 25: "I am responsible for what is going to happen tomorrow"/"Я відповідаю за те, що буде завтра"/The "Strike Poster" 243
Figure 26: "The Ukrainian nightmare"/The "Strike Poster" 243
Figure 27: "This is Not for Europe, But: For the future of our kids...for roads without pits...This is not for Europe but for medicine in the hospitals; This is not for Europe but for courts without bribes; This is not for Europe but against bribes in the kindergartens; This is not for Europe but for police without bribes; This is not against Russia but against the corrupt state authorities"/The "Strike Poster" 244
Figure 28: "Changing the country. We apologize for the inconvenience"/"Змінюємо країну. Перепрошуємо за незручності"/The "Strike Poster" 244
Figure 29: "March 2014"/The "Strike Poster" 245
Figure 30: "The Leninfall"/"Ленінопад"/The "Strike Poster". 245
Figure 31: Petrov, Egor. "I am a drop in the ocean" 246
Figure 32: Petrov, Egor. "I am a drop in the ocean" 246
Figure 33: Petrov, Egor. "I am a drop in the ocean" 247
Figure 34: Petrov, Egor. "I am a drop in the ocean" 247

Figure 35: Petrov, Egor. "I am a drop in the ocean. Art making the revolution"/"Я- крапля в океані. Мистецтво робить революцію" 248
Figure 36: Petrov, Egor. "I am a drop in the ocean" 248
Figure 37: Petrov, Egor. "I am a drop in the ocean" 249
Figure 38: "Obtained dignity – Let us protect the state!"/"Здобули гідність-- захистимо державу!" 249
Figure 39: "Friend! Have you signed up for the National Guard of Ukraine?"/"Друже! Ти записався до Національної гвардії України?" 250
Figure 40: "Heroes do not die!"/"Герої не вмирають!" 250
Figure 41: "60 000 of the best patriots have already signed the contract. Become the best!"/"60 000 найкращих патріотів вже підписали контракт. Стань найкращим!" 251
Figure 42: "National Guard of Ukraine: The service by the contract and the call of the heart -Serhij Shkabadura, the Printer"/"Національна Гвардія України: Служба за контрактом та покликом серця -Сергій Шкабадура, Друкар" 251
Figure 43: "Obtained the eternal life in a fight"/"Здобув вічне життя в бою" 252
Figure 44: "Army! Language! Faith! We are walking our own path! We are Ukraine- Petro Poroshenko"/"Армія! Мова! Віра! Ми йдемо своїм шляхом! Ми-Україна. Петро Порошенко" 252
Figure 45: "The army is saving, protecting, helping"/"Армія рятує, захищає, допомогає" 253
Figure 46: "The army is saving, protecting, helping"/"Армія рятує, захищає, допомогає" 253
Figure 47: "The army is saving, protecting, helping"/"Армія рятує, захищає, допомогає" 254
Figure 48: "The army is saving, protecting, helping"/"Армія рятує, захищає, допомогає" 254
Figure 49: "The army is saving, protecting, helping"/"Армія рятує, захищає, допомогає" 255

Figure 50: "The perished in way based on months as of 21.01.2016"/"Загиблі по місяцях війни станом на 21.06.2016" 255
Figure 51: "The army is saving, protecting, helping"/"Армія рятує, захищає, допомогає" 256
Figure 52: "Projectio" 256
Figure 53: "Projectio" 257
Figure 54: "Projectio" 257
Figure 55: "Projectio" 258
Figure 56: "Projectio" 258
Figure 57: "Projectio" 259
Figure 58: "Projectio" 259
Figure 59: Grassroots-made posters 260
Figure 60: "Father, will you protect?"/Тату, ти захистиш?" 260
Figure 61: "For each of us death has a bullet"/"На каждого из нас у смерти есть по пуле" 261
Figure 62: "ATO should begin from Verkhovna Rada"/"АТО нужно начинать с верховной рады" 261
Figure 63: "The shocking socio-economic therapy which isuselessly taking place during 15-20 years is obtaining all signs of the genocide. The secret plan of zionistic- satanistic regime of Petro Poroshenko and Putin becomes obvious"'/"Шокова соціально-економічна терапія, що безрезультатно триває протягом 15-20 років, набуває усіх ознак геноциду. Таємний план сіоністсько-натанинського режиму Порошенко-Путіна стає явним" 262
Figure 64: "19.02.2017. 14.00. Maidan. This political power emerged on the blood of the heroes"/"19.02.2017. 14.00. Майдан. Ця влада прийшла на крові героїв" 262
Figure 65: "Death to Putin! Death to Yanukovych! Death to Poroshenko!"/"Смерть Путіну! Смерть Януковичу! Смерть Параше!" 263
Figure 66: Poster memorial, "Skryabin," "Kuzma" 263

Figure 67: "We were simply dumped. Like mugs behind the backs, did their things, flushed us"/"Нас просто кинули. Як лохів розвели за спинами, діла свої зробили. Злили нас" 264
Figure 68: "A thief has stolen a mace from a thief" 264
Figure 69: "Toppled Lenin" 265
Figure 70: "Bessarabka Lenin. Pedestal" 265
Figure 71: "Darth Vader" 266
Figure 72: "Lenin the Cossack" 266
Figure 73: "In vino Veritas?" 267
Figure 74: "Lenin pedestal"/"Torturer"/ "Кат" 267
Figure 75: "Pedestal of Lenin" 268
Figure 76: "Eternal Memory"/"Вічна пам'ять" 268
Figure 77: "Pedestal of Lenin. Kyiv" 269
Figure 78: Belorussets, Yevgenia. "Let's Put Lenin's Head Back Together" Photograph. Pinchuk Art Center, Kyiv, January 13, 2016. By Anna Kutkina. 269
Figure 79: Belorussets, Yevgenia. "Let's Put Lenin's Head Back Together". Photograph. Pinchuk Art Center, Kyiv, January 13, 2016. By Anna Kutkina. 270
Figure 80: Graffiti on the wall. "Stop Nationalism". Photograph. Pinchuk Art Center, Kyiv, January 13, 2016. By Anna Kutkina. 270
Figure 81: "Shchors monument" 271
Figure 82: "To the border guards who died as a result of the military confrontations during the time of guarding of the border at the east of Ukraine. The pain and sorrow are in our hearts forever. We bow to you, the protectors of the border of Ukraine; may the eternal memory be yours! Glory to the heroes!" 271
Figure 83: "To the protectors of the border of the motherland of all generations" 272
Figure 84: "The state service of the border of Ukraine. An avenue of the border control" 272
Figure 85: Maidan Nezalezhnosti Square: The protestors helmets and slogans of Maidan 273
Figure 86: "Porter Pub" 273

Figure 87: "Porter Pub" 274
Figure 88: "Fire does not burn the fierce ones" / "Вогонь запехлих не пече" 274
Figure 89: "Lviv has not calmed down yet," "Glory to Heroes," "You are forever alive in a heated heart"/"Львів не заспокоївся ще," "Героям слава," "Ви вічно живі в гарячому серці" 275
Figure 90: "Sofiivska square" 275
Figure 91: "Knygarnya E" 276
Figure 92: "Knygarnya E" 276
Figure 93: "Knygarnya E" 277
Figure 94: "Knygarnya E" 277
Figure 95: "A movie by Oles Yanchuk. *The Secret Diary of Symon Petlura*"/"Фільм Олеся Янчука. Таємний Щоденник Симона Петлюри" 278
Figure 96: The "Right Sector" flag... 278
Figure 97: The "Right Sector" flag... 279
Figure 98: "The Right Sector: if not me, then who? If not now, then when?"/"Як не я-то хто? Як не тепер-то коли?" 279
Figure 99: "Language' (in Ukrainian) and not 'Language' (in Russian)?"/"Мова а не язык" 280
Figure 100: "No to war. Yes to Nazism" ("Нет войне. Да нацизму")/"Junta will be! Yes to Nazism" ("Хунта буде. Да нацизму") 280
Figure 101: "If wherever you look is darkness and color-black that means you fell asleep and tomorrow will be better" 281
Figure 102: "OUN - Power, Honor!"/"ОУН – Сила, Честь!" 281
Figure 103: "Glory to Ukraine"/"Слава Україні" 282
Figure 104: "Freedom or death"/"Воля або смерть" 282
Figure 105: "West and East are together forever. P.R.O. -- D. Shukhevych"/"Захід і схід разом назавжди. П.Р.О. Д. Шухевич" 283
Figure 106: "Return your Crimea"/"Поверни свій Крим" 283
Figure 107: "Street of the Heroes of the Heavenly Hundred"/"Вул. Героїв Небесної Сотні............... 284

APPENDIX

Figure 108: "The Republic of Maidan: Honor versus lawlessness" 284
Figure 109: "The Republic of Maidan: Honor versus lawlessness" 285
Figure 110: "Made in Russia"/"Вироблено в Росії" 285
Figure 111: The "100 years of Fighting for Freedom" 286
Figure 112: The "100 years of Fighting for Freedom" 286
Figure 113: The "100 years of Fighting for Freedom" 287
Figure 114: The "100 years of Fighting for Freedom" 287
Figure 115: The "100 years of Fighting for Freedom" 288
Figure 116: The "100 years of Fighting for Freedom" 288
Figure 117: The "100 years of Fighting for Freedom" 289
Figure 118: The "100 years of Fighting for Freedom" 289
Figure 119: The "100 years of Fighting for Freedom" 290
Figure 120: The "100 years of Fighting for Freedom" 290
Figure 121: The "100 years of Fighting for Freedom" 291
Figure 122: The "100 years of Fighting for Freedom" 291
Figure 123: "For your and our freedom 1968-2018"/"За вашу і нашу свободу 1968-2018" 292
Figure 124: "For your and our freedom 1968-2018"/"За вашу і нашу свободу 1968-2018" 292
Figure 125: "For your and our freedom 1968-2018"/"За вашу і нашу свободу 1968-2018" 293
Figure 126: "For your and our freedom 1968-2018"/"За вашу і нашу свободу 1968-2018" 293
Figure 127: "For your and our freedom 1968-2018"/"За вашу і нашу свободу 1968-2018" 294
Figure 128: "Maidan: Landscape of Memory" 294
Figure 129: "Maidan: Landscape of Memory" 295
Figure 130: "Maidan: Landscape of Memory" 295
Figure 131: "Information stand" 296
Figure 132: "Information stand" 296
Figure 133: "Commemorative board: the participants of the Euromaidan Revolution" 297
Figure 134: "Commemorative board: the participants of the Euromaidan Revolution" 297

Figure 135: "Commemorative board: The participant of the Euromaidan Revolution. Donetsk State University" 298
Figure 136: "Commemorative board: The participants of the pro-Ukrainian march in Kharkiv" 298
Figure 137: "Commemorative board: The participants of the Euromaidan Revolution in Kharkiv" 299
Figure 138: "Heroes do not die. Glory to Ukraine!"/"Герої не вмирають. Героям Слава!" 299

APPENDIX 231

Figure 1: "Stalin's Monument"
HZ. *The Stalin Monument and Pedestal, viewed from the west*. Photograph. Wikipedia. August 30, 2021.
https://en.wikipedia.org/wiki/Stalin_Monument_(Prague)#/media/File:PomnikStalina-Praga1.jpg

Figure 2: "Unified Country"/"Єдина країна/Единая страна"
A poster (fabric) placed on the wall of the Central Department Store. Photo: Anna Kutkina, Khreshchatyk Street, Kyiv, May 14 2014.

Figure 3: "I love Ukraine"/"Я люблю Україну"
Grassroots graffiti. Photo: Anna Kutkina, Maidan Nezalezhnosti square, Kyiv, May 17 2014.

Figure 4: "Ukraine is not Russia!"/"Україна не Россія"
Grassroots graffiti. Photo: Anna Kutkina, Maidan Nezalezhnosti square, Kyiv, May 17 2014.

Figure 5: "We are the brotherhood with Russians blood-wise, butare never as brotherly-slavery, Sevastopolian"/"Мы с русскими по крови—братство, но никогда — по братству рабства-Севастополец"

Grassroots poster. Photo: Anna Kutkina, Maidan Nezalezhnosti square, Kyiv, May 18 2014.

Figure 6: "Go home!"

Grassroots poster to object to Russia's intervention in Ukraine. Photo: Anna Kutkina, Maidan Nezalezhnosti square, Kyiv, May 18 2014.

Figure 7: "No to War!"/"Нет войне!"

Grassroots poster to object to the military activities in Donbas. Photo: Anna Kutkina, Maidan Nezalezhnosti square, Kyiv, May 21 2014.

Figure 8: "No to War!"/"Нет войне!"

Grassroots poster to object to the military activities in Donbas. Photo: Anna Kutkina, Maidan Nezalezhnosti square, Kyiv, May 21 2014.

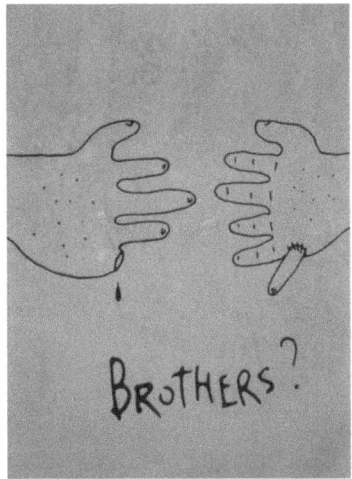

Figure 9: "Brothers?"

Grassroots poster to object to the occupation of Crimea by the Russian Federation. Photo: Anna Kutkina, Maidan Nezalezhnosti square, Kyiv, May 21 2014.

Figure 10: "Human Rights"/"Права людини"

Grassroots poster placed on the wall of the building. Photo: Anna Kutkina, Khreshchatyk Street, Kyiv, May 28 2014.

Figure 11: "Love Russians despise Putin"/"Любим русских презираем Путина"

Grassroots poster placed on the carcass of the Christmas tree. Photo: Anna Kutkina, Maidan Nezalezhnosti square, Kyiv, May 13 2014.

Figure 12: "People, think"/"Люди, задумайтесь"

Grassroots graffiti painted by the participant(s) of the Euromaidan revolution. Source: Anna Kutkina, Maidan Nezalezhnosti square, Kyiv, May 12 2014.

Figure 13: "We need a Ukrainian President. PS: A Banderovite"/"Нам потрібний президент українець. ПС: Бандерівець"

Grassroots graffiti painted by the participant(s) of the Euromaidan revolution.
Photo: Anna Kutkina, Maidan Nezalezhnosti square, Kyiv, April 10 2014.

Figure 14: "To Europe without Yalynkovych!"/"В Європу без Ялинковича!"

Artistic installation of the participant(s) of the Euromaidan revolution.
Photo: Anna Kutkina, Khreshchatyk Street, Kyiv, May 10 2014.

Figure 15: "The Communist party"/"Компартия"
Artistic installation of the participant(s) of the Euromaidan revolution.
Photo: Anna Kutkina, Khreshchatyk Street, Kyiv, May 12 2014.

Figure 16: The "Strike Poster" exhibition
Grassroots public artistic installation. Photo: Anna Kutkina, Maidan Nezalezhnosti square, Kyiv, February 17 2015.

Figure 17: "Я крапля в океані"/"I am a drop in the ocean"/The "Strike Poster"

Grassroots public artistic installation. Photo: Anna Kutkina, Maidan Nezalezhnosti square, Kyiv, February 17 2015.

Figure 18: "Euromaidan is the best thing that could have happened to Ukraine"/"Евромайдан- лучшее, что могло случиться с Украиной"/The "Strike Poster"

Grassroots public artistic installation. Photo: Anna Kutkina, Maidan Nezalezhnosti square, Kyiv, February 17 2015.

Figure 19: "The Yanukovych Nose"/"Ніс Януковича"/The "Strike Poster"

Grassroots public artistic installation. Photo: Anna Kutkina, Maidan Nezalezhnosti square, Kyiv, February 17 2015.

Figure 20: "We are being beaten at our own expense"/"Нас бьют за наши деньги"/ The "Strike Poster"

Grassroots public artistic installation. Photo: Anna Kutkina, Maidan Nezalezhnosti square, Kyiv, February 17 2015.

Figure 21: "We do not need such hockey"/"Такой хоккей нам не нужен"/The "Strike Poster"

Grassroots public artistic installation. Photo: Anna Kutkina, Maidan Nezalezhnosti square, Kyiv, February 17 2015.

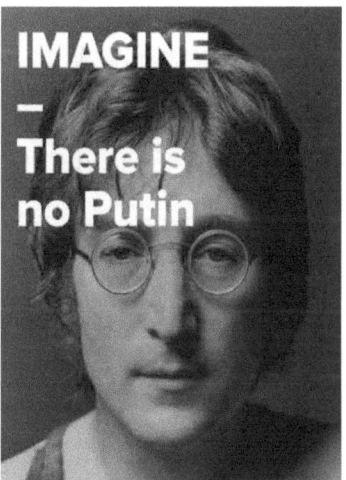

Figure 22: "Imagine – there is no Putin"/The "Strike Poster"/The "Strike Poster"

Grassroots public artistic installation. Photo: Egor Petrov, The "Strike Poster" project. Image shared by the author during interview in Kyiv, May 5 2016. © copyright 2021 by Egor Petrov.

Figure 23: "Constitution of Ukraine (Article 5): The only source of power in Ukraine are the people"/"Коституція України стаття 5: Єдиним джерелом влади в Україні є народ"/The "Strike Poster"
Grassroots public artistic installation. Photo: Anna Kutkina, Maidan Nezalezhnosti square, Kyiv, February 17 2015.

Figure 24: "Shame for the entire world"/"Сором на весь світ"/The "Strike Poster"
Grassroots public artistic installation. Photo: Anna Kutkina, Maidan Nezalezhnosti square, Kyiv, February 17 2015.

APPENDIX   243

Figure 25: "I am responsible for what is going to happen tomorrow"/"Я відповідаю за те, що буде завтра"/The "Strike Poster"

Grassroots public artistic installation. Photo: Anna Kutkina, Maidan Nezalezhnosti square, Kyiv, February 17 2015.

Figure 26: "The Ukrainian nightmare"/The "Strike Poster"

Grassroots public artistic installation. Photo: Anna Kutkina, Maidan Nezalezhnosti square, Kyiv, February 17 2015.

Figure 27: "This is Not for Europe, But: For the future of our kids...for roads without pits...This is not for Europe but for medicine in the hospitals; This is not for Europe but for courts without bribes; This is not for Europe but against bribes in the kindergartens; This is not for Europe but for police without bribes; This is not against Russia but against the corrupt state authorities"/The "Strike Poster"
Grassroots public artistic installation. Photo: Anna Kutkina, Maidan Nezalezhnosti square, Kyiv, February 17 2015.

Figure 28: "Changing the country. We apologize for the inconvenience"/"Змінюємо країну. Перепрошуємо за незручності"/The "Strike Poster"
Grassroots public artistic installation. Photo: Anna Kutkina, Maidan Nezalezhnosti square, Kyiv, February 17 2015.

APPENDIX 245

Figure 29: "March 2014"/The "Strike Poster"
Grassroots public artistic installation. Photo: Anna Kutkina, Maidan Nezalezhnosti square, Kyiv, February 17 2015.

Figure 30: "The Leninfall"/"Ленінопад"/The "Strike Poster"
Grassroots public artistic installation. Photo: Anna Kutkina, Maidan Nezalezhnosti square, Kyiv, February 17 2015.

Figure 31: Petrov, Egor. "I am a drop in the ocean"
Poster posted across Ukraine as part of the "Strike Poster" project. Photograph. Image shared by the photographer during interview in Kyiv, May 5, 2016. © copyright 2021 by Egor Petrov.

Figure 32: Petrov, Egor. "I am a drop in the ocean"
Poster in Zaporizhzhya, Eastern Ukraine, as part of the "Strike Poster" project. Photograph. Image shared by the photographer during interview in Kyiv, May 5, 2016. © copyright 2021 by Egor Petrov.

APPENDIX 247

Figure 33: Petrov, Egor. "I am a drop in the ocean"
Hand-made posters "I am a drop in the ocean", as part of the "Strike Poster" project, being used during 'Maidan' protests in different regions of Ukraine. Photograph. Image shared by the photographer during interview in Kyiv, May 5, 2016. © copyright 2021 by Egor Petrov.

Figure 34: Petrov, Egor. "I am a drop in the ocean"
Poster placed in Paris, France as a statement of support of the Euromaidan revolution in Ukraine. Photograph. Image shared by the photographer during interview in Kyiv, May 5, 2016. © copyright 2021 by Egor Petrov.

Figure 35: Petrov, Egor. "I am a drop in the ocean. Art making the revolution"/"Я- крапля в океані. Мистецтво робить революцію"

Images of the "Strike Poster" project become part of the official state affairs. Photograph. Image shared by the photographer during interview in Kyiv, May 5, 2016. © copyright 2021 by Egor Petrov.

Figure 36: Petrov, Egor. "I am a drop in the ocean"

As part of the "Strike Poster" project, are set as a phone wallpaper. Photograph. Image shared by the photographer during interview in Kyiv, May 5, 2016. © copyright 2021 by Egor Petrov

Figure 37: Petrov, Egor. "I am a drop in the ocean"
Images of the "Strike Poster" project become part of ordinary citizens' daily space as covers for mobile phones. Photograph. Image shared by the photographer during interview in Kyiv, May 5, 2016. © copyright 2021 by Egor Petrov.

Figure 38: "Obtained dignity – Let us protect the state!"/ "Здобули гідність-- захистимо державу!"
Poster stand-board promoting conscription to fight in Donbas. Photo: Anna Kutkina, Khreshchatyk street, Kyiv, October 12 2015.

Figure 39: "Friend! Have you signed up for the National Guard of Ukraine?"/"Друже! Ти записався до Національної гвардії України?"

Poster stand-board promoting conscription to fight in Donbas. Photo: Anna Kutkina, Arsenala Street, Kyiv, May 2 2015.

Figure 40: "Heroes do not die!"/"Герої не вмирають!"

Photo: Anna Kutkina, Khreshchatyk Street, Kyiv, November 2 2015.

APPENDIX 251

Figure 41: "60 000 of the best patriots have already signed the contract. Become the best!"/"60 000 найкращих патріотів вже підписали контракт. Стань найкращим!"

Poster stand-board promoting conscription to fight in Donbas. Photo: Anna Kutkina, Arsenala Street, Kyiv, 26 2017.

Figure 42: "National Guard of Ukraine: The service by the contract and the call of the heart -Serhij Shkabadura, the Printer"/"Національна Гвардія України: Служба за контрактом та покликом серця -Сергій Шкабадура, Друкар"

Poster stand-board promoting conscription to fight in Donbas. Photo: Anna Kutkina, Vinnytsia, April 1 2017.

Figure 43: "Obtained the eternal life in a fight"/"Здобув вічне життя в бою"

Poster stand-board promoting conscription to fight in Donbas. Photo: Anna Kutkina, Peremohy Avenue, Kyiv. September 17 2018.

Figure 44: "Army! Language! Faith! We are walking our own path! We are Ukraine- Petro Poroshenko"/"Армія! Мова! Віра! Ми йдемо своїм шляхом! Ми-Україна. Петро Порошенко"

State-promoted poster/President Poroshenko election campaign. Photo: Anna Kutkina, Peremohy Avenue, Kyiv, September 17 2018.

Figure 45: "The army is saving, protecting, helping"/"Армія рятує, захищає, допомогає"

Public poster exhibition on war in Donbas. Photo: Anna Kutkina, Maidan Nezalezhnosti square, Kyiv, June 18 2016.

Figure 46: "The army is saving, protecting, helping"/"Армія рятує, захищає, допомогає"

Public poster exhibition on war in Donbas. Photo: Anna Kutkina, Maidan Nezalezhnosti square, Kyiv, June 18 2016.

Figure 47: "The army is saving, protecting, helping"/"Армія рятує, захищає, допомогає"

Public poster exhibition on war in Donbas. Photo: Anna Kutkina, Maidan Nezalezhnosti square, Kyiv, June 18 2016.

Figure 48: "The army is saving, protecting, helping"/"Армія рятує, захищає, допомогає"

Public poster exhibition on war in Donbas. Photo: Anna Kutkina, Maidan Nezalezhnosti square, Kyiv, June 18 2016.

Figure 49: "The army is saving, protecting, helping"/"Армія рятує, захищає, допомогає"

Public poster exhibition on war in Donbas. Photo: Anna Kutkina, Maidan Nezalezhnosti square, Kyiv, June 18 2016.

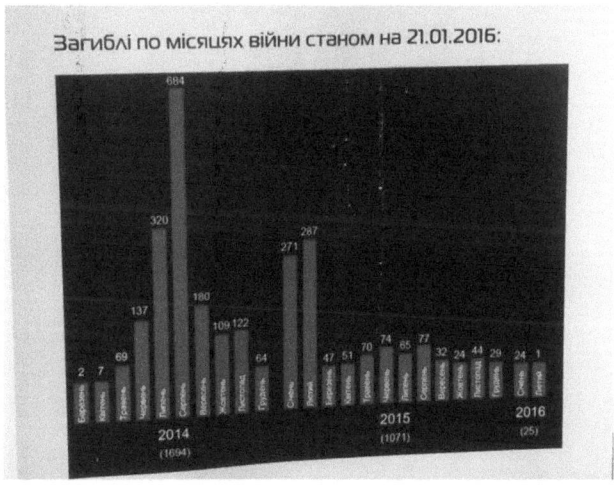

Figure 50: "The perished in way based on months as of 21.01.2016"/"Загиблі по місяцях війни станом на 21.06.2016"

Public poster stand on war in Donbas. Photo: Anna Kutkina, Maidan Nezalezhnosti square, Kyiv, June 18 2016.

Figure 51: "The army is saving, protecting, helping"/"Армія рятує, захищає, допомогає"

Public poster exhibition on war in Donbas. Photo: Anna Kutkina, Maidan Nezalezhnosti square, Kyiv, June 18 2016.

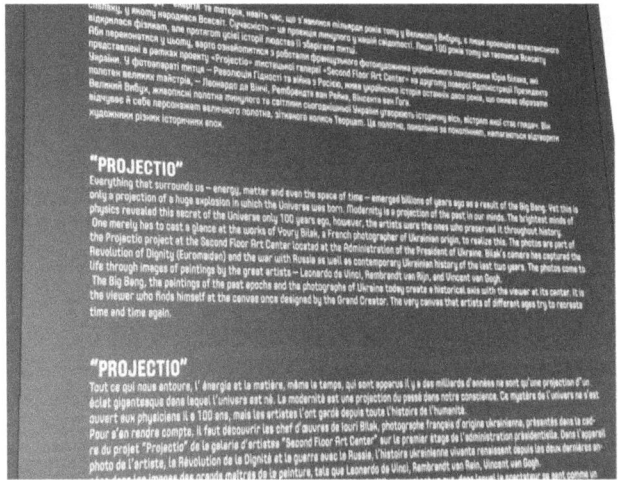

Figure 52: "Projectio"

Soldiers of war in Donbas 'as' art classics. Photo: Anna Kutkina, Boryspil International Airport, Kyiv, April 17 2017.

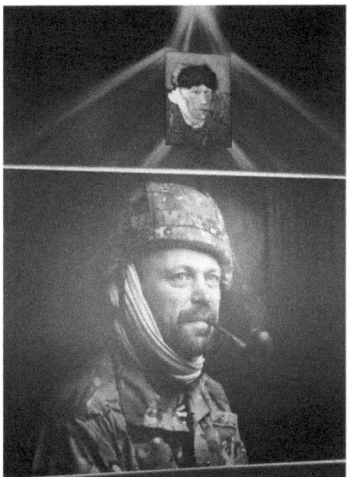

Figure 53: "Projectio"

Soldiers of war in Donbas 'as' art classics. Photo: Anna Kutkina, Boryspil International Airport, Kyiv, April 17 2017.

Figure 54: "Projectio"

Soldiers of war in Donbas 'as' art classics. Photo: Anna Kutkina, Boryspil International Airport, Kyiv, April 17 2017.

258   Between Lenin and Bandera

Figure 55: "Projectio"
Soldiers of war in Donbas 'as' art classics. Photo: Anna Kutkina, Boryspil International Airport, Kyiv, April 17 2017.

Figure 56: "Projectio"
Soldiers of war in Donbas 'as' art classics. Photo: Anna Kutkina, Boryspil International Airport, Kyiv, April 17 2017.

APPENDIX 259

Figure 57: "Projectio"
Soldiers of war in Donbas 'as' art classics. Photo: Anna Kutkina, Boryspil International Airport, Kyiv, April 17 2017.

Figure 58: "Projectio"
Soldiers of war in Donbas 'as' art classics. Photo: Anna Kutkina, Boryspil International Airport, Kyiv, April 17 2017.

Figure 59: Grassroots-made posters
Soldiers, artists and journalists who died in Donbas. Photo: Anna Kutkina, Maidan Nezalezhnosti square, Kyiv, February 12 2016.

Figure 60: "Father, will you protect?"/Тату, ти захистиш?"
Photo: Anna Kutkina, Maidan Nezalezhnosti square, Kyiv, February 4 2016.

APPENDIX 261

Figure 61: "For each of us death has a bullet"/"На каждого из нас у смерти есть по пуле"

Photo: Anna Kutkina, Maidan Nezalezhnosti square, Kyiv, February 4 2016.

Figure 62: "ATO should begin from Verkhovna Rada"/"ATO нужно начинать с верховной рады"

Grassroots graffiti. Photo: Anna Kutkina, Maidan Nezalezhnosti square, Kyiv, February 4 2017.

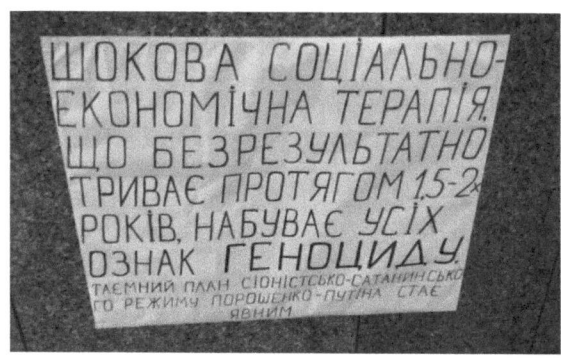

Figure 63: "The shocking socio-economic therapy which isuselessly taking place during 15-20 years is obtaining all signs of the genocide. The secret plan of zionistic- satanistic regime of Petro Poroshenko and Putin becomes obvious"'/"Шокова соціально-економічна терапія, що безрезультатно триває протягом 15-20 років, набуває усіх ознак геноциду. Таємний план сіоністсько-натанинського режиму Порошенко-Путіна стає явним"

Grassroots poster. Photo: Anna Kutkina, Maidan Nezalezhnosti square, Kyiv, November 18 2015.

Figure 64: "19.02.2017. 14.00. Maidan. This political power emerged on the blood of the heroes"/"19.02.2017. 14.00. Майдан. Ця влада прийшла на крові героїв"

Grassroots graffiti. Photo: Anna Kutkina, Lybidska, Kyiv. October 2 2017.

Figure 65: "Death to Putin! Death to Yanukovych! Death to Poroshenko!"/"Смерть Путіну! Смерть Януковичу! Смерть Параше!"

Grassroots graffiti. Photo: Anna Kutkina, Maidan Nezalezhnosti square, Kyiv, October 15 2016.

Figure 66: Poster memorial, "Skryabin," "Kuzma"

Photo: Anna Kutkina, Maidan Nezalezhnosti square, Kyiv, November 29 2015.

Figure 67: "We were simply dumped. Like mugs behind the backs, did their things, flushed us"/"Нас просто кинули. Як лохів розвели за спинами, діла свої зробили. Злили нас"

Grassroots poster citing lyrics of the song "Dumped"/the Ukrainian band "Skryabin". Photo: Anna Kutkina, Maidan Nezalezhnosti square, Kyiv, January 11 2016.

Figure 68: "A thief has stolen a mace from a thief"

Grassroots poster pointing at corruption of the post-Euromaidan political regime. Photo: Anna Kutkina, Maidan Nezalezhnosti square, Kyiv, January 11 2016.

APPENDIX 265

Figure 69: "Toppled Lenin"
BaseSat. *Toppled Lenin statue being broken into pieces for souvenirs.* Photograph.
Wikipedia. August 31, 2021. https://en.wikipedia.org/wiki/Demolition_of_
monuments_to_Vladimir_Lenin_in_Ukraine#/media/File:Euromaidan_in_Kyiv_e
arly_evening_2013-12-10_(013).JPG

Figure 70: "Bessarabka Lenin. Pedestal"
Photo: Anna Kutkina, Bessarabska Square, April 2 2014.

Figure 71: "Darth Vader"
© copyright 2021 by Niels Ackermann / Lundi13

Figure 72: "Lenin the Cossack"
© copyright 2021 by Niels Ackermann / Lundi13

APPENDIX 267

Figure 73: "In vino Veritas?"
© copyright 2021 by Sébastien Gobert / Daleko-Blisko

Figure 74: "Lenin pedestal"/"Torturer"/" "Кат"
© copyright 2021 by Dmytro Zamiatin

Figure 75: "Pedestal of Lenin"
Photo: Anna Kutkina, Lubny, June 8 2016.

Figure 76: "Eternal Memory"/"Вічна пам'ять"
Pedestal of Lenin statue painted into a commemorative symbol of the fallen heroes of WWII/protectors of the Ukrainian state. Photo: Anna Kutkina, Poltava, June 11 2016.

Figure 77: "Pedestal of Lenin. Kyiv"
Pedestal of the toppled statue of Lenin decorated with Ukrainian insignia. Photo: Anna Kutkina, Kyiv, October 7 2018.

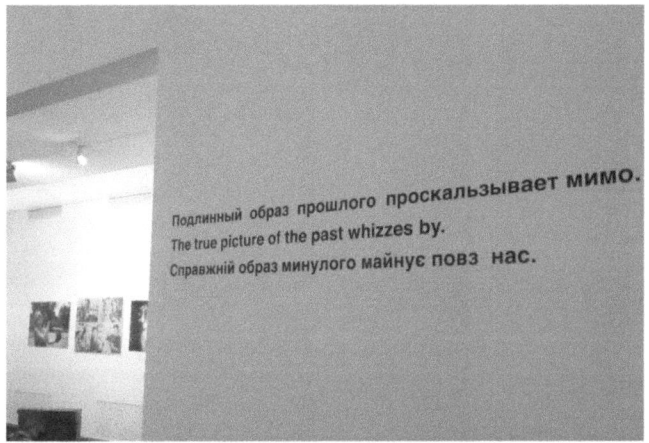

Figure 78: Belorussets, Yevgenia. "Let's Put Lenin's Head Back Together" Photograph. Pinchuk Art Center, Kyiv, January 13, 2016. By Anna Kutkina.

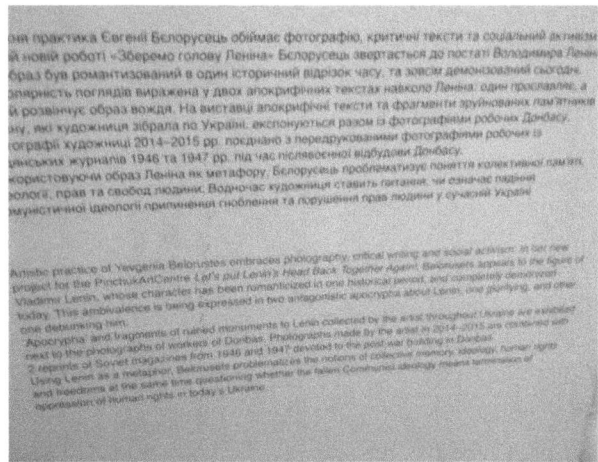

Figure 79: Belorussets, Yevgenia. "Let's Put Lenin's Head Back Together". Photograph. Pinchuk Art Center, Kyiv, January 13, 2016. By Anna Kutkina.

Figure 80: Graffiti on the wall. "Stop Nationalism". Photograph. Pinchuk Art Center, Kyiv, January 13, 2016. By Anna Kutkina.

Figure 81: "Shchors monument"
Photo: Anna Kutkina, Kyiv, September 17 2018.

Figure 82: "To the border guards who died as a result of the military confrontations during the time of guarding of the border at the east of Ukraine. The pain and sorrow are in our hearts forever. We bow to you, the protectors of the border of Ukraine; may the eternal memory be yours! Glory to the heroes!"

Commemorative plate. Photo: Anna Kutkina, Kyiv, April 5 2017.

Figure 83: "To the protectors of the border of the motherland of all generations"

Photo: Anna Kutkina, Kyiv, April 9 2017.

Figure 84: "The state service of the border of Ukraine. An avenue of the border control"

Photo: Anna Kutkina, Kyiv, April 5 2017.

APPENDIX 273

Figure 85: Maidan Nezalezhnosti Square: The protestors helmets and slogans of Maidan
Photo: Anna Kutkina, Kyiv, June 4 2014.

Figure 86: "Porter Pub"
Insignia of the Euromaidan revolution and war in Donbas is made part of the interior of the pub. Photo: Anna Kutkina, Kyiv, July 14 2016.

Figure 87: "Porter Pub"
Insignia of the Euromaidan revolution and war in Donbas is made part of the interior of the pub. Photo: Anna Kutkina, Kyiv, July 14 2016.

Figure 88: "Fire does not burn the fierce ones"/ "Вогонь запехлих не пече"
Grassroots graffiti. Photo: Anna Kutkina, Maidan Nezalezhnosti square, Kyiv, June 5 2014.

APPENDIX 275

Figure 89: "Lviv has not calmed down yet," "Glory to Heroes," "You are forever alive in a heated heart"/"Львів не заспокоївся ще," "Героям слава," "Ви вічно живі в гарячому серці"

A collage of the protestors' t-shirts. Photo: Anna Kutkina, Maidan Nezalezhnosti square, Kyiv, May 6 2014.

Figure 90: "Sofiivska square"

Commemorative board to the soldiers fallen in Donbas. Photo: Anna Kutkina, Kyiv, June 6 2015.

Figure 91: "Knygarnya E"
Bookshelves. Photo: Anna Kutkina, Khreshchatyk Street, Kyiv, June 12 2015.

Figure 92: "Knygarnya E"
Bookshelves. Photo: Anna Kutkina, Khreshchatyk Street, Kyiv, June 12 2015.

Figure 93: "Knygarnya E"
Bookshelves. Photo: Anna Kutkina, Khreshchatyk Street, Kyiv, June 12 2015.

Figure 94: "Knygarnya E"
Bookshelves. Photo: Anna Kutkina, Khreshchatyk Street, Kyiv, June 12 2015.

Figure 95: "A movie by Oles Yanchuk. *The Secret Diary of Symon Petlura*"/"Фільм Олеся Янчука. Таємний Щоденник Симона Петлюри"

Stand-board advertising. Photo: Anna Kutkina, Kyiv, September 17 2018.

Figure 96: The "Right Sector" flag

Photo: Anna Kutkina, Khreshchatyk Street, Kyiv, May 2 2014.

Figure 97: The "Right Sector" flag
Photo: Anna Kutkina, Maidan Nezalezhnosti, Kyiv, May 2 2014.

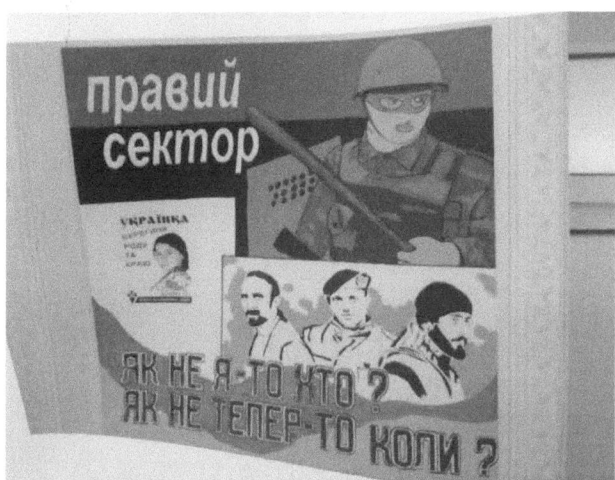

Figure 98: "The Right Sector: if not me, then who? If not now, then when?"/"Як не я-то хто? Як не тепер-то коли?"
Grassroots poster. Photo: Anna Kutkina, Kharkiv, June 27 2016.

Figure 99: "'Language' (in Ukrainian) and not 'Language' (in Russian)?"/"Мова а не язык"

Grassroots graffiti. Photo: Anna Kutkina, Zaporizhzhya, June 28 2014.

Figure 100: "No to war. Yes to Nazism" ("Нет войне. Да нацизму")/"Junta will be! Yes to Nazism" ("Хунта буде. Да нацизму")

Grassroots graffiti. Photo: Anna Kutkina, Lubny, June 25 2016.

Figure 101: "If wherever you look is darkness and color-black that means you fell asleep and tomorrow will be better"
Grassroots graffiti. Photo: Anna Kutkina, Lviv, February 1 2017.

Figure 102: "OUN - Power, Honor!"/"ОУН – Сила, Честь!"
Grassroots graffiti. Photo: Anna Kutkina, Kryvij Rih, November 18 2016.

Figure 103: "Glory to Ukraine"/"Слава Україні"
Grassroots graffiti. Photo: Anna Kutkina, Poltava, April 28 2015.

Figure 104: "Freedom or death"/"Воля або смерть"
Grassroots graffiti. Photo: Anna Kutkina, Maidan Nezalezhnosti square, Kyiv, May 2 2014.

Figure 105: "West and East are together forever. P.R.O. -- D. Shukhevych"/"Захід і схід разом назавжди. П.Р.О. Д. Шухевич"

Grassroots graffiti. Photo: Anna Kutkina, Poltava, April 2 2015.

Figure 106: "Return your Crimea"/"Поверни свій Крим"

Grassroots graffiti. Photo: Anna Kutkina, Khreshchatyk Street, Kyiv, November 11 2015.

Figure 107: "Street of the Heroes of the Heavenly Hundred"/"Вул. Героїв Небесної Сотні

Artistic renaming of the street. Photo: Anna Kutkina, Institytska street, Kyiv, June 3 2014.

Figure 108: "The Republic of Maidan: Honor versus lawlessness"

Grassroots posters. Photo: Anna Kutkina, Maidan Nezalezhnosti square, Kyiv, February 19 2016.

Figure 109: "The Republic of Maidan: Honor versus lawlessness"
Grassroots poster. Photo: Anna Kutkina, Maidan Nezalezhnosti square, Kyiv, February 19 2016.

Figure 110: "Made in Russia"/"Вироблено в Pocii"
Public campaign at the grocery stores not to buy products made in Russia. Photo: Anna Kutkina, Kryvij Rih, June 19 2016.

Figure 111: The "100 years of Fighting for Freedom"
Public exhibition. Photo: Anna Kutkina, Maidan Nezalezhnosti Square, Kyiv, October 2 2017.

Figure 112: The "100 years of Fighting for Freedom"
Public exhibition. Photo: Anna Kutkina, Maidan Nezalezhnosti Square, Kyiv, October 2 2017.

Figure 113: The "100 years of Fighting for Freedom"
Public exhibition. Photo: Anna Kutkina, Maidan Nezalezhnosti Square, Kyiv, October 2 2017.

Figure 114: The "100 years of Fighting for Freedom"
Public exhibition. Photo: Anna Kutkina, Maidan Nezalezhnosti Square, Kyiv, October 2 2017.

Figure 115: The "100 years of Fighting for Freedom"
Public exhibition. Photo: Anna Kutkina, Maidan Nezalezhnosti Square, Kyiv, October 2 2017.

Figure 116: The "100 years of Fighting for Freedom"
Public exhibition. Photo: Anna Kutkina, Maidan Nezalezhnosti Square, Kyiv, October 2 2017.

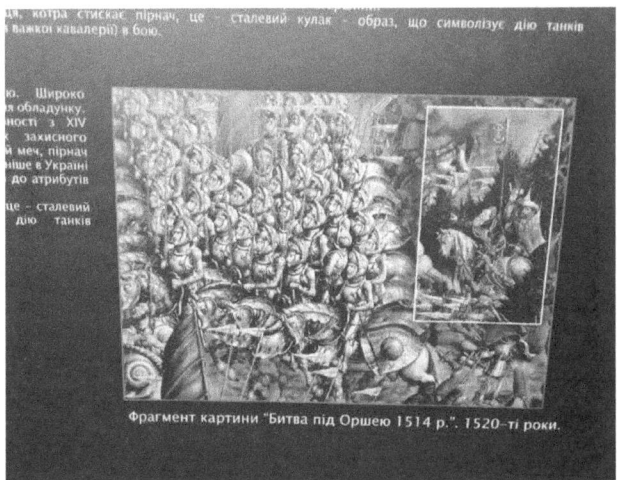

Figure 117: The "100 years of Fighting for Freedom"
Public exhibition. Photo: Anna Kutkina, Maidan Nezalezhnosti Square, Kyiv, October 2 2017.

Figure 118: The "100 years of Fighting for Freedom"
Public exhibition. Photo: Anna Kutkina, Maidan Nezalezhnosti Square, Kyiv, October 2 2017.

Figure 119: The "100 years of Fighting for Freedom"
Public exhibition. Photo: Anna Kutkina, Maidan Nezalezhnosti Square, Kyiv, October 2 2017.

Figure 120: The "100 years of Fighting for Freedom"
Public exhibition. Photo: Anna Kutkina, Maidan Nezalezhnosti Square, Kyiv, October 2 2017.

APPENDIX 291

Figure 121: The "100 years of Fighting for Freedom"
Public exhibition. Photo: Anna Kutkina, Maidan Nezalezhnosti Square, Kyiv, October 2 2017.

Figure 122: The "100 years of Fighting for Freedom"
Public exhibition. Photo: Anna Kutkina, Maidan Nezalezhnosti Square, Kyiv, October 2 2017.

Figure 123: "For your and our freedom 1968-2018"/"За вашу і нашу свободу 1968-2018"

Public exhibition. Photo: Anna Kutkina, Maidan Nezalezhnosti square, Kyiv, September 19, 2018.

Figure 124: "For your and our freedom 1968-2018"/"За вашу і нашу свободу 1968-2018"

Public exhibition. Photo: Anna Kutkina, Maidan Nezalezhnosti square, Kyiv, September 19, 2018.

APPENDIX 293

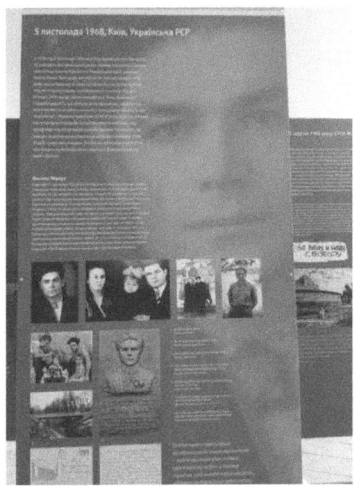

Figure 125: "For your and our freedom 1968-2018"/"За вашу і нашу свободу 1968-2018"
Public exhibition. Photo: Anna Kutkina, Maidan Nezalezhnosti square, Kyiv, September 19, 2018.

Figure 126: "For your and our freedom 1968-2018"/"За вашу і нашу свободу 1968-2018"
Public exhibition. Photo: Anna Kutkina, Maidan Nezalezhnosti square, Kyiv, September 19, 2018.

Figure 127: "For your and our freedom 1968-2018"/"За вашу і нашу свободу 1968-2018"
Public exhibition. Photo: Anna Kutkina, Maidan Nezalezhnosti square, Kyiv, September 19, 2018.

Figure 128: "Maidan: Landscape of Memory"
Public exhibition. Photo: Anna Kutkina, Maidan Nezalezhnosti square, Kyiv, September 19 2018.

Figure 129: "Maidan: Landscape of Memory"

Public exhibition. Photo: Anna Kutkina, Maidan Nezalezhnosti square, Kyiv, September 19 2018.

Figure 130: "Maidan: Landscape of Memory"

Public exhibition. Photo: Anna Kutkina, Maidan Nezalezhnosti square, Kyiv, September 19 2018.

Figure 131: "Information stand"
Photo: Anna Kutkina, Maidan Nezalezhnosti Square, Kyiv, October 5 2017.

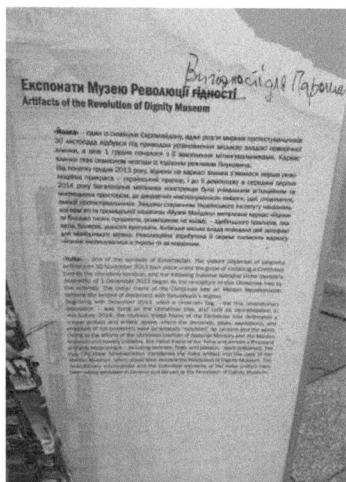

Figure 132: "Information stand"
Photo: Anna Kutkina, Maidan Nezalezhnosti Square, Kyiv, October 5 2017.

APPENDIX 297

Figure 133: "Commemorative board: the participants of the Euromaidan Revolution"

Photo: Anna Kutkina, Lviv, February 1 2017.

Figure 134: "Commemorative board: the participants of the Euromaidan Revolution"

Photo: Anna Kutkina, Vinnytsia, February 1 2017.

Figure 135: "Commemorative board: The participant of the Euromaidan Revolution. Donetsk State University"

Photo: Anna Kutkina, Vinnytsia, February 1 2017.

Figure 136: "Commemorative board: The participants of the pro-Ukrainian march in Kharkiv"

Photo: Anna Kutkina, Kharkiv, June 7 2016.

Figure 137: "Commemorative board: The participants of the Euromaidan Revolution in Kharkiv"

Photo: Anna Kutkina, Kharkiv, June 7 2016.

Figure 138: "Heroes do not die. Glory to Ukraine!"/"Герої не вмирають. Героям Слава!"

Photo: Anna Kutkina, Maidan Nezalezhnosti square, Kyiv, April 17 2015.

SOVIET AND POST-SOVIET POLITICS AND SOCIETY
Edited by Dr. Andreas Umland | ISSN 1614-3515

1   Андреас Умланд (ред.) | Воплощение Европейской конвенции по правам человека в России. Философские, юридические и эмпирические исследования | ISBN 3-89821-387-0

2   Christian Wipperfürth | Russland – ein vertrauenswürdiger Partner? Grundlagen, Hintergründe und Praxis gegenwärtiger russischer Außenpolitik | Mit einem Vorwort von Heinz Timmermann | ISBN 3-89821-401-X

3   Manja Hussner | Die Übernahme internationalen Rechts in die russische und deutsche Rechtsordnung. Eine vergleichende Analyse zur Völkerrechtsfreundlichkeit der Verfassungen der Russländischen Föderation und der Bundesrepublik Deutschland | Mit einem Vorwort von Rainer Arnold | ISBN 3-89821-438-9

4   Matthew Tejada | Bulgaria's Democratic Consolidation and the Kozloduy Nuclear Power Plant (KNPP). The Unattainability of Closure | With a foreword by Richard J. Crampton | ISBN 3-89821-439-7

5   Марк Григорьевич Меерович | Квадратные метры, определяющие сознание. Государственная жилищная политика в СССР. 1921 – 1941 гг | ISBN 3-89821-474-5

6   Andrei P. Tsygankov, Pavel A. Tsygankov (Eds.) | New Directions in Russian International Studies | ISBN 3-89821-422-2

7   Марк Григорьевич Меерович | Как власть народ к труду приучала. Жилище в СССР – средство управления людьми. 1917 – 1941 гг. | С предисловием Елены Осокиной | ISBN 3-89821-495-8

8   David J. Galbreath | Nation-Building and Minority Politics in Post-Socialist States. Interests, Influence and Identities in Estonia and Latvia | With a foreword by David J. Smith | ISBN 3-89821-467-2

9   Алексей Юрьевич Безугольный | Народы Кавказа в Вооруженных силах СССР в годы Великой Отечественной войны 1941-1945 гг. | С предисловием Николая Бугая | ISBN 3-89821-475-3

10 Вячеслав Лихачев и Владимир Прибыловский (ред.) | Русское Национальное Единство, 1990-2000. В 2-х томах | ISBN 3-89821-523-7

11 Николай Бугай (ред.) | Народы стран Балтии в условиях сталинизма (1940-е – 1950-е годы). Документированная история | ISBN 3-89821-525-3

12 Ingmar Bredies (Hrsg.) | Zur Anatomie der Orange Revolution in der Ukraine. Wechsel des Elitenregimes oder Triumph des Parlamentarismus? | ISBN 3-89821-524-5

13 Anastasia V. Mitrofanova | The Politicization of Russian Orthodoxy. Actors and Ideas | With a foreword by William C. Gay | ISBN 3-89821-481-8

14 Nathan D. Larson | Alexander Solzhenitsyn and the Russo-Jewish Question | ISBN 3-89821-483-4

15 Guido Houben | Kulturpolitik und Ethnizität. Staatliche Kunstförderung im Russland der neunziger Jahre | Mit einem Vorwort von Gert Weisskirchen | ISBN 3-89821-542-3

16 Leonid Luks | Der russische „Sonderweg"? Aufsätze zur neuesten Geschichte Russlands im europäischen Kontext | ISBN 3-89821-496-6

17 Евгений Мороз | История «Мёртвой воды» – от страшной сказки к большой политике. Политическое неоязычество в постсоветской России | ISBN 3-89821-551-2

18 Александр Верховский и Галина Кожевникова (ред.) | Этническая и религиозная интолерантность в российских СМИ. Результаты мониторинга 2001-2004 гг. | ISBN 3-89821-569-5

19 Christian Ganzer | Sowjetisches Erbe und ukrainische Nation. Das Museum der Geschichte des Zaporoger Kosakentums auf der Insel Chortycja | Mit einem Vorwort von Frank Golczewski | ISBN 3-89821-504-0

20 Эльза-Баир Гучинова | Помнить нельзя забыть. Антропология депортационной травмы калмыков | С предисловием Кэролайн Хамфри | ISBN 3-89821-506-7

21 Юлия Лидерман | Мотивы «проверки» и «испытания» в постсоветской культуре. Советское прошлое в российском кинематографе 1990-х годов | С предисловием Евгения Марголита | ISBN 3-89821-511-3

22 Tanya Lokshina, Ray Thomas, Mary Mayer (Eds.) | The Imposition of a Fake Political Settlement in the Northern Caucasus. The 2003 Chechen Presidential Election | ISBN 3-89821-436-2

23 Timothy McCajor Hall, Rosie Read (Eds.) | Changes in the Heart of Europe. Recent Ethnographies of Czechs, Slovaks, Roma, and Sorbs | With an afterword by Zdeněk Salzmann | ISBN 3-89821-606-5

24   *Christian Autengruber* | Die politischen Parteien in Bulgarien und Rumänien. Eine vergleichende Analyse seit Beginn der 90er Jahre | Mit einem Vorwort von Dorothée de Nève | ISBN 3-89821-476-1

25   *Annette Freyberg-Inan with Radu Cristescu* | The Ghosts in Our Classrooms, or: John Dewey Meets Ceauşescu. The Promise and the Failures of Civic Education in Romania | ISBN 3-89821-416-8

26   *John B. Dunlop* | The 2002 Dubrovka and 2004 Beslan Hostage Crises. A Critique of Russian Counter-Terrorism | With a foreword by Donald N. Jensen | ISBN 3-89821-608-X

27   *Peter Koller* | Das touristische Potenzial von Kam''janec'–Podil's'kyj. Eine fremdenverkehrsgeographische Untersuchung der Zukunftsperspektiven und Maßnahmenplanung zur Destinationsentwicklung des „ukrainischen Rothenburg" | Mit einem Vorwort von Kristiane Klemm | ISBN 3-89821-640-3

28   *Françoise Daucé, Elisabeth Sieca-Kozlowski (Eds.)* | Dedovshchina in the Post-Soviet Military. Hazing of Russian Army Conscripts in a Comparative Perspective | With a foreword by Dale Herspring | ISBN 3-89821-616-0

29   *Florian Strasser* | Zivilgesellschaftliche Einflüsse auf die Orange Revolution. Die gewaltlose Massenbewegung und die ukrainische Wahlkrise 2004 | Mit einem Vorwort von Egbert Jahn | ISBN 3-89821-648-9

30   *Rebecca S. Katz* | The Georgian Regime Crisis of 2003-2004. A Case Study in Post-Soviet Media Representation of Politics, Crime and Corruption | ISBN 3-89821-413-3

31   *Vladimir Kantor* | Willkür oder Freiheit. Beiträge zur russischen Geschichtsphilosophie | Ediert von Dagmar Herrmann sowie mit einem Vorwort versehen von Leonid Luks | ISBN 3-89821-589-X

32   *Laura A. Victoir* | The Russian Land Estate Today. A Case Study of Cultural Politics in Post-Soviet Russia | With a foreword by Priscilla Roosevelt | ISBN 3-89821-426-5

33   *Ivan Katchanovski* | Cleft Countries. Regional Political Divisions and Cultures in Post-Soviet Ukraine and Moldova | With a foreword by Francis Fukuyama | ISBN 3-89821-558-X

34   *Florian Mühlfried* | Postsowjetische Feiern. Das Georgische Bankett im Wandel | Mit einem Vorwort von Kevin Tuite | ISBN 3-89821-601-2

35   *Roger Griffin, Werner Loh, Andreas Umland (Eds.)* | Fascism Past and Present, West and East. An International Debate on Concepts and Cases in the Comparative Study of the Extreme Right | With an afterword by Walter Laqueur | ISBN 3-89821-674-8

36   *Sebastian Schlegel* | Der „Weiße Archipel". Sowjetische Atomstädte 1945-1991 | Mit einem Geleitwort von Thomas Bohn | ISBN 3-89821-679-9

37   *Vyacheslav Likhachev* | Political Anti-Semitism in Post-Soviet Russia. Actors and Ideas in 1991-2003 | Edited and translated from Russian by Eugene Veklerov | ISBN 3-89821-529-6

38   *Josette Baer (Ed.)* | Preparing Liberty in Central Europe. Political Texts from the Spring of Nations 1848 to the Spring of Prague 1968 | With a foreword by Zdeněk V. David | ISBN 3-89821-546-6

39   *Михаил Лукьянов* | Российский консерватизм и реформа, 1907-1914 | С предисловием Марка Д. Стейнберга | ISBN 3-89821-503-2

40   *Nicola Melloni* | Market Without Economy. The 1998 Russian Financial Crisis | With a foreword by Eiji Furukawa | ISBN 3-89821-407-9

41   *Dmitrij Chmelnizki* | Die Architektur Stalins | Bd. 1: Studien zu Ideologie und Stil | Bd. 2: Bilddokumentation | Mit einem Vorwort von Bruno Flierl | ISBN 3-89821-515-6

42   *Katja Yafimava* | Post-Soviet Russian-Belarussian Relationships. The Role of Gas Transit Pipelines | With a foreword by Jonathan P. Stern | ISBN 3-89821-655-1

43   *Boris Chavkin* | Verflechtungen der deutschen und russischen Zeitgeschichte. Aufsätze und Archivfunde zu den Beziehungen Deutschlands und der Sowjetunion von 1917 bis 1991 | Ediert von Markus Edlinger sowie mit einem Vorwort versehen von Leonid Luks | ISBN 3-89821-756-6

44   *Anastasija Grynenko in Zusammenarbeit mit Claudia Dathe* | Die Terminologie des Gerichtswesens der Ukraine und Deutschlands im Vergleich. Eine übersetzungswissenschaftliche Analyse juristischer Fachbegriffe im Deutschen, Ukrainischen und Russischen | Mit einem Vorwort von Ulrich Hartmann | ISBN 3-89821-691-8

45   *Anton Burkov* | The Impact of the European Convention on Human Rights on Russian Law. Legislation and Application in 1996-2006 | With a foreword by Françoise Hampson | ISBN 978-3-89821-639-5

46   *Stina Torjesen, Indra Overland (Eds.)* | International Election Observers in Post-Soviet Azerbaijan. Geopolitical Pawns or Agents of Change? | ISBN 978-3-89821-743-9

47   *Taras Kuzio* | Ukraine – Crimea – Russia. Triangle of Conflict | ISBN 978-3-89821-761-3

48   *Claudia Šabić* | „Ich erinnere mich nicht, aber L'viv!" Zur Funktion kultureller Faktoren für die Institutionalisierung und Entwicklung einer ukrainischen Region | Mit einem Vorwort von Melanie Tatur | ISBN 978-3-89821-752-1

49 *Marlies Bilz* | Tatarstan in der Transformation. Nationaler Diskurs und Politische Praxis 1988-1994 | Mit einem Vorwort von Frank Golczewski | ISBN 978-3-89821-722-4

50 *Марлен Ларюэль (ред.)* | Современные интерпретации русского национализма | ISBN 978-3-89821-795-8

51 *Sonja Schüler* | Die ethnische Dimension der Armut. Roma im postsozialistischen Rumänien | Mit einem Vorwort von Anton Sterbling | ISBN 978-3-89821-776-7

52 *Галина Кожевникова* | Радикальный национализм в России и противодействие ему. Сборник докладов Центра «Сова» за 2004-2007 гг. | С предисловием Александра Верховского | ISBN 978-3-89821-721-7

53 *Галина Кожевникова и Владимир Прибыловский* | Российская власть в биографиях I. Высшие должностные лица РФ в 2004 г. | ISBN 978-3-89821-796-5

54 *Галина Кожевникова и Владимир Прибыловский* | Российская власть в биографиях II. Члены Правительства РФ в 2004 г. | ISBN 978-3-89821-797-2

55 *Галина Кожевникова и Владимир Прибыловский* | Российская власть в биографиях III. Руководители федеральных служб и агентств РФ в 2004 г.| ISBN 978-3-89821-798-9

56 *Ileana Petroniu* | Privatisierung in Transformationsökonomien. Determinanten der Restrukturierungs-Bereitschaft am Beispiel Polens, Rumäniens und der Ukraine | Mit einem Vorwort von Rainer W. Schäfer | ISBN 978-3-89821-790-3

57 *Christian Wipperfürth* | Russland und seine GUS-Nachbarn. Hintergründe, aktuelle Entwicklungen und Konflikte in einer ressourcenreichen Region| ISBN 978-3-89821-801-6

58 *Togzhan Kassenova* | From Antagonism to Partnership. The Uneasy Path of the U.S.-Russian Cooperative Threat Reduction | With a foreword by Christoph Bluth | ISBN 978-3-89821-707-1

59 *Alexander Höllwerth* | Das sakrale eurasische Imperium des Aleksandr Dugin. Eine Diskursanalyse zum postsowjetischen russischen Rechtsextremismus | Mit einem Vorwort von Dirk Uffelmann | ISBN 978-3-89821-813-9

60 *Олег Рябов* | «Россия-Матушка». Национализм, гендер и война в России XX века | С предисловием Елены Гощило | ISBN 978-3-89821-487-2

61 *Ivan Maistrenko* | Borot'bism. A Chapter in the History of the Ukrainian Revolution | With a new Introduction by Chris Ford | Translated by George S. N. Luckyj with the assistance of Ivan L. Rudnytsky | Second, Revised and Expanded Edition ISBN 978-3-8382-1107-7

62 *Maryna Romanets* | Anamorphosic Texts and Reconfigured Visions. Improvised Traditions in Contemporary Ukrainian and Irish Literature | ISBN 978-3-89821-576-3

63 *Paul D'Anieri and Taras Kuzio (Eds.)* | Aspects of the Orange Revolution I. Democratization and Elections in Post-Communist Ukraine | ISBN 978-3-89821-698-2

64 *Bohdan Harasymiw in collaboration with Oleh S. Ilnytzkyj (Eds.)* | Aspects of the Orange Revolution II. Information and Manipulation Strategies in the 2004 Ukrainian Presidential Elections | ISBN 978-3-89821-699-9

65 *Ingmar Bredies, Andreas Umland and Valentin Yakushik (Eds.)* | Aspects of the Orange Revolution III. The Context and Dynamics of the 2004 Ukrainian Presidential Elections | ISBN 978-3-89821-803-0

66 *Ingmar Bredies, Andreas Umland and Valentin Yakushik (Eds.)* | Aspects of the Orange Revolution IV. Foreign Assistance and Civic Action in the 2004 Ukrainian Presidential Elections | ISBN 978-3-89821-808-5

67 *Ingmar Bredies, Andreas Umland and Valentin Yakushik (Eds.)* | Aspects of the Orange Revolution V. Institutional Observation Reports on the 2004 Ukrainian Presidential Elections | ISBN 978-3-89821-809-2

68 *Taras Kuzio (Ed.)* | Aspects of the Orange Revolution VI. Post-Communist Democratic Revolutions in Comparative Perspective | ISBN 978-3-89821-820-7

69 *Tim Bohse* | Autoritarismus statt Selbstverwaltung. Die Transformation der kommunalen Politik in der Stadt Kaliningrad 1990-2005 | Mit einem Geleitwort von Stefan Troebst | ISBN 978-3-89821-782-8

70 *David Rupp* | Die Rußländische Föderation und die russischsprachige Minderheit in Lettland. Eine Fallstudie zur Anwaltspolitik Moskaus gegenüber den russophonen Minderheiten im „Nahen Ausland" von 1991 bis 2002 | Mit einem Vorwort von Helmut Wagner | ISBN 978-3-89821-778-1

71 *Taras Kuzio* | Theoretical and Comparative Perspectives on Nationalism. New Directions in Cross-Cultural and Post-Communist Studies | With a foreword by Paul Robert Magocsi | ISBN 978-3-89821-815-3

72 *Christine Teichmann* | Die Hochschultransformation im heutigen Osteuropa. Kontinuität und Wandel bei der Entwicklung des postkommunistischen Universitätswesens | Mit einem Vorwort von Oskar Anweiler | ISBN 978-3-89821-842-9

73 *Julia Kusznir* | Der politische Einfluss von Wirtschaftseliten in russischen Regionen. Eine Analyse am Beispiel der Erdöl- und Erdgasindustrie, 1992-2005 | Mit einem Vorwort von Wolfgang Eichwede | ISBN 978-3-89821-821-4

74 Alena Vysotskaya | Russland, Belarus und die EU-Osterweiterung. Zur Minderheitenfrage und zum Problem der Freizügigkeit des Personenverkehrs | Mit einem Vorwort von Katlijn Malfliet | ISBN 978-3-89821-822-1

75 Heiko Pleines (Hrsg.) | Corporate Governance in post-sozialistischen Volkswirtschaften | ISBN 978-3-89821-766-8

76 Stefan Ihrig | Wer sind die Moldawier? Rumänismus versus Moldowanismus in Historiographie und Schulbüchern der Republik Moldova, 1991-2006 | Mit einem Vorwort von Holm Sundhaussen | ISBN 978-3-89821-466-7

77 Galina Kozhevnikova in collaboration with Alexander Verkhovsky and Eugene Veklerov | Ultra-Nationalism and Hate Crimes in Contemporary Russia. The 2004-2006 Annual Reports of Moscow's SOVA Center | With a foreword by Stephen D. Shenfield | ISBN 978-3-89821-868-9

78 Florian Küchler | The Role of the European Union in Moldova's Transnistria Conflict | With a foreword by Christopher Hill | ISBN 978-3-89821-850-4

79 Bernd Rechel | The Long Way Back to Europe. Minority Protection in Bulgaria | With a foreword by Richard Crampton | ISBN 978-3-89821-863-4

80 Peter W. Rodgers | Nation, Region and History in Post-Communist Transitions. Identity Politics in Ukraine, 1991-2006 | With a foreword by Vera Tolz | ISBN 978-3-89821-903-7

81 Stephanie Solywoda | The Life and Work of Semen L. Frank. A Study of Russian Religious Philosophy | With a foreword by Philip Walters | ISBN 978-3-89821-457-5

82 Vera Sokolova | Cultural Politics of Ethnicity. Discourses on Roma in Communist Czechoslovakia | ISBN 978-3-89821-864-1

83 Natalya Shevchik Ketenci | Kazakhstani Enterprises in Transition. The Role of Historical Regional Development in Kazakhstan's Post-Soviet Economic Transformation | ISBN 978-3-89821-831-3

84 Martin Malek, Anna Schor-Tschudnowskaja (Hgg.) | Europa im Tschetschenienkrieg. Zwischen politischer Ohnmacht und Gleichgültigkeit | Mit einem Vorwort von Lipchan Basajewa | ISBN 978-3-89821-676-0

85 Stefan Meister | Das postsowjetische Universitätswesen zwischen nationalem und internationalem Wandel. Die Entwicklung der regionalen Hochschule in Russland als Gradmesser der Systemtransformation | Mit einem Vorwort von Joan DeBardeleben | ISBN 978-3-89821-891-7

86 Konstantin Sheiko in collaboration with Stephen Brown | Nationalist Imaginings of the Russian Past. Anatolii Fomenko and the Rise of Alternative History in Post-Communist Russia | With a foreword by Donald Ostrowski | ISBN 978-3-89821-915-0

87 Sabine Jenni | Wie stark ist das „Einige Russland"? Zur Parteibindung der Eliten und zum Wahlerfolg der Machtpartei im Dezember 2007 | Mit einem Vorwort von Klaus Armingeon | ISBN 978-3-89821-961-7

88 Thomas Borén | Meeting-Places of Transformation. Urban Identity, Spatial Representations and Local Politics in Post-Soviet St Petersburg | ISBN 978-3-89821-739-2

89 Aygul Ashirova | Stalinismus und Stalin-Kult in Zentralasien. Turkmenistan 1924-1953 | Mit einem Vorwort von Leonid Luks | ISBN 978-3-89821-987-7

90 Leonid Luks | Freiheit oder imperiale Größe? Essays zu einem russischen Dilemma | ISBN 978-3-8382-0011-8

91 Christopher Gilley | The 'Change of Signposts' in the Ukrainian Emigration. A Contribution to the History of Sovietophilism in the 1920s | With a foreword by Frank Golczewski | ISBN 978-3-89821-965-5

92 Philipp Casula, Jeronim Perovic (Eds.) | Identities and Politics During the Putin Presidency. The Discursive Foundations of Russia's Stability | With a foreword by Heiko Haumann | ISBN 978-3-8382-0015-6

93 Marcel Viëtor | Europa und die Frage nach seinen Grenzen im Osten. Zur Konstruktion ‚europäischer' Identität' in Geschichte und Gegenwart | Mit einem Vorwort von Albrecht Lehmann | ISBN 978-3-8382-0045-3

94 Ben Hellman, Andrei Rogachevskii | Filming the Unfilmable. Casper Wrede's 'One Day in the Life of Ivan Denisovich' | Second, Revised and Expanded Edition | ISBN 978-3-8382-0044-6

95 Eva Fuchslocher | Vaterland, Sprache, Glaube. Orthodoxie und Nationenbildung am Beispiel Georgiens | Mit einem Vorwort von Christina von Braun | ISBN 978-3-89821-884-9

96 Vladimir Kantor | Das Westlertum und der Weg Russlands. Zur Entwicklung der russischen Literatur und Philosophie | Ediert von Dagmar Herrmann | Mit einem Beitrag von Nikolaus Lobkowicz | ISBN 978-3-8382-0102-3

97 Kamran Musayev | Die postsowjetische Transformation im Baltikum und Südkaukasus. Eine vergleichende Untersuchung der politischen Entwicklung Lettlands und Aserbaidschans 1985-2009 | Mit einem Vorwort von Leonid Luks | Ediert von Sandro Henschel | ISBN 978-3-8382-0103-0

98 Tatiana Zhurzhenko | Borderlands into Bordered Lands. Geopolitics of Identity in Post-Soviet Ukraine | With a foreword by Dieter Segert | ISBN 978-3-8382-0042-2

99 *Кирилл Галушко, Лидия Смола (ред.)* | Пределы падения – варианты украинского будущего. Аналитико-прогностические исследования | ISBN 978-3-8382-0148-1

100 *Michael Minkenberg (Ed.)* | Historical Legacies and the Radical Right in Post-Cold War Central and Eastern Europe | With an afterword by Sabrina P. Ramet | ISBN 978-3-8382-0124-5

101 *David-Emil Wickström* | Rocking St. Petersburg. Transcultural Flows and Identity Politics in the St. Petersburg Popular Music Scene | With a foreword by Yngvar B. Steinholt | Second, Revised and Expanded Edition | ISBN 978-3-8382-0100-9

102 *Eva Zabka* | Eine neue „Zeit der Wirren"? Der spät- und postsowjetische Systemwandel 1985-2000 im Spiegel russischer gesellschaftspolitischer Diskurse | Mit einem Vorwort von Margareta Mommsen | ISBN 978-3-8382-0161-0

103 *Ulrike Ziemer* | Ethnic Belonging, Gender and Cultural Practices. Youth Identitites in Contemporary Russia | With a foreword by Anoop Nayak | ISBN 978-3-8382-0152-8

104 *Ksenia Chepikova* | ‚Einiges Russland' - eine zweite KPdSU? Aspekte der Identitätskonstruktion einer postsowjetischen „Partei der Macht" | Mit einem Vorwort von Torsten Oppelland | ISBN 978-3-8382-0311-9

105 *Леонид Люкс* | Западничество или евразийство? Демократия или идеократия? Сборник статей об исторических дилеммах России | С предисловием Владимира Кантора | ISBN 978-3-8382-0211-2

106 *Anna Dost* | Das russische Verfassungsrecht auf dem Weg zum Föderalismus und zurück. Zum Konflikt von Rechtsnormen und -wirklichkeit in der Russländischen Föderation von 1991 bis 2009 | Mit einem Vorwort von Alexander Blankenagel | ISBN 978-3-8382-0292-1

107 *Philipp Herzog* | Sozialistische Völkerfreundschaft, nationaler Widerstand oder harmloser Zeitvertreib? Zur politischen Funktion der Volkskunst im sowjetischen Estland | Mit einem Vorwort von Andreas Kappeler | ISBN 978-3-8382-0216-7

108 *Marlène Laruelle (Ed.)* | Russian Nationalism, Foreign Policy, and Identity Debates in Putin's Russia. New Ideological Patterns after the Orange Revolution | ISBN 978-3-8382-0325-6

109 *Michail Logvinov* | Russlands Kampf gegen den internationalen Terrorismus. Eine kritische Bestandsaufnahme des Bekämpfungsansatzes | Mit einem Geleitwort von Hans-Henning Schröder und einem Vorwort von Eckhard Jesse | ISBN 978-3-8382-0329-4

110 *John B. Dunlop* | The Moscow Bombings of September 1999. Examinations of Russian Terrorist Attacks at the Onset of Vladimir Putin's Rule | Second, Revised and Expanded Edition | ISBN 978-3-8382-0388-1

111 *Андрей А. Ковалёв* | Свидетельство из-за кулис российской политики I. Можно ли делать добро из зла? (Воспоминания и размышления о последних советских и первых послесоветских годах) | With a foreword by Peter Reddaway | ISBN 978-3-8382-0302-7

112 *Андрей А. Ковалёв* | Свидетельство из-за кулис российской политики II. Угроза для себя и окружающих (Наблюдения и предостережения относительно происходящего после 2000 г.) | ISBN 978-3-8382-0303-4

113 *Bernd Kappenberg* | Zeichen setzen für Europa. Der Gebrauch europäischer lateinischer Sonderzeichen in der deutschen Öffentlichkeit | Mit einem Vorwort von Peter Schlobinski | ISBN 978-3-89821-749-1

114 *Ivo Mijnssen* | The Quest for an Ideal Youth in Putin's Russia I. Back to Our Future! History, Modernity, and Patriotism according to Nashi, 2005-2013 | With a foreword by Jeronim Perović | Second, Revised and Expanded Edition | ISBN 978-3-8382-0368-3

115 *Jussi Lassila* | The Quest for an Ideal Youth in Putin's Russia II. The Search for Distinctive Conformism in the Political Communication of Nashi, 2005-2009 | With a foreword by Kirill Postoutenko | Second, Revised and Expanded Edition | ISBN 978-3-8382-0415-4

116 *Valerio Trabandt* | Neue Nachbarn, gute Nachbarschaft? Die EU als internationaler Akteur am Beispiel ihrer Demokratieförderung in Belarus und der Ukraine 2004-2009 | Mit einem Vorwort von Jutta Joachim | ISBN 978-3-8382-0437-6

117 *Fabian Pfeiffer* | Estlands Außen- und Sicherheitspolitik I. Der estnische Atlantizismus nach der wiedererlangten Unabhängigkeit 1991-2004 | Mit einem Vorwort von Helmut Hubel | ISBN 978-3-8382-0127-6

118 *Jana Podßuweit* | Estlands Außen- und Sicherheitspolitik II. Handlungsoptionen eines Kleinstaates im Rahmen seiner EU-Mitgliedschaft (2004-2008) | Mit einem Vorwort von Helmut Hubel | ISBN 978-3-8382-0440-6

119 *Karin Pointner* | Estlands Außen- und Sicherheitspolitik III. Eine gedächtnispolitische Analyse estnischer Entwicklungskooperation 2006-2010 | Mit einem Vorwort von Karin Liebhart | ISBN 978-3-8382-0435-2

120 *Ruslana Vovk* | Die Offenheit der ukrainischen Verfassung für das Völkerrecht und die europäische Integration | Mit einem Vorwort von Alexander Blankenagel | ISBN 978-3-8382-0481-9

121 *Mykhaylo Banakh* | Die Relevanz der Zivilgesellschaft bei den postkommunistischen Transformationsprozessen in mittel- und osteuropäischen Ländern. Das Beispiel der spät- und postsowjetischen Ukraine 1986-2009 | Mit einem Vorwort von Gerhard Simon | ISBN 978-3-8382-0499-4

122 *Michael Moser* | Language Policy and the Discourse on Languages in Ukraine under President Viktor Yanukovych (25 February 2010–28 October 2012) | ISBN 978-3-8382-0497-0 (Paperback edition) | ISBN 978-3-8382-0507-6 (Hardcover edition)

123 *Nicole Krome* | Russischer Netzwerkkapitalismus Restrukturierungsprozesse in der Russischen Föderation am Beispiel des Luftfahrtunternehmens „Aviastar" | Mit einem Vorwort von Petra Stykow | ISBN 978-3-8382-0534-2

124 *David R. Marples* | 'Our Glorious Past'. Lukashenka's Belarus and the Great Patriotic War | ISBN 978-3-8382-0574-8 (Paperback edition) | ISBN 978-3-8382-0675-2 (Hardcover edition)

125 *Ulf Walther* | Russlands „neuer Adel". Die Macht des Geheimdienstes von Gorbatschow bis Putin | Mit einem Vorwort von Hans-Georg Wieck | ISBN 978-3-8382-0584-7

126 *Simon Geissbühler (Hrsg.)* | Kiew – Revolution 3.0. Der Euromaidan 2013/14 und die Zukunftsperspektiven der Ukraine | ISBN 978-3-8382-0581-6 (Paperback edition) | ISBN 978-3-8382-0681-3 (Hardcover edition)

127 *Andrey Makarychev* | Russia and the EU in a Multipolar World. Discourses, Identities, Norms | With a foreword by Klaus Segbers | ISBN 978-3-8382-0629-5

128 *Roland Scharff* | Kasachstan als postsowjetischer Wohlfahrtsstaat. Die Transformation des sozialen Schutzsystems | Mit einem Vorwort von Joachim Ahrens | ISBN 978-3-8382-0622-6

129 *Katja Grupp* | Bild Lücke Deutschland. Kaliningrader Studierende sprechen über Deutschland | Mit einem Vorwort von Martin Schulz | ISBN 978-3-8382-0552-6

130 *Konstantin Sheiko, Stephen Brown* | History as Therapy. Alternative History and Nationalist Imaginings in Russia, 1991-2014 | ISBN 978-3-8382-0665-3

131 *Elisa Kriza* | Alexander Solzhenitsyn: Cold War Icon, Gulag Author, Russian Nationalist? A Study of the Western Reception of his Literary Writings, Historical Interpretations, and Political Ideas | With a foreword by Andrei Rogatchevski | ISBN 978-3-8382-0589-2 (Paperback edition) | ISBN 978-3-8382-0690-5 (Hardcover edition)

132 *Serghei Golunov* | The Elephant in the Room. Corruption and Cheating in Russian Universities | ISBN 978-3-8382-0570-0

133 *Manja Hussner, Rainer Arnold (Hgg.)* | Verfassungsgerichtsbarkeit in Zentralasien I. Sammlung von Verfassungstexten | ISBN 978-3-8382-0595-3

134 *Nikolay Mitrokhin* | Die „Russische Partei". Die Bewegung der russischen Nationalisten in der UdSSR 1953-1985 | Aus dem Russischen übertragen von einem Übersetzerteam unter der Leitung von Larisa Schippel | ISBN 978-3-8382-0024-8

135 *Manja Hussner, Rainer Arnold (Hgg.)* | Verfassungsgerichtsbarkeit in Zentralasien II. Sammlung von Verfassungstexten | ISBN 978-3-8382-0597-7

136 *Manfred Zeller* | Das sowjetische Fieber. Fußballfans im poststalinistischen Vielvölkerreich | Mit einem Vorwort von Nikolaus Katzer | ISBN 978-3-8382-0757-5

137 *Kristin Schreiter* | Stellung und Entwicklungspotential zivilgesellschaftlicher Gruppen in Russland. Menschenrechtsorganisationen im Vergleich | ISBN 978-3-8382-0673-8

138 *David R. Marples, Frederick V. Mills (Eds.)* | Ukraine's Euromaidan. Analyses of a Civil Revolution | ISBN 978-3-8382-0660-8

139 *Bernd Kappenberg* | Setting Signs for Europe. Why Diacritics Matter for European Integration | With a foreword by Peter Schlobinski | ISBN 978-3-8382-0663-9

140 *René Lenz* | Internationalisierung, Kooperation und Transfer. Externe bildungspolitische Akteure in der Russischen Föderation | Mit einem Vorwort von Frank Ettrich | ISBN 978-3-8382-0751-3

141 *Juri Plusnin, Yana Zausaeva, Natalia Zhidkevich, Artemy Pozanenko* | Wandering Workers. Mores, Behavior, Way of Life, and Political Status of Domestic Russian Labor Migrants | Translated by Julia Kazantseva | ISBN 978-3-8382-0653-0

142 *David J. Smith (Eds.)* | Latvia – A Work in Progress? 100 Years of State- and Nation-Building | ISBN 978-3-8382-0648-6

143 *Инна Чувычкина (ред.)* | Экспортные нефте- и газопроводы на постсоветском пространстве. Анализ трубопроводной политики в свете теории международных отношений | ISBN 978-3-8382-0822-0

144　*Johann Zajaczkowski* | Russland – eine pragmatische Großmacht? Eine rollentheoretische Untersuchung russischer Außenpolitik am Beispiel der Zusammenarbeit mit den USA nach 9/11 und des Georgienkrieges von 2008 | Mit einem Vorwort von Siegfried Schieder | ISBN 978-3-8382-0837-4

145　*Boris Popivanov* | Changing Images of the Left in Bulgaria. The Challenge of Post-Communism in the Early 21st Century | ISBN 978-3-8382-0667-7

146　*Lenka Krátká* | A History of the Czechoslovak Ocean Shipping Company 1948-1989. How a Small, Landlocked Country Ran Maritime Business During the Cold War | ISBN 978-3-8382-0666-0

147　*Alexander Sergunin* | Explaining Russian Foreign Policy Behavior. Theory and Practice | ISBN 978-3-8382-0752-0

148　*Darya Malyutina* | Migrant Friendships in a Super-Diverse City. Russian-Speakers and their Social Relationships in London in the 21st Century | With a foreword by Claire Dwyer | ISBN 978-3-8382-0652-3

149　*Alexander Sergunin, Valery Konyshev* | Russia in the Arctic. Hard or Soft Power? | ISBN 978-3-8382-0753-7

150　*John J. Maresca* | Helsinki Revisited. A Key U.S. Negotiator's Memoirs on the Development of the CSCE into the OSCE | With a foreword by Hafiz Pashayev | ISBN 978-3-8382-0852-7

151　*Jardar Østbø* | The New Third Rome. Readings of a Russian Nationalist Myth | With a foreword by Pål Kolstø | ISBN 978-3-8382-0870-1

152　*Simon Kordonsky* | Socio-Economic Foundations of the Russian Post-Soviet Regime. The Resource-Based Economy and Estate-Based Social Structure of Contemporary Russia | With a foreword by Svetlana Barsukova | ISBN 978-3-8382-0775-9

153　*Duncan Leitch* | Assisting Reform in Post-Communist Ukraine 2000–2012. The Illusions of Donors and the Disillusion of Beneficiaries | With a foreword by Kataryna Wolczuk | ISBN 978-3-8382-0844-2

154　*Abel Polese* | Limits of a Post-Soviet State. How Informality Replaces, Renegotiates, and Reshapes Governance in Contemporary Ukraine | With a foreword by Colin Williams | ISBN 978-3-8382-0845-9

155　*Mikhail Suslov (Ed.)* | Digital Orthodoxy in the Post-Soviet World. The Russian Orthodox Church and Web 2.0 | With a foreword by Father Cyril Hovorun | ISBN 978-3-8382-0871-8

156　*Leonid Luks* | Zwei „Sonderwege"? Russisch-deutsche Parallelen und Kontraste (1917-2014). Vergleichende Essays | ISBN 978-3-8382-0823-7

157　*Vladimir V. Karacharovskiy, Ovsey I. Shkaratan, Gordey A. Yastrebov* | Towards a New Russian Work Culture. Can Western Companies and Expatriates Change Russian Society? | With a foreword by Elena N. Danilova | Translated by Julia Kazantseva | ISBN 978-3-8382-0902-9

158　*Edmund Griffiths* | Aleksandr Prokhanov and Post-Soviet Esotericism | ISBN 978-3-8382-0903-6

159　*Timm Beichelt, Susann Worschech (Eds.)* | Transnational Ukraine? Networks and Ties that Influence(d) Contemporary Ukraine | ISBN 978-3-8382-0944-5

160　*Mieste Hotopp-Riecke* | Die Tataren der Krim zwischen Assimilation und Selbstbehauptung. Der Aufbau des krimtatarischen Bildungswesens nach Deportation und Heimkehr (1990-2005) | Mit einem Vorwort von Swetlana Czerwonnaja | ISBN 978-3-89821-940-2

161　*Olga Bertelsen (Ed.)* | Revolution and War in Contemporary Ukraine. The Challenge of Change | ISBN 978-3-8382-1016-2

162　*Natalya Ryabinska* | Ukraine's Post-Communist Mass Media. Between Capture and Commercialization | With a foreword by Marta Dyczok | ISBN 978-3-8382-1011-7

163　*Alexandra Cotofana, James M. Nyce (Eds.)* | Religion and Magic in Socialist and Post-Socialist Contexts. Historic and Ethnographic Case Studies of Orthodoxy, Heterodoxy, and Alternative Spirituality | With a foreword by Patrick L. Michelson | ISBN 978-3-8382-0989-0

164　*Nozima Akhrarkhodjaeva* | The Instrumentalisation of Mass Media in Electoral Authoritarian Regimes. Evidence from Russia's Presidential Election Campaigns of 2000 and 2008 | ISBN 978-3-8382-1013-1

165　*Yulia Krasheninnikova* | Informal Healthcare in Contemporary Russia. Sociographic Essays on the Post-Soviet Infrastructure for Alternative Healing Practices | ISBN 978-3-8382-0970-8

166　*Peter Kaiser* | Das Schachbrett der Macht. Die Handlungsspielräume eines sowjetischen Funktionärs unter Stalin am Beispiel des Generalsekretärs des Komsomol Aleksandr Kosarev (1929-1938) | Mit einem Vorwort von Dietmar Neutatz | ISBN 978-3-8382-1052-0

167　*Oksana Kim* | The Effects and Implications of Kazakhstan's Adoption of International Financial Reporting Standards. A Resource Dependence Perspective | With a foreword by Svetlana Vlady | ISBN 978-3-8382-0987-6

168 *Anna Sanina* | Patriotic Education in Contemporary Russia. Sociological Studies in the Making of the Post-Soviet Citizen | With a foreword by Anna Oldfield | ISBN 978-3-8382-0993-7

169 *Rudolf Wolters* | Spezialist in Sibirien Faksimile der 1933 erschienenen ersten Ausgabe | Mit einem Vorwort von Dmitrij Chmelnizki | ISBN 978-3-8382-0515-1

170 *Michal Vít, Magdalena M. Baran (Eds.)* | Transregional versus National Perspectives on Contemporary Central European History. Studies on the Building of Nation-States and Their Cooperation in the 20th and 21st Century | With a foreword by Petr Vágner | ISBN 978-3-8382-1015-5

171 *Philip Gamaghelyan* | Conflict Resolution Beyond the International Relations Paradigm. Evolving Designs as a Transformative Practice in Nagorno-Karabakh and Syria | With a foreword by Susan Allen | ISBN 978-3-8382-1057-5

172 *Maria Shagina* | Joining a Prestigious Club. Cooperation with Europarties and Its Impact on Party Development in Georgia, Moldova, and Ukraine 2004–2015 | With a foreword by Kataryna Wolczuk | ISBN 978-3-8382-1084-1

173 *Alexandra Cotofana, James M. Nyce (Eds.)* | Religion and Magic in Socialist and Post-Socialist Contexts II. Baltic, Eastern European, and Post-USSR Case Studies | With a foreword by Anita Stasulane | ISBN 978-3-8382-0990-6

174 *Barbara Kunz* | Kind Words, Cruise Missiles, and Everything in Between. The Use of Power Resources in U.S. Policies towards Poland, Ukraine, and Belarus 1989–2008 | With a foreword by William Hill | ISBN 978-3-8382-1065-0

175 *Eduard Klein* | Bildungskorruption in Russland und der Ukraine. Eine komparative Analyse der Performanz staatlicher Antikorruptionsmaßnahmen im Hochschulsektor am Beispiel universitärer Aufnahmeprüfungen | Mit einem Vorwort von Heiko Pleines | ISBN 978-3-8382-0995-1

176 *Markus Soldner* | Politischer Kapitalismus im postsowjetischen Russland. Die politische, wirtschaftliche und mediale Transformation in den 1990er Jahren | Mit einem Vorwort von Wolfgang Ismayr | ISBN 978-3-8382-1222-7

177 *Anton Oleinik* | Building Ukraine from Within. A Sociological, Institutional, and Economic Analysis of a Nation-State in the Making | ISBN 978-3-8382-1150-3

178 *Peter Rollberg, Marlene Laruelle (Eds.)* | Mass Media in the Post-Soviet World. Market Forces, State Actors, and Political Manipulation in the Informational Environment after Communism | ISBN 978-3-8382-1116-9

179 *Mikhail Minakov* | Development and Dystopia. Studies in Post-Soviet Ukraine and Eastern Europe | With a foreword by Alexander Etkind | ISBN 978-3-8382-1112-1

180 *Aijan Sharshenova* | The European Union's Democracy Promotion in Central Asia. A Study of Political Interests, Influence, and Development in Kazakhstan and Kyrgyzstan in 2007–2013 | With a foreword by Gordon Crawford | ISBN 978-3-8382-1151-0

181 *Andrey Makarychev, Alexandra Yatsyk (Eds.)* | Boris Nemtsov and Russian Politics. Power and Resistance | With a foreword by Zhanna Nemtsova | ISBN 978-3-8382-1122-0

182 *Sophie Falsini* | The Euromaidan's Effect on Civil Society. Why and How Ukrainian Social Capital Increased after the Revolution of Dignity | With a foreword by Susann Worschech | ISBN 978-3-8382-1131-2

183 *Valentyna Romanova, Andreas Umland (Eds.)* | Ukraine's Decentralization. Challenges and Implications of the Local Governance Reform after the Euromaidan Revolution | ISBN 978-3-8382-1162-6

184 *Leonid Luks* | A Fateful Triangle. Essays on Contemporary Russian, German and Polish History | ISBN 978-3-8382-1143-5

185 *John B. Dunlop* | The February 2015 Assassination of Boris Nemtsov and the Flawed Trial of his Alleged Killers. An Exploration of Russia's "Crime of the 21st Century" | ISBN 978-3-8382-1188-6

186 *Vasile Rotaru* | Russia, the EU, and the Eastern Partnership. Building Bridges or Digging Trenches? | ISBN 978-3-8382-1134-3

187 *Marina Lebedeva* | Russian Studies of International Relations. From the Soviet Past to the Post-Cold-War Present | With a foreword by Andrei P. Tsygankov | ISBN 978-3-8382-0851-0

188 *Tomasz Stępniewski, George Soroka (Eds.)* | Ukraine after Maidan. Revisiting Domestic and Regional Security | ISBN 978-3-8382-1075-9

189 *Petar Cholakov* | Ethnic Entrepreneurs Unmasked. Political Institutions and Ethnic Conflicts in Contemporary Bulgaria | ISBN 978-3-8382-1189-3

190 *A. Salem, G. Hazeldine, D. Morgan (Eds.)* | Higher Education in Post-Communist States. Comparative and Sociological Perspectives | ISBN 978-3-8382-1183-1

191 *Igor Torbakov* | After Empire. Nationalist Imagination and Symbolic Politics in Russia and Eurasia in the Twentieth and Twenty-First Century | With a foreword by Serhii Plokhy | ISBN 978-3-8382-1217-5

192 *Aleksandr Burakovskiy* | Jewish-Ukrainian Relations in Late and Post-Soviet Ukraine. Articles, Lectures and Essays from 1986 to 2016 | ISBN 978-3-8382-1210-4

193 *Natalia Shapovalova, Olga Burlyuk (Eds.)* | Civil Society in Post-Euromaidan Ukraine. From Revolution to Consolidation | With a foreword by Richard Youngs | ISBN 978-3-8382-1216-6

194 *Franz Preissler* | Positionsverteidigung, Imperialismus oder Irredentismus? Russland und die „Russischsprachigen", 1991–2015 | ISBN 978-3-8382-1262-3

195 *Marian Madeła* | Der Reformprozess in der Ukraine 2014-2017. Eine Fallstudie zur Reform der öffentlichen Verwaltung | Mit einem Vorwort von Martin Malek | ISBN 978-3-8382-1266-1

196 *Anke Giesen* | „Wie kann denn der Sieger ein Verbrecher sein?" Eine diskursanalytische Untersuchung der russlandweiten Debatte über Konzept und Verstaatlichungsprozess der Lagergedenkstätte „Perm'-36" im Ural | ISBN 978-3-8382-1284-5

197 *Alla Leukavets* | The Integration Policies of Belarus and Ukraine vis-à-vis the EU and Russia. A Comparative Case Study Through the Prism of a Two-Level Game Approach | ISBN 978-3-8382-1247-0

198 *Oksana Kim* | The Development and Challenges of Russian Corporate Governance I. The Roles and Functions of Boards of Directors | With a foreword by Sheila M. Puffer | ISBN 978-3-8382-1287-6

199 *Thomas D. Grant* | International Law and the Post-Soviet Space I. Essays on Chechnya and the Baltic States | With a foreword by Stephen M. Schwebel | ISBN 978-3-8382-1279-1

200 *Thomas D. Grant* | International Law and the Post-Soviet Space II. Essays on Ukraine, Intervention, and Non-Proliferation | ISBN 978-3-8382-1280-7

201 *Slavomír Michálek, Michal Štefansky* | The Age of Fear. The Cold War and Its Influence on Czechoslovakia 1945–1968 | ISBN 978-3-8382-1285-2

202 *Iulia-Sabina Joja* | Romania's Strategic Culture 1990–2014. Continuity and Change in a Post-Communist Country's Evolution of National Interests and Security Policies | With a foreword by Heiko Biehl | ISBN 978-3-8382-1286-9

203 *Andrei Rogatchevski, Yngvar B. Steinholt, Arve Hansen, David-Emil Wickström* | War of Songs. Popular Music and Recent Russia-Ukraine Relations | With a foreword by Artemy Troitsky | ISBN 978-3-8382-1173-2

204 *Maria Lipman (Ed.)* | Russian Voices on Post-Crimea Russia. An Almanac of Counterpoint Essays from 2015–2018 | ISBN 978-3-8382-1251-7

205 *Ksenia Maksimovtsova* | Language Conflicts in Contemporary Estonia, Latvia, and Ukraine. A Comparative Exploration of Discourses in Post-Soviet Russian-Language Digital Media | With a foreword by Ammon Cheskin | ISBN 978-3-8382-1282-1

206 *Michal Vít* | The EU's Impact on Identity Formation in East-Central Europe between 2004 and 2013. Perceptions of the Nation and Europe in Political Parties of the Czech Republic, Poland, and Slovakia | With a foreword by Andrea Pető | ISBN 978-3-8382-1275-3

207 *Per A. Rudling* | Tarnished Heroes. The Organization of Ukrainian Nationalists in the Memory Politics of Post-Soviet Ukraine | ISBN 978-3-8382-0999-9

208 *Kaja Gadowska, Peter Solomon (Eds.)* | Legal Change in Post-Communist States. Progress, Reversions, Explanations | ISBN 978-3-8382-1312-5

209 *Paweł Kowal, Georges Mink, Iwona Reichardt (Eds.)* | Three Revolutions: Mobilization and Change in Contemporary Ukraine I. Theoretical Aspects and Analyses on Religion, Memory, and Identity | ISBN 978-3-8382-1321-7

210 *Paweł Kowal, Georges Mink, Adam Reichardt, Iwona Reichardt (Eds.)* | Three Revolutions: Mobilization and Change in Contemporary Ukraine II. An Oral History of the Revolution on Granite, Orange Revolution, and Revolution of Dignity | ISBN 978-3-8382-1323-1

211 *Li Bennich-Björkman, Sergiy Kurbatov (Eds.)* | When the Future Came. The Collapse of the USSR and the Emergence of National Memory in Post-Soviet History Textbooks | ISBN 978-3-8382-1335-4

212 *Olga R. Gulina* | Migration as a (Geo-)Political Challenge in the Post-Soviet Space. Border Regimes, Policy Choices, Visa Agendas | With a foreword by Nils Muižnieks | ISBN 978-3-8382-1338-5

213 *Sanna Turoma, Kaarina Aitamurto, Slobodanka Vladiv-Glover (Eds.)* | Religion, Expression, and Patriotism in Russia. Essays on Post-Soviet Society and the State. ISBN 978-3-8382-1346-0

214 *Vasif Huseynov* | Geopolitical Rivalries in the "Common Neighborhood". Russia's Conflict with the West, Soft Power, and Neoclassical Realism | With a foreword by Nicholas Ross Smith | ISBN 978-3-8382-1277-7

215 *Mikhail Suslov* | Geopolitical Imagination. Ideology and Utopia in Post-Soviet Russia | With a foreword by Mark Bassin | ISBN 978-3-8382-1361-3

216 *Alexander Etkind, Mikhail Minakov (Eds.)* | Ideology after Union. Political Doctrines, Discourses, and Debates in Post-Soviet Societies | ISBN 978-3-8382-1388-0

217 *Jakob Mischke, Oleksandr Zabirko (Hgg.)* | Protestbewegungen im langen Schatten des Kreml. Aufbruch und Resignation in Russland und der Ukraine | ISBN 978-3-8382-0926-5

218 *Oksana Huss* | How Corruption and Anti-Corruption Policies Sustain Hybrid Regimes. Strategies of Political Domination under Ukraine's Presidents in 1994-2014 | With a foreword by Tobias Debiel and Andrea Gawrich | ISBN 978-3-8382-1430-6

219 *Dmitry Travin, Vladimir Gel'man, Otar Marganiya* | The Russian Path. Ideas, Interests, Institutions, Illusions | With a foreword by Vladimir Ryzhkov | ISBN 978-3-8382-1421-4

220 *Gergana Dimova* | Political Uncertainty. A Comparative Exploration | With a foreword by Todor Yalamov and Rumena Filipova | ISBN 978-3-8382-1385-9

221 *Torben Waschke* | Russland in Transition. Geopolitik zwischen Raum, Identität und Machtinteressen | Mit einem Vorwort von Andreas Dittmann | ISBN 978-3-8382-1480-1

222 *Steven Jobbitt, Zsolt Bottlik, Marton Berki (Eds.)* | Power and Identity in the Post-Soviet Realm. Geographies of Ethnicity and Nationality after 1991 | ISBN 978-3-8382-1399-6

223 *Daria Buteiko* | Erinnerungsort. Ort des Gedenkens, der Erholung oder der Einkehr? Kommunismus-Erinnerung am Beispiel der Gedenkstätte Berliner Mauer sowie des Soloveckij-Klosters und -Museumsparks | ISBN 978-3-8382-1367-5

224 *Olga Bertelsen (Ed.)* | Russian Active Measures. Yesterday, Today, Tomorrow | With a foreword by Jan Goldman | ISBN 978-3-8382-1529-7

225 *David Mandel* | "Optimizing" Higher Education in Russia. University Teachers and their Union "Universitetskaya solidarnost'" | ISBN 978-3-8382-1519-8

226 *Mikhail Minakov, Gwendolyn Sasse, Daria Isachenko (Eds.)* | Post-Soviet Secessionism. Nation-Building and State-Failure after Communism | ISBN 978-3-8382-1538-9

227 *Jakob Hauter (Ed.)* | Civil War? Interstate War? Hybrid War? Dimensions and Interpretations of the Donbas Conflict in 2014–2020 | With a foreword by Andrew Wilson | ISBN 978-3-8382-1383-5

228 *Tima T. Moldogaziev, Gene A. Brewer, J. Edward Kellough (Eds.)* | Public Policy and Politics in Georgia. Lessons from Post-Soviet Transition | With a foreword by Dan Durning | ISBN 978-3-8382-1535-8

229 *Oxana Schmies (Ed.)* | NATO's Enlargement and Russia. A Strategic Challenge in the Past and Future | With a foreword by Vladimir Kara-Murza | ISBN 978-3-8382-1478-5

230 *Christopher Ford* | Ukapisme – Une Gauche perdue. Le marxisme anti-colonial dans la révolution ukrainienne 1917-1925 | Avec une préface de Vincent Présumey | ISBN 978-3-8382-0899-2

231 *Anna Kutkina* | Between Lenin and Bandera. Decommunization and Multivocality in Post-Euromaidan Ukraine | With a foreword by Juri Mykkänen | ISBN 978-3-8382-1506-8

232 *Lincoln E. Flake* | Defending the Faith. The Russian Orthodox Church and the Demise of Religious Pluralism | With a foreword by Peter Martland | ISBN 978-3-8382-1378-1

233 *Nikoloz Samkharadze* | Russia's Recognition of the Independence of Abkhazia and South Ossetia. Analysis of a Deviant Case in Moscow's Foreign Policy | With a foreword by Neil MacFarlane | ISBN 978-3-8382-1414-6

234 *Arve Hansen* | Urban Protest. A Spatial Perspective on Kyiv, Minsk, and Moscow | With a foreword by Julie Wilhelmsen | ISBN 978-3-8382-1495-5

235 *Eleonora Narvselius, Julie Fedor (Eds.)* | Diversity in the East-Central European Borderlands. Memories, Cityscapes, People | ISBN 978-3-8382-1523-5

236 *Regina Elsner* | The Russian Orthodox Church and Modernity. A Historical and Theological Investigation into Eastern Christianity between Unity and Plurality | With a foreword by Mikhail Suslov | ISBN 978-3-8382-1568-6

237 *Bo Petersson* | The Putin Predicament. Problems of Legitimacy and Succession in Russia | With a foreword by J. Paul Goode | ISBN 978-3-8382-1050-6

***ibidem**.eu*